WIN 'EM OVER!
GET HIRED!

JOB INTERVIEWS
THAT PRODUCE JOB OFFERS

■■■

IRV JASINSKI

Copyright 2007

Published by CAREER ADVANCEMENT PUBLICATIONS
Post Office Box 300431
Escondido, CA 92030 U.S.A.

Printed in the United States of America
Library of Congress Catalog Card Number: 2007922612
ISBN-0-942195-02-7 Softcover

Cover design by George Foster.
Interior design by www.abacusgraphics.com.
Illustrations by Aldo Garrido.
Copyediting by Judy Meyer, Editorial Services.
Indexing by Ken DellaPenta.

DEDICATED TO LEE

My wife, my best friend,
and the most important person in my life

**AND TO OUR
WONDERFUL CHILDREN**

Steve, Randy, Kevin and Jane

CONTENTS

Introduction and Overview x

About the Author xii

PART ONE: Crucial Preparation Before Your Interview

1   How the Hiring Game is Played 1
    Hires versus Non-Hires. Interviewer 'Roles.' Common
    Misconceptions. Advice From Friends. Your Game Objective.

2   They're Looking for Strong Job Proficiency 6
    Performance Factors. Other Performance Reflections.
    Keep Up-to-Date. Quiz Time. Answer to Quiz.
    Need for New Tools.

3   They Want 'Impressive Individuals'
    With Strong Growth Potential 12
    Positive Attitude('Positude'). Love of Your Job Field.
    Determination to Succeed. Leadership Potential. Performing
    Well Under stress. Team Oriented. Learning Ability.
    Professionalism. Self-Confidence. Adaptability and Flexibility.
    Well-Rounded and Personable. Ability to Influence Others.
    Communication Skills. Sense of Humor.
    Past, Present, and Future Oriented.

4   Research the Company 21
    Things You Should Investigate, Sources of Information.
    Firsthand Exposure.

5   References and Recommendations 25
    Employers. Educators. Peers. Customers. Contacting
    Reference Sources and Recommendation Letters. Sample Letters.

CONTENTS

6   The Screening, Interviewing, and Assessment Process 33
*Phone Prescreening Interviews. Job Fair Screening. Campus
Screening. Written Tests. Human Resources (HR). Hiring
Department. Panel/board Interviews. Interviews With Your
Spouse. Group-on-Group Interviews. Courtesy Interviews.
Interviewer Objectives. Directive Interviewing Approaches.
Non-Directive Interviewing Approaches.
Patterned/Structured Interviewing Approaches.
Medical Department. Background Investigations.*

7   Understanding What Interviews Are All About 52
*Fundamental Misunderstandings. Going Beyond Basic
Qualifications. Those They Don't Hire. Your Image.
Communication Skills. Body Language. Career Field
Commitment. Factors Weighed. What Can Hurt You.
Interviews are Vocal Essay Tests. Top Performers.*

8   You Must Sell Yourself 59

9   Interviewing for a 'Promotional' Job Opportunity 62
*Competing with Others 'Inside/Outside' the Company.
Choosing Your Best Selling Points. Concluding the Interview.*

10 Intelligence, Emotion, and Intuition 66
*Defining Intelligence. The Role Emotion Plays. Your Brain
and Mind at Work. The Power of Your Subconscious Mind.
Thought-Feeling Chain Reactions. Intuition.
Tapping into Your Subconscious.*

11 Measuring Your Situational Awareness 76
*What Is Situational Awareness?
How It Applies to Answering Questions.*

12 Preparing for the Interview: An Overview 79
*The Preparation Strategy. Plan Ahead. Prepare 'Your Own'
Answers. Don't Memorize Your Answers. Offer Them More Than
the Other Candidates Can. Show You Sincerely Want the Job.
Present Your People Skills. Highlight Your Decision-Making
Skills. Consider the Career Choices You've Made. Prove You're
More Than Just Another Job Candidate. Look to Your Future.*

13 Questions You Should Ask Yourself 86
This Particular Company. My Career. Interview-Specific Skills. General Communication Skills. My Background and Personal Life.

14 Questions Interviewers Ask 92
Establishing Rapport. Other Companies. The Interviewing Company. Diversified Hiring. Work Locations. Salary. How You Got Started in Your Profession. Civilian Work Background. Military Background. Education and Training. Legal Offenses and Convictions. Medical. Technical Expertise. The Available Position. Job Responsibilities. Positions Held. Periods of Unemployment. Overall Qualifications/Employment. Conflicts/Disagreements. Constructive Criticism. Accomplishments and Disappointments. Strengths and Weaknesses. Handling Stress. Professionalism/Situational Awareness. Decision-Making and Problem-Solving. Leadership. Hypothetical Role-Playing Scenarios. Job Situations Faced. Employee/Management Relations. Customer Concerns/Needs. Career Goals and Progression. Personality and Character. Free Time. The Future. Questions for Them. Wrapping Up.

15 The Psychologist's Evaluation 129
Questions Asked. Assessing 'What Makes You Tick.'

16 Underkill Versus Overkill 135

17 Insights into Building Terrific Answers 137
Tap Into Your Source Material. Be Comprehensive. Give Key Points and Supportive Points. Show Them How You Think. Bone Up. Know Their Company. Put 'People' First. Show Follow-Through. Be Loyal. Add Value to Their Company. Impress Them with Your Preparation. Pick Your Most and Least Favorite Jobs. Say It: "I'm One of the Best!" Make It Fresh. Establish a Positive Image of Yourself. Handle the 'Bad Stuff' Well. Fill Your Reserve Tank. Aim for Perfection.

18 How Long Should Your Answers Be? 152

19 Choosing Your Best Examples of
'Situational-Based Behavior' Experiences 154
Using the 'SPSRP' Approach.
Being Placed in a Role-Playing Situation.

20 Assessments Made During Group Participation 160
Candidates Address Group. Role-Playing Problem Situations.

21 Your Strengths 163
Professional Strengths. Practical Job Strengths. Intellectual.
Character and Values. Personality and People Skills.
Physical Attributes. Personal Life.

22 Your Weaknesses 178
Too Good. Goals you Haven't Yet Reached. A Soft Touch.
Too Humble. Inconsequential Faults.
Common Personal Weaknesses.

23 Military Job Candidates 184
Tips for the Military Job Candidates.

24 Interview Coaches and Prep Sheets 187

25 Selecting, Practicing and Perfecting Your Final Answers .. 190

26 Paperwork to Bring to Your Interview 193

27 Traveling to Your Interview 195

PART TWO: Presenting Yourself Impressively During Your Interview

28 It's Showtime! Reporting In for Your Interview 201

29 Bringing It All Together for Your Interview 203
Take Center Stage. Sell Yourself. Keep It Positive.
Relax...But Not Too Much. Know the Questioning Approaches
You'll Face. Develop the Art of Fielding Questions.
Use Your Key Points and Supporting Points. Be Specific.
Be Concise. Demonstrate Convictions and Compromise.
Expect the Unexpected. Make a Rapid Recovery.
Handle the 'Bad Stuff.' A Final Word of Incentive.

30   **Crucial First Five Minutes of Your Interview** **218**
Snap Decision. Setting the Tone.
What They Can 'Quickly' Learn About You.

31   **Dressing Appropriately for Your Interview** **226**
Men. Women. Additional Dress Insights (Men and Women).

32   **Your Voice and Delivery** **235**

33   **Speaking with the Right 'Body Language'** **237**
Please Be Seated. Express Yourself. Make Eye Contact.
Practice, Practice, Practice.

34   **The Messages You're Sending to Interviewers** **242**

35   **Tactful versus Tactless—Comments and Answers** **244**

36   **Handling Stress** **252**

37   **Displaying Your Sense Of Humor** **256**

38   **Your Relationship with the Interviewer,**
Understanding the Interaction **258**
The Interviewer's Knowledge Advantage. The Jitters.
Let's Be Friends. Interviewer Bias. Stay Focused. Tough Tactics.

39   **Handling Negative Questions** **267**

40   **Questions to Ask Interviewers** **270**

41   **Some "Don'ts"** **275**

42   **Some More "Do's"** **279**

43   **Review: The Key Steps to a Successful Interview** **284**

44   **Interviewer Reactions to Applicants** **286**
First Impressions. Interview Preparation. Handling Questions.
Personality and Character. Attitude. Delivery. Confidence Level.
People Skills. Self-Promotion. Interest in Their Profession.
Past Employment. Military or Civilian. Technical Expertise.
Education. Leadership. Integrity. Questions for the Interviews.
The Total Person. The 'Closing.'

45   **Wrapping Up Their Interview With You** **327**
A Final Caution.

46   **Making Their Final Selection** **329**

PART THREE: What To Do After Your Interview

47   **Recapping Your Interviews** 333
Reviewing Your Interview Performance.
Do You Still Want the Job?

48   **Job Offers and Salary Negotiations** 338
Content of Job Offers. What If They Don't Offer You a Job?
Company's Perspective on Your Job Worth. Your Perspective on
Your Job Worth. Negotiating for the Highest Starting Salary.
Salary Negotiations, 'A Case Study.' Choosing the Best Job Offer.

A Final Word from the Author 360

INTRODUCTION AND OVERVIEW

You have a very important job interview coming up. It's for a position you really want—with a great company. You're determined to do 'whatever it takes' to land a job offer. This book will show you everything you need to do to make it happen!

There are three major phases of a job interview. Each is crucial to getting hired.

- Preparing yourself, in every way possible, *before* you show up for the job interview.
- Presenting and selling yourself successfully *during* the interview.
- Follow up *after* your interview, to ensure that you will receive a job offer at the highest starting salary possible, and a very extensive benefits package.

Looking at job interviews from a broad perspective, everything you do and say will be carefully observed, analyzed, and evaluated. Getting hired depends on more than your technical qualifications for the position. There is no doubt that looking good on paper can open the door to obtaining an interview. However, from that point on, your success depends on how well you prepare for and present yourself under the pressure of an intense interview. When an employer decides who will get hired, your performance during the interview is the key factor. Just one or two seemingly insignificant mistakes could jeopardize the outcome of an interview and your future career. The competition for the 'best jobs' is intense. You need an edge over the other well-qualified job candidates.

Companies change their screening and selection processes from time to time. They will interview one-on-one for awhile, then switch to an interviewing panel/board. Questions asked can change or be rotated from one interview to another. New people will be conducting the interviews; they may hold lower or higher positions within Human Relations or the hiring department. Some companies may decide to use a psychologist to evaluate job applicants for higher level positions; others will drop the practice. Some add more testing…others drop certain tests. You get the picture. Keep abreast.

Together, we will thoroughly cover each of the three major phases of your upcoming interviews. You'll gain a greater understanding of what interviews are really about. You'll learn to anticipate and successfully meet interviewer expectations, stay calm and focused, handle tough questions and tactics, and build your own unique answers step by step—all the things you need to know about and do in order to get hired.

Once you receive a job offer, you want to carefully evaluate it—especially in today's atmosphere of companies freezing salaries, eliminating pension plans, reducing benefit coverage, passing on a bigger share of their increasing insurance costs to their employees, and engaging in outsourcing, down-sizing, buyouts, layoffs, and replacing full time employees with part-timers. Your take home pay becomes increasingly important. You have to almost view yourself as self-employed—moving from company to company, throughout your career.

You need to sell them on offering you the highest starting salary figure you can come up with, for which you can provide sound logic to support your receiving it. We will also discuss how to best accomplish this. Through applying effective salary negotiation skills which focus on your unique job expertise and qualifications, you will find out your 'true salary worth.' If you're very fortunate, you may receive more than one job offer and need to decide which would be best for you. I'll point out all the factors you should consider and how to go about making a sound decision.

Browse through the chapter titles to get a full perspective on how much you will learn by reading *Win 'Em Over! Get Hired!* You'll find they are short and filled with many straight to the point ideas and suggestions. Use this book as a job interview reference resource to quickly find the answers and information you're looking for to be successful in moving ahead in your career. The time to prepare for your next job interview is now!

■ ■ ■

ABOUT THE AUTHOR

Irv Jasinski has held Human Resources (HR) managerial positions in Employment, Compensation, and Training with TRW/Northrop Grumman, IBM, Flying Tigers/Federal Express, Sperry Rand/Honeywell, and Admiral. He is author of *Airline Pilot Interviews,* best-selling book among civilian and military pilot job applicants who want to fly for the airlines.

As head of Airline Pilot Employment Advisors (APEA), Irv has coached and counseled thousands of pilots and other professionals/managers in effective interview techniques. He has conducted these sessions in person (San Diego area) and by phone (throughout the country).

Irv is a contributing writer to the *Airline Pilot Careers* magazine—a leading publication in aviation for aspiring pilots throughout the country. His articles provide insights to pilots into how to best prepare and present themselves to airlines in job interviews in one of the most competitive professions in the world.

In his coaching sessions, he conducts mock interviews geared to the particular position sought and company offering it. Irv focuses on questions typically asked by HR and the hiring departments, physicians, and psychologists (if involved). He critiques the job applicant's answers, pointing out all the ways the applicant can create a better image of themselves in the minds of the interviewers.

Irv brings many years of experience in the interviewer's chair to his coaching. As manager of employment and recruitment for several major companies, he has personally screened, interviewed, assessed, and selected thousands of job candidates for hundreds of positions ranging from managers, engineers, business administrators, financial analysts, and sales representatives to computer analysts, programmers, machinists, nurses, and administrative assistants. He organized teams to recruit 'on site' at major cities across the country and internationally. Irv also led college recruitment teams in conducting campus interviews at major universities and colleges nationwide.

Irv trained managers, supervisors and HR personnel in the art of interviewing and conducting performance appraisals. He designed the employment application and screening procedures as well as the interviewing methods used by those responsible for the selection of job applicants. He developed many of the questions applicants are asked, chose the factors to be considered in assessing job candidates, and played a key role in the final selection process.

Irv served as equal employment opportunity (EEO) manager for several companies while heading their employment department. He interacted closely with the hiring staffs of other major companies and compared notes on reasons for hiring or not hiring job applicants.

The Birth of this Book

Over the years, Irv has observed what successful job candidates who were hired did that won them the jobs—and what those who weren't hired did that cost them the jobs. He wrote this book to share his findings and provide the guidance that job candidates need to be successful. His candid revelations, insights, and recommendations will help *you* succeed in getting hired.

While working as manager of employment, Irv also taught courses in interviewing techniques and career development at University of California Extension locations throughout the state. He has taught programs on performance assessment, employee counseling, team building, and management by objectives. In addition, Irv has conducted seminars in effective job-search and applicant interviewing techniques at several other universities and at major cities across the country. He tailored these programs for outplacement centers at several military bases. He worked closely with physicians, psychologists and psychiatrists. Irv represented 'business and industry' on the Board for the Accreditation of Colleges and High Schools in the Western United States. He was chairperson of Hire the Handicapped Mayor's Committee for the City of Phoenix, Arizona. He served as an advisor to business and education development groups. He also consulted several minority, female, and ethnic groups on hiring practices followed by employers.

Irv holds a bachelor's degree in psychology/personnel/business management and has taken advanced courses in these fields.

■ ■ ■

■ ■ ■

*Conduct a career audit of where you've been,
where you are now, and where you want to go—
then 'make it happen.'*

■ ■ ■

PART ONE

Crucial Preparation
Before Your Interview

■ ■ ■

Aspiring people always maintain proficiency
in their job interviewing skills.

■ ■ ■

1

HOW THE HIRING GAME IS PLAYED

O n the surface, an interview may seem straightforward—questions asked, answers given. Underneath though, there are many wheels and gears turning—interviewers weighing this and that, consciously and subconsciously. It's a game with high stakes—your future career.

This book was written to help you gain more insight into how the game is played. We'll cover the entire hiring, screening, interviewing, evaluation, and selection process. I will tell you what to do—and not to do—to score points with interviewers in order to win the game and get hired. As you read, you should begin to think deeply about yourself and how you can present all that you have going for you in the best possible light.

You will be surprised to learn how many things you do have going for you. There are many qualities you never realized you possessed. On the other hand, you may find that what you *thought* were the right things to do during an interview may have already cost you some excellent career opportunities. You will learn better ways of approaching your interviews including *what* to say, and *how* and *when* to say it. You will not only be more prepared for your interviews, but also more relaxed and confident when they happen.

Hires versus Non-Hires

If you were to look, right now, at two stacks of resumes—one of applicants who were hired, the other of applicants *not* hired—you probably wouldn't be able to tell them apart. The candidates in both stacks may appear to be qualified 'technically.' Perhaps some would not have been hired because of the employer's concern about the results of their written tests, medical examination, or background investigation. However, most who were turned down actually failed somewhere in their interview(s). For some reason they just didn't score high enough with the HR people, the hiring department, or someone else involved in the selection process. There could have been a number of things that went wrong or just one thing in particular that blew their chance for a great career. They may be aware of what happened, or they may not have a clue. Without further insight or advice, they would most likely repeat the same mistakes in future interviews.

Interviewer 'Roles'

Some interviewers play the role of both *interviewer* and *interrogator* in the hiring game. They can be friendly and easy to talk to at times. At other times, they can be quite blunt and irritating as they probe the applicant's background for hidden problem areas. They will keep looking longer and harder until they find something of concern, or are convinced there's nothing to find.

Common Misconceptions

Let's clear up some misconceptions common among job applicants.

"My getting hired or rejected will be based *primarily* on my technical qualifications for the job for which I'm applying" and "Those with the heaviest technical qualifications get the jobs."

To reiterate what was said in the Introduction and Overview, you can count on your technical qualifications only to get you called in for a job interview. From that point on, your getting hired depends on *how well* you perform in the interview process and throughout all of the other phases of applicant assessment. Think about it: If your qualifications spoke for themselves, employers would not have to test and interview you. They could just run your qualifications through their computers and send you either a job offer or a rejection.

Other misconceptions are:

"They will have to prove to me that I'm not qualified" and "They will have to find out what's wrong with me in order to turn me down."

Contrary to these assumptions, *you* will have to prove to *them* that you are well qualified. They will be determined to find out what's right with you before they will consider hiring you. It's a lot like winning a football game. You go into the game with no points on the board. Your objective is to score enough points to win. If you play too defensive a game, the other team can beat you with a three-point field goal.

Advice from Friends

Carefully critique any interviewing advice you get from those around you. Some will provide realistic insight—others may provide opinions which aren't backed up with sound logic. For example, some have said: "Don't ramble on, you might say something wrong." Rambling means continuing to talk and repeat yourself about something you already covered well. Making more good points in other important areas is not rambling. When you know what you're talking about and are concise, you don't have to worry about saying too much. You will be wrong in leaving out something important. The key is to be concise and condensed in what you have to say.

Some people who have been hired assume that the way they handled the interview is the best way to go. They say, "This is the way I did it—and they hired me!" Emulating them could cost you the job. Maybe they made a few mistakes that were outweighed by many positive things they did. It could be that they were interviewed by a new, relatively inexperienced person who was getting his or her first exposure to screening, interviewing, and evaluating candidates for that particular position. Their interviewer may have been more lenient in his or her assessment criteria than a heavily experienced, critical interviewer. Perhaps the answers given were very appropriate for that candidate's particular qualifications and background, but not for other candidates with different education, training, and experience.

Your friend might have had a strong 'in' with someone very influential in the company who put a lot of pressure on the interviewer to hire his or her friend. It could have been a borderline hiring decision that went your friend's way. Maybe the interviewer was in an especially good mood that day and interpreted answers more favorably than usual.

Take such advice with caution. Analyze all you hear, consider the source and ask yourself, "Does it make sense?"

Your Game Objective

You need to approach your interviews thinking *'What will it take for me to win this game?'* Throughout the interview, the interviewers are constantly assessing you. You make points, fail to make points, or lose points. To win the position for which you're being interviewed, you have to acquire as many points as possible in your interview. You must play this game offensively all the way through. If you sit back, speak as little as you think is necessary to answer questions, and put only minimum effort into trying to prove to those interviewing you that you are more capable and qualified than the other candidates, then you are not going to be hired. It's that simple! Just a point or two difference between you and another well-qualified job candidate can determine who wins the game and gets the job.

In the chapters ahead, I'll show you how to develop a winning game plan and put it into action.

■ ■ ■

The more you look inside yourself,
the clearer things look outside.

■ ■ ■

"Don't laugh! This is how I got my last three jobs!"

2

THEY'RE LOOKING FOR STRONG JOB PROFICIENCY

When a company sizes up a job candidate, they're looking for someone with strong job proficiency. They expect that you have performed well in every position you have held, even if it was temporary, and they expect that you will continue to do so with them if hired.

Performance Factors

You should be ready to address each of these important performance-related areas with the interviewer:

- How well you know your job and perform in it—your job proficiency
- The extent to which your education and training (both civilian and military) are applicable to your present and past positions— and to their job opening
- The breadth and depth of your knowledge and understanding of what's currently happening in your career field
- The strength and quality of your job skills, abilities, and techniques in your present position
- Your major job accomplishments and achievements
- Completion of your job assignments, goals, and objectives 'on time' or ahead of due dates
- The number of compliments or complaints received as a result of your job performance
- How many times you've been promoted and if you were ever involuntarily terminated
- What your supervisors have to say about you in their job performance appraisals

- The extent to which you are considered truly professional in your job and field by management
- Your job performance reputation and image among your peers, associates, supervisors, and customers
- Whether your supervisors consider you an outstanding, excellent, good, average, fair, or poor performer—based primarily upon your performance appraisals and salary reviews

Do everything possible, in preparing yourself for your interviews, to bring out how well you know your job and how well you perform in every job assignment given. Provide the best examples of your 'performance in action' to support the points you make during your interviews.

A track record of upward job progression over the years, with quick mastery of new job assignments, is convincing evidence that you can learn quickly and apply that knowledge successfully. Whatever compelling evidence you can present, the interviewer must feel assured that you have what it takes to successfully complete their job training program and/or step into the new job without any significant problems. Otherwise, you will not be hired.

Other Performance Reflections

You'll gain additional points during your interviews by demonstrating your knowledge of, and interest in, the business end of the company and your ability to successfully interact with all types and levels of people—both inside and outside the company. These skills increase your job effectiveness and value to their company.

Proficiency in performance is also reflected by the grades you made in job-related courses and overall educational training programs. When it comes to grades, to be in the running, employers expect you to have an overall grade point average (GPA) of at least 2.3 (C)—preferably much higher, depending on the job level and complexities of the position for which you are being considered. Candidates with a low GPA must work hard to convince the interviewers that their GPA doesn't truly reflect their learning ability. If this is one of your problem concerns, you need to prepare an effective response in this area of discussion. Perhaps you worked your way through college, excelled in sports, were active in community service, belonged to a fraternity/sorority, were active in social clubs, or ROTC—pursuits that took time away from your studies, but made you a more well-rounded person. If you made better grades in classes and programs that related closely to the position for which you are applying, be certain to point this out.

Let's say that the job opening calls for someone with strong mechanical aptitude. Point out your strength in this area 'off the job' as well. For example, mentioning that you maintain your own automobile, do your own home decorating and remodeling, or landscaping, or enjoy working with wood or metal—all reflect upon this aptitude.

Keep Up-to-Date

As you attain additional qualifications that significantly increase your job proficiency, send an update letter to the HR department manager of your target companies.

It should basically say: "I am a job candidate on file with your company for the position of ... Please update your records to reflect the following change(s) ... I am continuing to increase my job skills, knowledge, and accomplishments in my career field and look forward to hearing from you." Follow each employer's particular policy for update submissions.

PRESTO≡

"My third argument with my captain wasn't nearly as bad as the first two."

Quiz Time

This visual quiz may be familiar to you. It has been around, but it still makes an extremely important key point. It is directly applicable to people preparing for job interviews.

Try connecting all nine cities with only four straight, connected lines (no backtracking).

LOS ANGELES	LAS VEGAS	DENVER
KANSAS CITY	CHICAGO	DETROIT
CLEVELAND	BUFFALO	NEW YORK

Give up? Turn to the next page for the answer.

Answer to Quiz

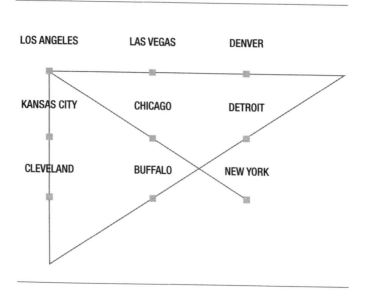

LOS ANGELES	LAS VEGAS	DENVER
KANSAS CITY	CHICAGO	DETROIT
CLEVELAND	BUFFALO	NEW YORK

Simple, isn't it? Why don't most of us come up with the answer on our *first* try? We think that we must somehow solve the problem 'within the square'—the corners of which are Los Angeles, Denver, Cleveland, and New York. We can solve the problem only when we go outside the square and our 'self-imposed' restrictions.

Applying this same thought process to the challenge of getting a job offer, we could consider the square area as that encompassed by *quantitative attributes* such as jobs held, years of experience, promotions, number of degrees and certifications, licenses, training programs completed and so forth. We can think of the area *beyond* the square (into which we must extend ourselves in order to attain our goal) as *qualitative attributes* such as love of your job and career field, leadership, professionalism, image, concern for customer needs, attitude, personality, character and values.

Need for New Tools

Most of us have learned to solve our problems using the same tools over and over, because they have always worked for us. We're sure that all the right answers lie in front of us, as they always have. When we come to a new problem or challenge that these tools don't seem capable of solving, it's time to look elsewhere for *new* tools. This applies to job interviews as well. You can't afford to lose opportunities to advance in your career because you stubbornly adhere to 'old tools' that have worked in past interviews. During your interviews, you must possess and display all your attributes both *within and outside the square* (quantitative and qualitative) in the most favorable light possible. We'll discuss these in more depth in the chapters ahead.

■ ■ ■

Tough times never last — tough people do.

■ ■ ■

3

THEY WANT 'IMPRESSIVE INDIVIDUALS' WITH STRONG GROWTH POTENTIAL

An impressive record of job performance will open doors, but you'll win the job by showing them the 'outside the square' attributes that companies hope to find in a job candidate. These should include: a strong concern for a focus on quality in everything he or she pursues, an awareness of cost concerns and willingness to play a part in controlling costs, and an emphasis on teamwork, customers, and people in general. Employers want a person who enjoys their job and the people he or she works with, someone who wants to move ahead in his or her job skills and abilities in order to advance to a more responsible position. They want an individual who has a desire to help others, an employee who is completely loyal to their company, a 'nice person' who can get along with anyone, on and off the job. Do you consider yourself an impressive individual and employee? Do you think that you have what it takes to develop into one of their best job performers? Do you have the attributes it requires to advance to a senior level? And later move up into supervision? Many interviewers feel that your effectiveness on the job has a great deal to do with your personality, character traits, and values. Let's take a look at some of them.

Positive Attitude ('Positude')

One of the most important ingredients necessary to build an impressive personal image is a strong positive attitude. I combine these into what I consider 'positude.' Do you view a new and complex situation as an opportunity for improvement or as an unwanted problem? Do you display 'positude' in your approach and interaction with everyone you work with, day in and day out?

You may wonder whether an intangible such as attitude is really that important. Well, consider this statement made by the head of a major leading company:

> "We can 'give some' on a job candidate who doesn't have heavy technical expertise in his or her job field or who perhaps didn't do as well as he or she should have in their grades in college. But we will not give one inch to any candidate who doesn't have a good attitude! We can train and retrain a person in areas of job knowledge much easier than we can change that person's attitude. We are not in the business of changing people's attitudes. It's too difficult and time-consuming! We have to accept job candidates as we view them in the attitude that they reflect to us in their contact with our company, and throughout our entire job applicant assessment process. That attitude has to be good!"

Love of Your Job Field

You may or may not be completely satisfied with your present position but having a pure love of your profession and career field is considered by many hiring department interviewers to be crucial to establishing a highly successful career in any occupation or profession. This correlates closely with staying current in the field you are in and doing your best at what you most enjoy. It may well be one of the key reasons why some individuals are more impressive in their job performance than others who are more technically qualified. Employers would like to feel that the job candidate whom they have chosen has a desire to perform in the job which is greater than his or her desire for any other type of good job in another field. This desire is the compelling force that makes a person apply all of his or her energy, ability, and potential toward performing better in every respect. It nurtures a very strong pride in doing 'what he or she does' and being able to earn a living doing something they enjoy.

Determination to Succeed

A strong determination to succeed which permeates everything you do is considered by many hiring department managers as the most important attribute an employee can possess. Employment interviewers and hiring department supervisors look closely for evidence of this attribute: your record of having consistent, high quality performance; feedback from prior employers on your demonstration of job conscientiousness; your taking the initiative to discuss what is important to job success during your interview, and pointing out how your major strengths coincide with these success factors.

Leadership Potential

Leadership potential is of vital importance to every employer—whether displayed in inspiring peers and associates as a member of a work team—or in supervising others directly. Interviewers are evaluating you not only from the perspective of how successful you will be in performing all of your job responsibilities for their company, but also in how successful you will be in leading others around you. It's part of your 'job worth'—the ability to have a positive impact upon everyone you come in contact with each day. Do you consistently exercise good judgment in your decision-making? Are you good at motivating others around you? Do you show strong integrity? Can you relate well to customers, department employees, and management personnel throughout the company? Interviewers look at your record of leadership accomplishments in your various job responsibilities, training, schooling, and so on. They also observe the way you handle yourself during the interview—how you act, what you say, and how you say it. Let them know that you have a strong desire to not only perform well on the job if hired, but to advance into more responsible positions involving leadership roles. Point out that you will make every effort to earn those job opportunities through building an impressive performance record in your current position and displaying your skills at motivating people.

Performing Well Under Stress

Employers also look for individuals who can perform well under stress and pressure. When the going gets tough, an employee must not become frustrated or defensive, or overreact to situations. He or she must not intimidate or belittle colleagues. In your interview, be prepared for stress-producing questions and scenarios. Interviewers will closely observe your reactions and responses. Some interviewers can be very subtle in their approach—others quite direct. For example, they could ask you if you have ever tried smoking marijuana. Should you answer "no", the interviewer will continue to question you on the same issue to note whether you lose your cool or change your story...if you do, it will jeopardize your credibility. Other stressful situations and questions will be covered later in the chapter entitled 'Handling Stress.'

Team Oriented

Companies are also looking for a strongly team-oriented person—someone who can get along very well with the people he or she works with, directly and indirectly. They want an employee who places team success above individual recognition, helping and backing up fellow members of their department in every way possible. In conversation, team-oriented people often make reference to "we," "our," and "us." Candidates who lack this team orientation frequently identify with "I," "my," and "me." If an accomplishment was a team effort, say "we!" If it was primarily the result of your achievements and attributes, then "I" is appropriate. Interviewers watch for these identifying signs during the interview and in your written presentations (such as cover letters and correspondence).

Learning Ability

Demonstrated learning ability is an important asset. It helps to assure HR interviewers, hiring department supervisors, and management that you can successfully complete their company's training programs and on-the-job instruction, and then go on to master every task and job assignment. Your past grades and class standings are one indicator. Another is your progression in salary and job promotions. Is it beyond the norm for people in your profession? Have the projects you've been given gotten bigger and more complex? Do your performance appraisals reflect how quickly and how well you've handled each? The way you adapt to the interview itself also reflects your learning ability. Do you quickly pick up on the mood of the interviewers, understand their questions, and gain insight into what they are looking for? Do you perceive how much time they are likely to spend on each question/answer and know when they want to hear more, or when it's time for you to stop talking?

Professionalism

Employers who have job openings in professional, supervisory, and management positions especially want someone who *looks, acts, dresses,* and *speaks professionally.* They want someone who handles people, job assignments, and situations in a professional manner, and someone who creates a good public image with strong growth potential. In fact, they feel that no matter what job you have, you should be professional in how you perform. People notice the level of professionalism in everyone they come in contact with in conducting business-related matters. How many times have you heard people ask, "And what do you do for a living...Who do you work for?" In what ways do you project professionalism and how can you improve your personal image?

Self-Confidence

Self-confidence is another highly-desired trait. Employers want people who believe in themselves, people who are convinced that they can do an outstanding job for their company. Do you seem proud of what you have accomplished and project confidence that you will succeed if given the opportunity to work for them?

Adaptability and Flexibility

Interviewers look for evidence of adaptability and flexibility. They would like to hire someone who can successfully adapt to *any* situation, whether it be a less desirable work assignment, an unexpected layoff, or a family crisis. They seek individuals who can handle frustrations and readily adapt to new schedules, people, places, things, and ideas. They don't want employees who get too comfortable with the 'status quo.' They want those who view change as being 'for the better.'

Well-Rounded and Personable

Employers also want *well-rounded, personable* individuals. This ties in closely with attitude, adaptability, and flexibility. Employees have to inter-act daily with many other employees within and outside their department who have different attitudes, work habits, mannerisms, and outlooks on their job future. Many employees have to deal directly with their company's customers, clients, and the public. The interviewer wants to know how compatible and conversant you would be in discussions with them on matters relating to the company's products and services as well as the company itself. Can you take the lead at times? Do you listen attentively when others are speaking? Would you be considered an informative, interesting, congenial, open, honest, receptive person to talk to who is concerned with helping them in any way you can, with the focus on customer satisfaction?

All these skills are important because when people are comfortable interacting with you and believe that you are truly receptive to their needs, concerns, problems, and situations they must deal with, they will extend themselves to help you and do things for you that go beyond their typical job responsibilities. They will make an extra effort to please and help you. You will cultivate strong, mutual respect for one another that will pay off in many ways.

Ability to Influence Others

An employee's ability to influence other people has significant bearing upon his or her total contribution and worth to the employer. You have only so much ability and potential of your own; being able to have a strong, positive influence on others is an added force that can do more for the company than you could do alone. You can help others apply their abilities more effectively and recognize the full latitude of their potentials. When others observe you, do you appear enthusiastic about yourself, the company, and the future? Are you an example of a person who enjoys coming to work? Do you stimulate and inspire others? This ability to influence both individual and team performance in many positive ways is difficult to measure, yet we all recognize it when we spot it in people. For a leader, this ability to influence others is an essential asset, which is crucial to team success. You must directly or indirectly display your share of it in your job interviews.

Conversely, we all know a few people who just seem to make those around them feel uncomfortable. If you convey that 'uncomfortable' feeling in a job interview, it could kill your chances of getting hired. An interviewer will not recommend someone with whom he or she would not personally be at ease interacting with on a daily basis.

Communication Skills

The ability to communicate effectively can add many points to your total score in the minds of those assessing you. How well do you convey what you are trying to say to interviewers in your choice of words, use of your voice, facial expressions, and so on? Are your answers and statements clear and concise? Could you further expand your vocabulary, choose more descriptive words in answering questions, and more effectively control the volume, pitch, and speed of your voice? Do you communicate too much (not knowing when to stop) or not enough (leaving your listener waiting for more)? Are you easily understood? How do you sound to your peers and friends? Are you impressive? Do you connect with your listeners every time you interact?

Sense of Humor

A good sense of humor contributes a great deal to achieving success in any position you are in. One of the most effective methods of preventing a disagreement from turning into a heated argument is to diffuse it with humor. It's difficult to become angry with someone who has just said something funny to you. Having a good sense of humor can help to establish many lasting working relationships and friendships, as well as prevent 'run-ins'. People are more comfortable and at ease around those with a sense of humor. This really counts. Plus, it has been proven medically to enhance your health.

Demonstrate your sense of humor during your interviews. When the interviewers kid one another or you, they observe your reaction. Do they catch you smiling—or looking at them as though they've experienced a 'brain disconnect.' Can you take good-natured kidding and laugh at yourself? If you have been told by many people that you are very 'witty', display it tactfully at opportune times during your interview. It can earn you additional points in the interview scoring game.

Having a sense of humor is one of the most important assets you can have for being successful in your job, career field, marriage, and other very close friendships and relationships.

Past, Present, and Future Oriented

Companies seek job candidates who are past, present, and future oriented—not focused on just one of those areas. During an interview, do you talk primarily about what you *have* accomplished and relatively little about what you *are* currently accomplishing? Or do you do an impressive job of relating to your past and present achievements but fail to bring out any *future* plans to improve yourself? Are you goal oriented? You must remember that the ultimate hiring decision rests on the extent to which the interviewers view you as being successful 'in the future' in the position for which you are being considered. Certainly, your past and present achievements and attitude will strongly influence your future successes. In addition, however, companies want some further indication and insight from you as to what you intend to do in the future.

You need to convince the interviewer that you will do all of the following:
- Apply a great percentage of what you have learned in college and training programs to increasing your job skills and overall job capabilities

- Be very successful performing all your job responsibilities and assignments
- Accept full responsibility for your—and your department's— actions and decisions
- Get along well with your boss and the people you work with on a day-to-day basis
- Communicate clearly and concisely
- Make a strong contribution to the team
- Place customer satisfaction and effective teamwork as top priorities
- See the big picture
- Be goal oriented
- Think ahead
- Display your strong analytical skills
- Be cost, profit and quality oriented
- Listen well and serve as a sounding board, when needed, for those around you
- Recognize and compliment good performance, never claiming credit for the accomplishments of others on the team
- Be diplomatic and tactful at all times, making people feel at ease when talking with you
- Show a sincere interest and trust in everyone around you
- Be a good role model
- Help develop others
- Reflect a 'positive tone' throughout the day
- Work well with people at all levels within the company and your industry
- Be receptive to new ideas and constructive criticism
- Bring out the very best performance in yourself and those you can influence
- Lead by example
- Delegate well
- Be an effective instructor and counselor
- Be proficient at team building
- Be a good facilitator, planner, and organizer
- Demonstrate integrity, patience, loyalty, assertiveness, enthusiasm, and decisiveness
- Avoid bias, inconsistency, or a dictatorial approach

- Focus on satisfying the needs of the customers, whether they are the users of your company's products and services or other employees who rely on your services to get their jobs done successfully
- Never belittle others
- Give your subordinates and peers the benefit of what you've learned over the years
- Welcome questions, concerns, and issues
- Be willing to compromise when the situation calls for it
- Apply a great percentage of what you've learned in college to increasing your job skills and overall job capabilities
- Be company-oriented, presenting a positive image of your company at all times

**"About how long will this take?
I've got a hot buyer for my Ipod waiting for me."**

4

RESEARCH THE COMPANY

Early in your interview, you may be asked, "How much do you know about our company?" or "Why would you rather work for us than one of our competitors?" You should be prepared to provide some specific answers to these questions. The interviewer wants to know that you are interested enough in *their* particular company to have taken the time to find out from a number of people and a variety of sources as much as you possibly could about them from a number of perspectives. The depth of your research on their company shows the extent to which you are motivated to work for them. Also, the more you know, the more you can slant your presentation and answers in an interview to 'fit in' with them/their team. This helps you to also come up with some good questions for them.

Things You Should Investigate
Your knowledge of this particular organization and other organizations in their field helps you to determine which one would be most compatible with your personal and career interests, needs, and goals. What type of information should you look for? What are the factors that you can compare? These are some of the things you should investigate:

- Company's area of expertise; major accomplishments, progress and projects; company standards and stability
- Company's history—significant milestones
- Overall reputation among people in the industry—especially those who work for them
- All of the products and services they provide, including new products and services coming out
- Their parent company and subsidiaries

- Individual treatment and recognition—especially through having bought their products or used their services
- Caliber and friendliness of the people, as well as employee morale
- Very recent, significant changes; innovations in their field
- Expansion plans and rate of growth; new orders
- Track record of their performance over all their years in business—customer satisfaction
- Employee-management relations (past and present)
- Caliber of their top management and reputation in the industrial and business world—their image and corporate culture
- Leadership achievements, innovations over competing companies and ranking among principle competitors
- Likelihood of downsizing, outsourcing, acquisition, unwanted takeover or merger
- Probability of layoffs in the future and for what length of time
- Financial status—sales, revenues, earnings, debts and profit trends; equity-to-debt ratio, cash reserves, and total assets; business outlook for the next five years
- Current price of their stock
- Size and number of locations throughout the country/world
- Total number of people employed—number at the location you are seeking
- Names and titles of their top officials and those key people running the department you're interested in
- Job title/description/requirements/requisites of the position sought
- Starting salary and the length of time it takes to advance to higher positions in the job family
- Job and salary structure and progression
- Training provided
- Employee benefits
- Present retirement program—how 'secure'
- Impact of all of these on your spouse and family

Your individual goals and values should coincide with and complement those of the company you are hoping to join. They should be in sync. The atmosphere that you enjoy working in should be the atmosphere that exists throughout their organization. Find out their 'personality'—you don't want to have a personality conflict with your employer.

Sources of Information

You can obtain all the information you seek from many available sources:

- Internet coverage/company's own website and others which provide in-depth company information; networking with on-line discussion groups
- Industry and trade directories published by each state
- General business directories, magazines and periodicals: *Business Week, Encyclopedia of Associations, Thomas Register of American Manufacturers, Forbes, Readers' Guide to Periodical Literature, The Wall Street Journal, US Industrial Outlook, Newsweek, US News and World Report* and reports from Dun & Bradstreet, Moody's Investor Services, and Standard & Poor's
- Company marketing materials: 'hotlines', in-house newsletters, promotional brochures, and other handouts
- Annual and quarterly reports issued by the public relations department of the companies you're interested in
- Stockbrokers and stock reports
- Stockholder meetings (purchase a few shares of stock in the company that interests you, and you'll be invited to these annual events)
- College and university libraries and career/placement centers; professional organizations
- Executive search firms, outplacement organizations, 'head-hunters', employment consultants and agencies
- Consulting services which serve as a career information resource for professionals, providing in-depth coverage of all major companies
- Books written about their industry
- TV and radio business programs and news items
- Major and local newspaper press releases
- Firsthand insights from people who work for the company— especially those in the position you're seeking and retirees
- Family, neighbors, and friends who may be knowledgeable in the company's history and current status

The more of these sources you utilize, the more confident you will be in your choice of the company you would most enjoy working for…and the more impressive you will be during an interview, having this knowledge.

Meeting someone from the hiring department of the company you're interviewing with can be very productive. It provides you an opportunity to get to know the person well enough to ask questions about his or her company, job, department, supervisor, and how he or she enjoys working there. You get a chance to talk about yourself, your interest in the job opening and company, and your job qualifications. At the same time, you're selling yourself as a likeable person whom he or she would enjoy working with and getting to know better. The person you're conversing with will usually volunteer to 'put in a good word' for you, if you were successful in projecting a likable image of yourself. You might want to invite the person to have lunch or coffee.

Don't focus completely on one company in preparing yourself for interviews. Prepare for your two runners-up as well. You might be unexpectedly called in to interview with another impressive organization. How are they different from the others? Do they ask different questions? Do they have a different personality? How do you plan to answer certain questions based upon that difference? Will you feel challenged and thoroughly enjoy your daily interactions with personnel on all levels? Is this the type of company with which you want to identify yourself for many years to come?

Firsthand Exposure

You should consider taking advantage of opportunities to be interviewed by several reputable companies even if they aren't at the top of your list. You'll gain more insight into what to look for in a company and the challenges of being interviewed will provide a learning experience that will increase your effectiveness as a job applicant and, in turn, the chances of obtaining the position you really want. Shoot for interviews with at least three companies and receiving job offers from two. This will allow you a choice as to which company is best for you and your family.

■ ■ ■

Stress occurs when you won't accept the possibility of failure.

■ ■ ■

5

REFERENCES AND RECOMMENDATIONS

Many people have been able to obtain job interviews—and enhanced their chances of being hired—through the recommendations of prior employers and customers, and peers whom they knew well and who are currently employed with the company that has the job opening. They carry a lot of weight with HR and the hiring department and they can vouch for your character. Show your willingness to have your current employer contacted to check out job references with them *after* you receive a job offer—and that job offer being contingent on their receiving strong positive feedback on your job performance.

Employers

Prior employers have had a firsthand opportunity to observe and evaluate your total performance as a technically-skilled professional in your field and as an employee interacting with other employees throughout their company. It's ideal to get recommendation letters from those to whom you reported directly, most recently, and for long periods of time. A letter of recommendation from a supervisor you have only worked for a very short period of time won't carry nearly as much weight.

Some superiors, in composing a letter of recommendation, water down positive statements to the point that they appear lukewarm and have no real value. Others come on so strongly that they seem unbelievable. Some speak in such generalities that potential employers can't tell exactly what the person is trying to say. Don't submit letters like these. Reference letters must be both truly supportive of you and believable.

You could be asked why you haven't given them, nor have they received, a letter of recommendation from one of your prior employers. Even if you left that company because you felt that you were not treated fairly, don't badmouth them. Interviewers feel that if you do, you might do the same regarding them. Try to find some redeeming values about that company and how you were treated.

Even if you haven't requested a letter of recommendation from a particular past employer, it would be wise to contact them to 'smooth things over' in case your prospective employer decides to phone them. Point out your appreciation of their giving you the opportunity work for them and although things didn't work out as well as you both had hoped, you're still grateful for having the chance to prove yourself to them—and wish you had succeeded. Place the accountability squarely on your shoulders. You have little to lose and a lot to gain.

Educators

Recent college graduates should obtain letters of recommendation and endorsements from department heads, professors, counselors, advisors, students tutored, part-time employers, community and charitable organizations served, career-oriented clubs actively participated in, and so forth. Any major drive, program, or project in which you significantly contributed to would warrant a letter of recommendation from the person who headed it. If you did a good job, get credit for it!

Peers

Friends who are employed with the company to which you're applying have credibility with those conducting the interviewing and selection assessment process. Also, the company believes that their employees will be honest with them, and that they will not risk their reputation with their employer unless they are certain that—considering their company's standards and mode of operation—you would work out well if hired.

Your friends should have passed their probation period and earned credibility by working for their company one to two years. These friends can 'hand walk' your resume and employment application and their written endorsement of you to the hiring department manager and/or HR. They can say a few words expressing their sincere support of you. Some of them may prefer to speak to HR and hiring department interviewers directly rather than compose a letter of recommendation. It's best to support the approach with which they are most comfortable.

You can also ask for letters of recommendation from friends with whom you've worked (both civilian and military) who have a good reputation in the industry. The bottom line is that your references and letters of recommendation must come from people who are viewed as quality sources. If your friends enjoy the status and seem willing to support you, call and ask them for their support!

Customers

Gain extra points by submitting letters of recommendation from one or two of the key customers you serviced (outside or within your previous employers). They should reflect how well you provided them with the services they needed and how they personally enjoyed interacting with you.

Contacting Reference Sources for Recommendation Letters

You should contact your chosen references to request a letter/statement of recommendation before you submit your resume and report for your job interview. They will appreciate the 'heads up' and be prepared for phone inquiries from prospective employers as well. If they agree, discuss the type of performance coverage that you believe would be most important to your prospective employer. If some individuals are very willing to support you but not sure exactly what to say and how to say it, or can't recall all the details and circumstances, offer to provide a draft that they can adapt or expand. A weak or poorly prepared letter of recommendation is worse than no recommendation at all.

Letters of recommendation should include the following:

- The writer's position, department, and organization as well as length of employment
- His or her relationship with you
- When and for how long that relationship existed
- Your position and major responsibilities at that time
- How long you occupied that position
- Your key skills, strengths, attributes, qualities, and how well you applied them 'across the board'
- Your strong technical knowledge in your position and field
- Major accomplishments, key projects, programs, and assignments
- Your equally strong people skills
- The person's contact information should the company wish to ask any questions or desire additional information

If you have any doubts about whether the person you have asked to submit a letter of recommendation will strongly support you—especially if the person appears hesitant to write such a letter—withdraw your request. Don't take a chance on this.

Phone each person who wrote a letter of recommendation or gave a phone endorsement supporting you and thank them for doing so. You may need another letter and/or endorsement from him or her in the future.

Make it clear to company screening personnel and job interviewers that you are proud of your track record of performance and the extent to which people have gone out of their way to write letters of support. Point out how you would more than welcome their contact with each reference and that you would be willing to provide additional endorsers, if need be.

**"This is quite an impressive letter of recommendation
from your last parole officer."**

Sample Letter of Recommendation (Civilian)

Kristina Parrish
2812 W. Fairmont Avenue
Atlanta, GA 31270-5143

(date)

Mr. Jason Conard
Human Resources
Deluxe Airlines
P.O. Box 14801
Atlanta, GA 38192-4915

Dear Mr. Conard:

Jane Schwarz has applied for a flight officer's position with our airline and I would like to highly recommend her to you.

While I was flying as captain for Skyward Airlines from [month/year] to [month/year], Jane was my first officer on numerous flights. Her attitude, flight skills, and ability to interact well with flight crews were impressive. She displayed a great in-depth knowledge of the aircraft's systems and strong operational skills. She supported me in every possible way and frequently volunteered to help others around her. Jane followed check-lists and flight procedures very closely. Her dress, grooming, and behavior were of the highest professional standards. She has good timing; she knows when to be serious and when it's okay to kid around (showing a great sense of humor).

Jane Schwarz also had a positive influence on those with whom she worked and let it be known that safety was her top priority in everything she did. She went out of her way to speak with passengers and was very customer-oriented. Jane hit it off well with ground crews. She always spoke well of the company and her fellow employees, personifying warmth, friendliness, and professionalism.

It's no wonder that Jane quickly upgraded to captain before I left Skyward to join Deluxe. She possesses all the leadership and technical flight skills necessary to motivate a flight crew to perform at its best.

Having spent two years with our airline, interacting with many flight crew members, I'm certainly impressed with the caliber of our people. Jane Schwarz would fit right in with everyone.

Feel free to contact me at work, at home: (404) 581-9162, or by e-mail: kparrish@aol.com.

Sincerely,

Kristina "Stien" Parrish
First Officer, Deluxe Airlines

■ ■ ■

'Feelings' can be your best friend,
and your worst enemy.

■ ■ ■

Sample Letter of Recommendation (Military)

Christopher Thompson
1017 S. Spring Street
Portland, OR 97208-1019

(date)

Southern Airlines
People Employment Department
Ms. Katherine Conard
P.O. Box 36491
Dallas, TX 74398-1563

Dear Ms. Conard:

I *strongly* endorse Carlos Gonzales for employment as a flight officer for your airline. Mr. Gonzales was assigned to my F/A-18 squadron from [month/year] to [month/year]. As his commanding officer, I had many opportunities to observe Carlos perform under a myriad of challenging flight operations.

In comparing the manner in which he performed numerous flight assignments with others in a similar position under my command, I would rate him in the top ten percent of his peer group.

Carlos was a proven strike-fighter pilot; a highly-gifted aviator with out-standing flying and people skills. His aeronautical knowledge and tactical expertise were unquestioned. He provided exceptional leadership, guidance, and counsel to those under him, significantly enhancing safety and professionalism throughout the squadron.

Carlos consistently displayed very keen insight, sound judgment, and impressive team interaction in combat missions and other tactical flights.

I could always count on him to volunteer for the toughest missions and display superior leadership, regardless of the challenges and complexities faced. He never let us down—always made the right decisions. Plus, he is very enjoyable to work with.

It is my opinion that Carlos Gonzales would be a very valuable addition to your flight team. You would never regret hiring him!

You are welcome to contact me for further details. You can reach me on duty at (503) 462-3099, at my home: (503) 379-8814, or by e-mail: cthompson@aol.com.

Sincerely,

Christopher Thompson
Commander, U.S. Navy

■ ■ ■

Many people don't really listen,
just wait their chance to talk.

■ ■ ■

6

THE SCREENING, INTERVIEWING
AND ASSESSMENT PROCESS

You have been successful in gaining the interest of the company you want to work for and expect to be contacted to discuss your interest in and qualifications for the position you're seeking. When can you expect that to happen? What is involved in the company's screening, interviewing, evaluation, and selection process? Larger companies have their HR and hiring departments handle this process. Small-sized employers usually have one person do it all. This is often the person who will be your supervisor.

It would benefit you to meet someone in their organization (as early as possible) who is familiar with how HR and the hiring department supervisors operate in the interviewing and assessment process. In talking with that individual, you can gain a great deal of insight into what to expect and what counts most.

There are a number of screening phases that you can expect to go through. How far you proceed will depend on how well you perform in each phase. It may take a few days to complete them all, or even a week or two. For the sake of discussion, let's conduct a walk-through of one company's screening process. The order of phases varies from one organization to another.

Phone Prescreening Interviews
Many companies are prescreening job candidates for key positions by phone, putting them through a mini-interview to determine whether they should be invited in for a comprehensive interview. The interview can last

15 to 20 minutes, or as long as 30 to 45 minutes—the greater their interest in you, the longer the interview. This approach is less costly to both the company and the job applicant in time spent and costs incurred than in-person interviews. You must be as thoroughly prepared for his type of abbreviated interview/rough screening as you would be for the 'full treatment' at their facilities.

Have a copy of your resume and employment application near the phone in order to readily recall pertinent facts relating to questions you may be asked. Also, have a calendar readily available that contains all your appointments in case the caller wishes to set up an in-person interview appointment with you. If nervous, walk around during the first five minutes of the conversation. Don't eat during the discussion; it's okay to take a small sip of water once or twice to clear your throat. Avoid background noises, TV, radio, stereo, and conversations taking place within close earshot. You may have to move to another room/area that is more conducive to a business conversation. Don't tape this call. Instead, have a writing pad nearby to take notes to recall your discussion. Jot down key points and supporting information you may wish to relate to the caller sometime during your conversation in anticipation of questions you are most likely to be asked—about yourself personally, your areas of technical expertise, important projects, programs, job assignments and responsibilities, education, and training.

The caller—usually from the HR or hiring department—will phone you unexpectedly one evening or weekend. Don't act rushed or startled to receive their call or seem to be taken off guard. Instead, say you were hoping to hear from him or her. [Obtain the correct pronunciation of his or her name]. He or she will ask you several questions covering your interest in the job opening, the highlights of your education, training, and employment. The caller may also ask a few questions pertaining to problem areas, such as low grades, lack of a degree, an involuntary termination, periods of unemployment, very short periods of employment, slow job and salary growth and progression. He or she wants to clarify *why* and *how* this happened and be on the lookout for inconsistencies. You may have left out some information on your employment application or resume that he or she thought was important to know about before inviting you in. He or she is looking for any 'red flags' that will alert him or her to a significant problem area. Hiring department supervisors/managers may ask one or two in-depth, technically-oriented questions to those who are heavily experienced in the field of the job opening. The fact that he or she wants to ask you many questions indicates a strong interest in you. Be prepared to have two or three *job-related questions* to ask the caller—primarily centered on key job responsibilities and accountabilities, typical job challenges and assignments, types of projects involved, where the position falls within its job family, job progression, and to whom the position reports. Include a question which will provide the opportunity for you to tie in your job attributes with those job skills and abilities they are seeking in finding the most qualified job candidate for the position.

The interviewer wants to get a feel for what you are like; your personality, attitude, character, style, open-mindedness, level of comprehension, sense of humor, and so on. Questions could touch upon your leadership skills and problem-solving approaches. Perhaps during this prescreening, the caller will uncover a hidden problem of some sort and wish to explore it thoroughly. In short, it's an efficient way to identify and eliminate those candidates who looked good on paper, but didn't live up to their employment package. It saves the time and effort expended in conducting a formal job interview.

Remember, the interviewer can't observe you face to face, so your 'voice' must reveal what they're looking for in prescreening you. When expecting a phone call from a particular employer, warm up your vocal chords early each morning by singing, talking to others, or even to yourself. Your voice should be strong and clear and you should speak with good diction. You want to sound sincere, warm, friendly, enthusiastic, and glad you received a phone call from them. Give them your best 'phone smile.' Listen closely to the caller's voice pattern and be compatible with it. Also, practice aloud what you plan to say in responding to expected questions. Answer questions with concise, brief statements; don't, however, sound abrupt.

Don't initiate any discussion on salary. If the interviewer brings it up, state that you are 'open' to discussion. Point out that you would be in a better position to arrive at a valid 'asking salary' figure *after* having a more in-depth understanding of the job. You need to learn more about job responsibilities, assignments, projects, programs, the company's salary structure, salary review schedule, and salary range for the position. All this should be brought up at the in-person interview.

If the interviewer is satisfied that there are no apparent problems and everything seems positive, you'll be scheduled for a job interview appointment. You may get the invitation at the close of the conversation or in the near future. Tactfully ask who you will be speaking with—his or her full name and title, and approximately how long the interview will last. Reaffirm the interview date, time, and place to report. Even if you aren't invited to an interview at that time, close the conversation in a positive manner; thank the caller for contacting you, and emphasize your interest in the position and company, and that you would look forward to the opportunity to meet him or her in the near future at their facilities.

Set up a file for each of your top five companies. Record not only key information gained through your research on them, but most importantly, all contact with them. Begin with that significant prescreening phone interview. Be certain you record the caller's name, job title, name of the company, telephone number, email address, fax number, job title of the open position, and the date you were contacted.

You might receive a call from a recruitment search firm which represents the employer or several employers with similar staffing needs. The line of questioning is similar. Your name may have come to their attention through your responding to an advertisement or perhaps someone reputable in your field of work knows you or heard good things about you. If the caller is impressed with your presentation and job qualifications and determines there is a job match, he or she will arrange for an interview at that employer's facilities—at the expense of the employer. There must be mutual interest. Many people have found rewarding careers and/or valuable experience going through such interviews. If you have the time, avail yourself of such opportunities.

Job Fair Screening

Many companies prescreen job applicants at job fairs. Their 'mini-interviews' are much shorter than phone interviews. The interviewers want to gain a thumbnail picture of what the applicant is like. They can determine if he or she is in the ballpark of what they're looking for—in terms of appearance, dress, attitude/personality, education, job experience, career interests, and salary needs. They accomplish this by quickly reviewing the applicant's resume and asking two or three pertinent questions—all within three to five minutes.

Your resume must be the result of many polishing touches—not a rough draft, and your pitch to the interviewer as professional as possible.

Approach those employers you are most interested in working for first. Be prepared to give a brief summary 'sales pitch' (30-45 seconds) wrapping up what you have to say. It should focus on one to two of your strongest selling points. Also remember to dress as you would for any important in-person job interview.

There isn't time for a lot of small talk. It will take considerable time to develop summary statements in each area of anticipated questions. Achieve this through practice prior to attending the fair.

The company representative will decide whether to be encouraging or discouraging to you. "Your qualifications appear to come close to fitting one of our current openings" or "We really don't have a current job opening in your area of job interests and qualifications." He or she may say that you could expect to hear from them shortly by phone (further prescreening) or be invited to an interview at one of their facilities.

Campus Screening

Employers conduct face-to-face prescreening mini-interviews on college university campuses in a similar manner as they do at job fairs. The main difference is that there are many job openings, in different fields and job levels that employers are concerned with filling at job fairs; on campus, they are most concerned with filling entry-level positions with graduates who express a strong desire to enter that field.

If you have established good relationships with job counselors and the career placement center staff, they will often go out of their way to 'put in a good word for you' with the employers coming to their school. This ensures you will fill an appointment slot on their tight schedule. The company representative may allot more time for you as a promising job prospect.

Should the company representative be impressed with you, expect to be contacted within a short period of time (a few days to a week). Don't press the representative to commit to an interview at their location. That will only make him or her defensive. The representative needs time to compare all the graduates interviewed. The decision as to who will be invited to interviews will come after their return to their home base.

It's encouraging to make it through this prescreening but keep your cool; the job's not yours just yet. You have simply gained the opportunity to be thoroughly evaluated through their *full* screening, interviewing, and assessment process. You are entered in the race—how well you run in it will be determined later.

Written Tests

Many companies put job candidates through extensive psychological, technical, and verbal testing; others put you through a few or none. The primary goal of most tests is to eliminate those 'most likely to fail' in the job/field/area for which the test was designed. These tests may seem irrelevant and intrusive, but employers would not use them unless they had been proven to accurately predict success on the job, and achieve consistent results when a candidate is retested. The tests themselves are rigorously evaluated for validity and reliability before they are adopted. Cutoff scores are established, and candidates who score below them are generally eliminated from further consideration. Those who score above this cutoff line are thought to have a good chance to succeed, although tests cannot predict to what *extent* or degree any individual will succeed.

Many tests are designed to measure performance skills, abilities, and technical expertise. Some cover areas of related knowledge in the science field, aptitudes and learning potential, abstract reasoning, memory, overall intelligence, career interests, and psychological makeup. They were developed to determine how easily trainable you are and how well you could adapt to any work situation.

Psychological tests are designed to measure how balanced and well-rounded you are in dealing with other individuals, both one-on-one and in groups. There are many things that they want to learn about you. What is the level of your integrity? How honest and reliable are you? What is your level of self-esteem? What are your logical skills, your ability to concentrate under pressure? How much pressure can you handle? Are you an introvert, extrovert, or ambivert? How 'open' are you? How argumentative, defensive, emotionally stable, empathetic, tolerant, and responsible are you? Do you have strong leadership attributes? Are you more of a loner or a joiner? How well can you control your impulses? Do you tend to look at things from a negative or positive viewpoint? How suitable are you to the profession and position? How closely do you adhere to rules? Any indications of serious mental problems? These tests measure how well you will adapt to others and handle people in every type of situation, your decision-making and consensus building styles and abilities; what your personality is like (behavioral patterns and characteristics), traits you possess, your character and value system. Remember, when taking tests, that we all have our normal weaknesses and negative thoughts from time to time—we're human—just don't go overboard. Don't pretend you're perfect either.

Don't get overly concerned about trying to prepare for psychological tests. Your personality is well-established by now and not likely to be modified significantly enough (before taking the tests) to raise your test scores. Don't second-guess yourself—you know who you are and you aren't going to change overnight. These tests are designed with built-in verification—asking the same question several times in different ways. Too many inconsistent, conflicting answers will invalidate your test results. Trying to outthink the designer of a psychological test could cost you a great job opportunity. Answer the questions from your perspective as a professional in your position, rather than how you feel and act in your personal life.

Depending on the job and level of position for which you are being considered, you could also be tested on eye/hand coordination, programming/computer skills, mathematics, physics, spatial orientation, abstract reasoning, mental alertness, motor abilities, mechanics, electrical and electronic applications, number sequence stress, recognition, perception, vocabulary, and listening skills. Other tests concentrate on your general knowledge in a variety of areas.

Some tests are designed to penalize you for wrong answers; others aren't. If you find out that wrong answers won't count against you in a particular test, by all means try to answer as many questions in the time allotted as possible—what have you got to lose?

You can take several other effective approaches to score higher on tests of knowledge:

- Avoid alcoholic or caffeinated beverages, smoking, eating heavily, and consuming large amounts of liquids a day or two before your interview. Get plenty of sleep.
- Do some stretching and light exercises to relax your entire body the morning of your interview.
- Think and feel as though you were at work, taking on a new job assignment.
- Answer the easy questions first; then go back over the tougher ones.
- Don't spend too much time on any one question—move on to the next.
- Your first, spontaneous reaction tends to be a valid one.
- Lean toward answers which project positive values and traits in describing yourself.
- Most questions asked with 'always' and 'never' modifiers are

intended to throw you off. Suggest that you don't agree with the statement because it is too absolute.

- Take reading courses, expand the types of materials you read, and increase your vocabulary. Exercise 'mentally.'
- Practice—if you have the chance to be tested at a college, university, business, industrial, or governmental employment placement/career counseling office, or a specialized test consulting service, do so. Take a variety of written tests. Studies show that the more you practice taking tests, the more likely you will reduce your level of anxiety and score well when tested by a prospective employer.

There is a great deal of controversy as to how valid tests designed to measure intelligence truly are. Most employers interpret the test results cautiously. Many experts disagree on what intelligence truly is and how to approach measuring it.

Human Resources (HR)

You are most likely to be interviewed at the company's facilities. At first by someone from the HR department—an employment or HR manager, employment representative or recruiter. If possible, schedule your interview for a Monday or Friday morning. Interviewers generally feel good on Fridays because they are looking forward to an enjoyable weekend. They are rested and more relaxed on Mondays, having been away from the stresses of work for two days.

You may be interviewed outside the company's facilities; a local restaurant, hotel lobby, at the airport (if you flew in for your interview), or career/placement center on-campus. Some employers conduct their interviews by video phone, employment consultant's business location, or at the site of a recognized organization supporting the interests of various EEO (Equal Employment Opportunity) groups. Video interviews allow several interviewers at different locations to interact with you at the same time. This method is generally used for managerial and executive-level job candidates who are under strong consideration.

The interview may be combined with breakfast, lunch, or dinner. Several interviewers could be present. You're expected to join in their conversations, listen carefully, and ask a few good job and company-related questions. Eat a light meal and refrain from having an alcoholic beverage. Treat the waiter/waitress with respect. Begin and end your meal as those interviewing you do. The interviewers expect you to be more relaxed in these settings and more likely to 'open up' and be less guarded in your responses to their questions. Be sure to thank them for the meal and the opportunity to meet with them. Never complain about the food or service.

Interviews at the company's facilities can last from fifteen minutes to as long as an hour. They cover a range of questions concerning your employment application and resume, verification of your technical job qualifications, education, training, employment record, personal data, and so on. Interviewers are concerned with validating your credentials. You may be asked if all the information provided is accurate and if you want to make any changes. The records you were asked to bring to your interview will be checked out. This time also provides an opportunity for the interviewers to find out what you are like from the company's perspective: Do you match the professional image they want to project throughout their company, to co-workers, supervisors, upper management, customers, and the public? Employers expect their employees to look, think, and act 'professional'—no matter what their position and job level is in the company. Are you customer-oriented or only concerned about performing your job tasks and being paid well?

You may be asked to express your ideas, insights, and opinions on a variety of job-related topics: How you happened to choose the profession and career field you are in; why you particularly want to work for *their* organization; your strengths, weaknesses, skills, qualities, and career goals. HR wants to gain an understanding of your personality, character, values, work ethics, likability, communication effectiveness, potential for development, team orientation, motivation, reliability, trust-worthiness, drive, energy level, assertiveness, listening ability, attention span, and ability to deal with people at all levels and under all types of situations. It's all part of their 'weeding out' process to save the hiring department from wasting their time interviewing people who do not meet both the company's standards of employability and its specific needs.

Some questions may appear on the surface to be unrelated to the job you're applying for or the one you currently hold. How many times have you thought to yourself, "Now why did they ask me that?" To the interviewers, all questions asked are directly or indirectly job related.

HR can eliminate you from continuing on in the selection process but can't hire you. It's up to the hiring department to decide whether or not to hire you. HR is expected to spot behavior concerns and other problems the company would be greatly concerned with and want to avoid.

Hiring Department

If you receive the HR/personnel department's endorsement, you will then most likely be interviewed by the hiring department's supervisor to whom the position will report. The hiring department supervisor wants to know two things about you: (1) Are you the 'best qualified' of all the interviewees, and (2) Do I like you and could I and others be able to work closely with you.

Your interview with the hiring department may take place the same day as your interview with HR, or the following day—even a week or two later. The interview may last from 30 minutes to an hour. Occasionally, another supervisor or manager from their department will join the hiring supervisor and participate in the questioning and subsequent evaluation of the job candidates.

Supervisors interviewing job applicants for positions reporting to them are generally not as thoroughly trained in interviewing techniques as HR interviewers are. Nevertheless, you must approach them as competent interviewers. Don't lower your guard.

I'll describe only the basic structure of the interview here. You'll find much more in the coming chapters.

Panel/Board Interviews

Occasionally, someone from the hiring department who holds the same type of position you seek or is a group leader may join in the interviewing. Companies will also rotate their interviewers. A manager from another department within the company may participate in the interviewing to offer another perspective on how well the applicant will fit into the company.

Being interviewed by several people (panel or review board) creates a 'team atmosphere' similar to what you would find working with others at their company. How well will you score with this particular team? Ideally, learn to identify each panel member's face with a name and position title. If you are unsure that you can, don't. You don't want to botch up his or her name or job title. Just answer his or her questions as you would speaking to one interviewer. Having several interviewers present at the same time has more validity than one-on-one interviews because they must reach agreement as a team. They take turns asking questions but are free to interrupt at any time with a comment or another question. They can throw a work-related problem at you to see how well you would handle it. You can be interrupted in the middle of a statement you were making to see how you handle it. They want to uncover all the reasons why you are interested in this particular job opening. Their goal is to determine the extent of your technical expertise in your field and profession, your leadership potential, your ability to plan and follow through effectively, and your personality, attitude, behavior, character, and values. Display your spontaneousness and warmth; your willingness to help others in the department on a voluntary basis. (The team will discuss each member's observations and assessments of you.) Such a close-knit team can more thoroughly discuss all aspects of your presentation and responses to their questions, as well as their insights and opinions of you—before reaching a group consensus on whether or not you should be hired.

Panel/board interviews are more stressful than one-on-one interviews because you have to read and size up several personalities and approaches rather than one—within a very short period of time. Be yourself. Your presentation must go over well with each panel member. If you follow the approaches suggested throughout this book, you will be successful in building a positive image of yourself in their eyes.

The topics discussed by the hiring department interviewer will be similar to those covered by the interviewer in HR. However, they are more technically oriented—geared to the job opening. They may also focus on the depth of your job expertise in a variety of areas directly related to your current and past experience.

Interviews with Your Spouse

Some companies, in different parts of the world, will want to talk to your spouse as well. It's really a brief mini-interview. They want to observe what he or she looks like in terms of grooming, dress, and overall appearance to determine if he or she will reflect a positive image of his or her spouse (if hired) when at company gatherings, and when actively engaged in community activities—which would reflect, in turn, upon the company, directly or indirectly.

A spouse's 'dress' does not have to meet as high a company standard as that of the job candidate. However, the spouse's grooming, dress, and appearance must be in good taste, appropriate for the occasion, and fit in comfortably with the 'dress culture' of that company, the local area, and dress codes for that country and its culture. Spouses should dress 'moderately'—err on the conservative side—with colors chosen to compliment his or her skin color and tone. Wear well-fitted clothing. Hair length and style should fit in with their company standards for domestic/foreign based employees. Wear your wedding ring.

Spouses should be prepared to answer several questions, such as: How do you feel about your husband/wife wanting to take this job? Our company? Moving to our area/country, living conditions? Do you work outside the home? What type of work do you do? Do you plan to continue working after you relocate to our area? What concerns do you have? Is there anything you would like to ask us?

All of your spouse's responses should be strong and positive, and supportive of you. Discuss what she or he is prepared to say when asked such questions in order to be in sync with answers the other plans to give. Again, practice before 'show time.'

Just as you plan to do, your spouse should smile off and on, maintain good eye contact with the interviewers, and never get defensive.

You must realize that other countries do not have all the laws that we do to protect the individual rights of job applicants. A company operating in a country that doesn't have protective laws such as ours, can ask you anything they choose to, on any subject.

Group-on-Group Interviews

Some employers have been known to screen/interview several job candidates at the same time in order to observe how they handle the stress of direct competition. They want to see which candidates 'turn them off,' which 'turn them on.' Sometimes job applicants in a group interview are eliminated from future consideration at this point.

During such interviews, those interviewing may brief the group on their company. They may also ask each candidate to stand up and introduce himself or herself to the group, and describe their employment background and training within a timeframe of two to three minutes. Each candidate is asked at least one question, with an occasional follow-up inquiry. The session ends with a question-and-answer period.

This is one of the very few times you will directly compete with other job candidates; in the same room, at the same time. Keep your focus free of distractions. Be friendly with everyone and remain calm. Don't try to copy what another candidate says or allow yourself to be intimidated. Don't attack anyone. Focus on the interviewer, the questions you're being asked, and the best answers you can give. Honor the confidentiality of the situation—don't repeat what other candidates said.

Courtesy Interviews

There are times when a company will interview someone when they don't intend to hire that person, perhaps out of courtesy to a well-regarded employee, customer, or prominent person who asked that his or her friend or relative be interviewed. Either there isn't a job opening or if there is one, the person to be interviewed doesn't have the job qualifications required. The interviewer conducts a very brief and courteous interview. Don't act offended if this should happen to you. Thank the interviewer for taking the time to speak to you and providing the opportunity to meet him or her. If the interviewer is impressed with you, this brief interaction could lead to a full interview for a specific job that may become open later.

Career Selection

Find out what it's really like working in the profession/career field that interests you most by talking to people who are working in it. As such, you will be interviewing the people you meet and obtaining their insights and perspectives on what to expect should you enter this profession. Choose people at entry, intermediate, advanced, and supervisory job levels. Assure them that your discussions will be confidential.

Consider asking some of the following questions:

- What interested you in this particular profession?
- What appealed most?
- What research did you conduct?
- What sources were the most productive?
- How did you obtain your first position in this profession?
- What were the required qualifications, job responsibilities, and types of job assignments?
- How long were you in it?
- Why did you leave it?
- What was your next position?
- How would you describe it and the department?
- What did you like most and least? Why?
- What was it like working with your boss, peers, and co-workers?
- What is your current position?
- How did you obtain it?

- What are your main job responsibilities, and typical job assignments?
- What knowledge, skills, and abilities do you utilize?
- How would you describe the job family/organization make-up?
- How would you describe your typical day?
- What types of problems, obstacles, and challenges do you face?
- Do you lead or directly supervise others?
- How do you motivate them?
- What is the typical job progression in both time and salary?
- What type of individual would be most suited for your profession?
- If you had to do it over again, what would you have done differently?
- Can you suggest others I should talk to who could also provide a picture of what it's like working in your profession?

Thank each person emphatically at the close of your conversation for taking time out of their busy schedule to help you in determining your future career direction. Send a thank you note the following day.

Job Leads

Whether you are seeking an entry level or advanced position, you want to obtain job leads from successful people in your profession/career field, or someone very familiar with it; in other cases, someone who has lots of contacts with people who could be of help. Since nearly half of all job openings and newly created positions are not advertised, you can significantly increase your chances of landing a highly-desirable job in your profession by using this approach.

You want to identify these people through your contacts with career centers, past college professors, alumni, associations and clubs in your profession, job search firms, prior bosses and peers, friends who are in your career field, networking, gaining pertinent information on internet websites, and business directories recommended by your local reference librarians.

You should also seek companies with excellent reputations who either employ people in your profession or know of others who do. Find out the job title, name, and phone number of someone in HR, PR, or the line department who would most likely be 'in the know' as to who might be currently recruiting or planning to hire someone with your job qualifications in the near future. One referral will lead to another, which in turn can result in a job interview and job offer.

Phone or drop by the person's office, introduce yourself, and tactfully ask for five minutes of their time to gain the benefit of their advice in helping you to advance your career. If you win 'em over—using all the approaches and techniques of selling yourself that we've discussed—and he or she likes you, it's quite likely the conversation will last fifteen to thirty minutes. When a person feels that your are sincere and truly value their help, that person will extend themselves to help you. Your goal is to end up with a job lead—directly or indirectly leading to a job interview.

You must make this person feel very comfortable with you from the moment he or she meets you. Offer to answer any questions they might have about who you are, your background, how and why you chose to speak to them. Be honest, straight forward, and sincere. In today's world of 'spin experts', people crave authenticity.

Among the questions you might want to ask are:

- Do you know of any company/organization which is currently recruiting people in my profession or might be planning to in the near future?
- Who do you suggest that I contact?
- Can I use your name as my source of referral?
- Are there any companies opening new facilities in the area?
- What is the present status of hiring around town from your perspective?

Should your contact have additional time to spend with you, ask him or her about their professional background. You can also offer information on your background, along with your key career goals.

Interviewer Objectives

The interviewers want to learn as much about you as they possibly can in the time allotted, so help them in every way you can. Will your answers reflect the knowledge expected of you, considering your particular background and qualifications? Will you impress them by going beyond that? Their questions and the way in which they are asked can place you under a great deal of stress. Will you be able to remain relaxed, or will you become uptight? Will you display a high degree of maturity, calmness, and composure throughout the interview?

Interviewers want to gain an insight into how you plan, prioritize, communicate, make decisions, solve problems, and organize what you're doing. How thoroughly did you prepare for your interview with them? What's your general attitude? How well do you sell yourself? How in depth are your thoughts, ideas, and opinions? How much research have you done on their company? Do they detect quality in your answers, as well as an impressive choice of content? Do you have any fresh concepts and perceptions? They want to take a close look at you as a whole person—not just your job knowledge and expertise. They will record their key impression of each person they interview in a written summary.

When you are interviewed several times by different interviewers and asked the same question, be consistent in your answers. Interviewers will check with one another. Also, don't try to 'pin down' an interviewer if he or she was (in your opinion) being evasive or did not fully cover a point that was made. You may win the battle but will certainly lose the war.

Hiring department supervisors, as well as HR interviewers, have very busy schedules and don't have time to answer *numerous* questions by job applicants during interviews and post-interview followups. Too many questions could turn them off. They may think you're a pain to deal with and the type who, if hired, will want extra attention and be too aggressive in dealing with others.

Directive Interviewing Approaches

Some interviewers like to *lead* you directly in the conversation, asking you specific questions about all areas of your qualifications. They want detailed, direct responses. For example, they may ask, "Exactly why did you leave your last job?" or "How long do you plan to stay with us if hired?" It's their way of pinning you down on information they wish to uncover and to also clear up any concerns they may have about you.

Non-Directive Interviewing Approaches

There are interviewers who like to see how *you* think, approach, and analyze each area of your background and job qualifications—without being led by the hand. There is little guidance given in what you should say and how you wish to approach the subject. For example, they may ask, "What are your thoughts about your job history?" or "Where do you want to go from here in your career?" You can start and end your comments whenever and wherever you choose. You might wish to tell an interesting story or two to bring out favorable points about yourself.

Patterned/Structured Interviewing Approaches

Many interviewers like to ask the *same* questions of all job applicants. They feel that this structured/patterned approach is fairer to all candidates, consistent, and increases the validity of their interviewing techniques. You may be asked for 'specifics' or 'freelance' responses, such as, "Why and how did you choose the career field you're in?" or "How would you resolve this problem which could occur in the job we have open?" The interviewer, through past experience is aware of the most effective solutions devised. He or she measures how close you came to the ideal solutions and scores you accordingly in their notes.

Medical Department

At this point or later in the screening process (if you are still on 'go' for continued assessment), you will receive a medical examination. The higher the position level, the more extensive the examination. Large companies have their own medical staff; smaller companies use private physicians/medical staff to conduct their pre-employment examinations. The physician is concerned with any existing or highly potential physical, mental, or emotional conditions that could significantly impair your ability to perform all the job tasks and assignments of the position for which you are being considered.

The examination may include height and weight measurements; urinalysis; tests for glaucoma, diabetes, or hypertension; assessment of your blood pressure, eyesight (testing for color blindness), hearing, blood, and heart (EKG), and x-rays (chest, abdomen, back). Bring along whatever documents you have that relate to any current or past significant medical condition.

The physician will have the opportunity to get to know you and form an assessment of your overall health. Think of this person as another interviewer. What you say during your discussions is 'on the record.' In most cases, the exam will not follow the pattern of your previous interviews since it is not firmly structured or programmed to cover a wide range of topics and questions. Nevertheless, it is an interview and carries a certain amount of weight in the assessment process. Be tactful in responding to questions; you are still being critiqued.

Throughout your medical examination and conversations with the physician and medical staff, show that you are an alert, professional person, can handle stress well, care about your appearance and personal hygiene, and are proud of your accomplishments and what you intend to achieve if given the opportunity to work for the company.

The company's physician is expected to provide valuable insight into the current health of each job applicant examined, and whether or not the applicant meets the minimum health requirements for the position sought. You may pass the medical examination but be borderline on some of the test results. You may be predisposed to a serious health condition. Considering this, when asked for your family medical history, you should not *volunteer* significant negative information (such as cancer, heart problems, diabetes, or hypertension) in the health history of your parents, grandparents, brothers, sisters, aunts, and uncles. If asked directly on a medical questionnaire, however, be truthful. Similarly, don't raise the issue of your poor eating and sleeping habits or drinking or smoking to excess. Don't volunteer the fact that you were adopted; an unknown family health history can pose a possible future health risk.

With the advent of the Americans with Disabilities Act (ADA), employers have become more cautious in their medical assessments. The burden of proof for rejections for medical reasons is placed on the employer, not the job candidate. Employers must be prepared to prove, if confronted legally, that the person rejected for medical reasons would not be able to perform all the tasks and responsibilities required of him or her as defined by the company's job description for the job opening. In most cases, you have to pass a medical examination before being made a job offer. You must do so before going on the company's payroll and starting to work.

Background Investigation

Most larger companies conduct an extensive background investigation to verify such things as your education accomplishments, degrees, diplomas, certificates, grades, training, employment history (including exact dates of employment), positions held, your job responsibilities, and your overall performance. Under the Freedom of Information Act, state labor codes (covering inspection of personnel files by employees), and other disclosure laws, you can obtain a great deal of information from government organizations and from your present and previous employers. For example, you can check out your credit record, available law enforcement data, and military information. Employers will also check with the National Driver Register and various law enforcement agencies.

You should be prepared to tell the interviewer who they can check with to verify what you have told them with reference to your prior job experience (names, company and e-mail addresses, business phone numbers of your last three immediate supervisors, and so on). Let them also know, if possible, who they should directly contact to verify your college degree and other educational/training accomplishments.

Employers must be able to obtain positive reinforcement and verification of your technical job qualifications and the level of your performance in each job held. If they can't contact key people to verify information that you've provided, you are not likely to get hired. Mix-ups in names and other data have happened and can be costly. Providing the correct information can speed up your background investigation and expedite your chances of being hired.

Some employers may continue to gather verification information during your training and probationary/trial period in order to complete every aspect of their background investigation. Should there be any significant discrepancies or undisclosed, negative information, the employer has the right to terminate you before you complete your probation.

Companies have used both inside and outside investigative agencies to conduct background checks on job candidates. [Some job applicants have had themselves checked out by an investigative agency to see if there are any surprises or misinformation presented.] You are asked to sign information release forms in which you authorize and approve the release of information about you to the inquiring employer. Try to smooth things out with former employers (where there was some friction) before the background check begins.

Keep in mind that most employers are primarily for-profit organizations and as such are highly concerned with their return on investment. For every dollar they spend on recruitment, salaries, benefits, and training, there must be more than a dollar earned through the employee's contribution on the job.

■ ■ ■

Don't confuse 'recognizing a problem exists'
with having solved it.

■ ■ ■

7

UNDERSTANDING WHAT INTERVIEWS ARE ALL ABOUT

We all would like simple answers to our questions about landing a new job. There are very few times that this happens. Life and work are very complex, with many shades and perspectives. It's like looking at the same multi-dimensional objects from five different views. Interviewers and job applicants have different views from their own perspectives. Getting hired isn't a simple problem to solve with simple solutions; otherwise, everyone could obtain a new job easily. It's like figuring out and putting together a puzzle: you study the 'picture' it will make on the box cover, then study the individual cut pieces, and determine which pieces match. Put them all together and you have the picture [job] you want.

The interviewing and assessment process is complex and comprehensive. A great deal happens—some of it visible and apparent to you, much of it invisible and mysterious. You are asked questions and give answers, but you don't know for certain what the interviewers are thinking as they listen to your responses. You're really not certain whether you are scoring or losing points.

The interviewer controls the interview—both the pace and what will be discussed. Be aware that some interviewers will lead you in a direction that can cause you to say something derogatory about one of the companies you worked for—either the job you held, a boss, co-worker, or customer. Don't go there.

The interview itself should be an open, enjoyable, friendly, productive conversation between two or more people—not an interrogation or debate. Interviewers and job applicants have both been known, at times, to be guilty of interrogating one another. Interviewers will ask negative types of questions to determine how well you handle pressure. Stay calm, gather your thoughts, and turn your response into an opportunity to say something positive, such as "Actually, it turned into a good thing that happened to me. Let me tell you about it, if I may."

Fundamental Misunderstanding

Many people have said to me, "I'm as qualified as the ones they just hired—why didn't they hire me? Why did they like the others better? I didn't screw up my answers; I didn't lie. I have the education, training, and job experience they require, so what's the problem?" These questions reflect a fundamental misunderstanding of what interviews are all about. All the job applicants who get called in for an interview meet the employer's job prerequisites—but only a very few get hired. Why is this? The answer to that question is the essence of this book.

Going Beyond Basic Qualifications

Employers call you in for an interview to learn much more about you than the information contained in your resume and employment application. Interviewers want to see what you look like, hear you talk, and learn how well you communicate with other people that want to get a feel for your personality, judgment calls, decision-making, character, and values. They want to know how well these fit in with their culture, atmosphere, and style. Your conduct during your interview gives them an indicator of your likely behavior on the job. They also want to know how much you know about their organization.

Job candidates who didn't make the cut often tell me: "I understood each question they asked and gave some good answers. How can they turn me down if I didn't say anything wrong?" The answer is simple: This candidate didn't come up with enough 'right' things to say. Most job applicants come up with *some* good answers. But the top 20 to 30 percent who get hired make *more* good points, and cover *more* important major areas, than those who aren't hired. They offer *fresh* observations, and they present them in a compelling way.

Your interviewers will be assessing you for factors they consider important in predicting success on the job. You must impress them with some skills (interviewing, for one) that may be relatively new for you. The interview is your chance to let them know all the good things about you that they're hoping you possess. If you don't open up, interviewers will choose someone else—a forthcoming candidate who they do come to know and understand, and who impresses them. It's difficult for an interviewer to turn down someone that he or she especially 'likes' who is well qualified for the job.

Those They Don't Hire

Those not hired are, in general, overconfident about how well they'll perform in their interviews. They believe they are relatively likeable; their resume and employment application reflect good technical job expertise. But they don't prepare for their interviews as well as they've worked on building their job qualification. They figure they have a good insight into what questions will be asked and won't have any problem coming up with reasonable answers.

When they get to the interview, they're only adequate. They offer the first responses that come to mind, and leave it at that. They're asked questions they didn't anticipate, and must come up with answers 'on the fly.'

Interviewers expect to hear answers that are honest, well thought out, and tactfully presented. Without these ingredients, your chances of getting hired are slim.

If you're ill-prepared and your answers are brief, the interview will certainly go more quickly. You may think (especially if you're feeling nervous and unsure) that a short interview is better all around: easier for you, and easier for the interviewer. This is not so! A short interview offers you fewer opportunities to score points—and fewer second chances to recover from any sketchy or unimpressive answers you give at the outset.

Your Image

Of all the factors important to interviewers, one of the most important is your image; that is, the way others perceive you, especially in initial encounters. This factor can be critical in a close race with another candidate. How's *your* image? How professional do you appear to people who meet you for the first time? Interviewers often reflect on that very *first* impression.

You can do ten things 'right' in your interview and one thing 'wrong' that's significant to the interviewer, and he or she will remember the latter a lot longer than the former. It could cost you the job. Stick to your game plan to prevent making such a mistake. Don't become overly spontaneous.

Focus on getting the interviewer to 'learn more about you' rather than learning more about the interviewer! Both are important but knowing who you are must take priority.

Communication Skills

Your communication skills are also of vital importance. How well do you impress the interviewer with your speech in the interview, as well as the written materials you provide (resume, cover letter, employment application, and so on)? Do you express yourself clearly and concisely, or are you often misunderstood? Do people enjoy conversing with you? The chapter "Your Voice and Delivery" addresses this topic specifically.

Body Language

Many research studies have found that our body language can make a stronger impression than our spoken words. Interviews are no exception. Watch one of the old silent films to observe how effectively people can communicate their thoughts and feelings through body movements and facial expressions. Body language wins over word statements if there is any doubt as to which to believe. Chapter 33 offers tips for making a positive impression in this area.

Career Field Commitment

While it's true that the interviewers can learn a great deal about you from your employment package, in the interview they will focus on how you present this information and respond to further questions regarding your job and career interests. In particular, when asking questions about your job experience, they are seeking something difficult to measure but vitally important: your love of what you do and the degree to which you are committed to advancing in your career field.

Are you beginning to get the idea? You're not just being scored on delivering the right answers—you're showing the interviewer who you are and how you think, feel, and respond. He or she will draw far-reaching conclusions from your ability to provide thoughtful, impressive answers to his or her questions. For example, if you appear to catch on quickly to what is being discussed, the interviewer may conclude that you'll be able to successfully comprehend and complete their on-the-job training programs without any difficulties.

Factors Weighed

Your performance in the interview will earn you a total score that will be ranked with the total scores of each competing job applicant. Your actions, comments, and answers will, to a great extent, determine the score you receive on numerous factors [discussed earlier], such as:

- Extent of interest in the position applied for and their company
- Degree of competence in current position held
- Potential for further advancement
- Overall attitude
- Level of maturity
- Likability
- Initiative and self-motivation
- Reasoning and analytical ability
- Openness to change and to conflicting opinions
- Ability to work effectively with all types and levels of people
- Ability to handle stress and pressure
- Cost and profit consciousness
- Customer orientation
- Loyalty to employers
- Long-term career goals

You're scored on each area of assessment, on a scale of one to five or one to ten—the higher the number, the higher the score. Each area will have a certain *weighted value,* which varies from company to company. Some organizations establish a formal ranking system; others subjectively evaluate and select.

If you view the interview as a test, you're right—but it's not a test of the true/false, right/wrong, multiple-choice type that can be tallied up to a specific percentage. It's not a simple matter of giving either 'right' or 'wrong' answers. While interviewers strive to be as objective as possible, each interviewer will assess you subjectively according to his or her own sensibilities and interviewing experience—rating each of your answers and the overall impression you make as outstanding, excellent, good, average, fair, or poor. To be among the top 20 to 30 percent who get hired, you must score many 'good, excellent, and outstanding' points.

In order to score high in each area, you must bring out experiences and accomplishments which gain the most points; especially those most important to employers.

What Can Hurt You

What you don't say *can* hurt you—if you were expected to say it. When you leave out important points, as far as the interviewer is concerned, you either didn't think those points were important enough to mention, or you didn't have the insight to recognize their importance and relevance to the question asked. The interviewer may conclude that you easily forget things when you're under any kind of stress (not just the stress of an interview).

You only get credit for what's in your head when it comes out of your mouth. Interviewers often think to themselves *Let's see what this candidate knows that's important to us.* If the candidate doesn't offer that in his or her answers, interviewers assume *It just isn't there to begin with...this person can't be too sharp.*

Interviews are Vocal Essay Tests

Think of the interview as a 'vocal essay test.' Just as in a written essay test, your answers reveal not just what you know, but your ability to *select and present* your knowledge. The more pertinent points you can make, the more you'll impress your evaluator. Too many job candidates think of a few impressive points, give those points, and leave it at that. They think, "If I came up with some that are okay, I pass." Wrong! You should present *all* the significant points you can muster. Cover every important major area with fresh, clear, concise answers.

An interview is not a speed test. Interviewers are more interested in the content and quality of your answers than how quickly you answer their questions. They want to hear your most significant, meaningful responses to open-ended questions. They will not be impressed if you seem to be striving to see how fast you can 'get them off your back.' Candidates with very little to say end up with a short interview—and in most cases, a rejection.

Candidates who are hired *stand out* in many ways. They cover more in the same period of time, and what they say has a positive impact—it sticks in the minds of their interviewers. They also come across as 'good company'—someone who would be enjoyable to work with, day in and day out. They know when to be serious and when to laugh and smile. They speak warmly about people they've worked with and experiences they've been through. They maintain good eye contact are relaxed and open. Their body language reflects this throughout the interview. They are the spark plugs of a smooth running, efficient engine: their department.

In a way, interviewing is like flying an airplane: your flight training prepared you to fly an airplane efficiently; your knowledge, training, and experience in interviewing prepared you to conduct yourself productively in an interview. How well you actually fly the aircraft, and how well you present yourself in an interview, are both measured by an evaluator. In either case, you may be well-qualified, but that in itself doesn't mean you can perform well.

Top Performers

Top performers do more than is expected of them on the job. Highly motivated job candidates do the same in preparing for their job interviews. They do more than just meet minimum expectations. 'Good' is not good enough: 'excellent' and 'outstanding' candidates get the job offers.

The better you understand the interviewing game, the better you can prepare to play it well. Practice builds expertise, which in turn instills a feeling of assurance that you will succeed. You must to go into your interviews with strong self-confidence gained from preparing a realistic game plan. The following chapters will help you do just that.

■ ■ ■

Your critics are really your friends—
they point out ways you can improve.

■ ■ ■

8

YOU MUST SELL YOURSELF

You have spent years—and perhaps thousands of dollars—building your qualifications in order to advance in your chosen career field. *You are your product.* You've designed and built it and packaged it in your resume and employment application. Now comes the time to sell yourself in your job interviews as a top-quality product. View interviewers as skeptical buyers who have to be really sold on why they should buy the product you are representing. Don't be intimidated by your competition. Try to be 'salesperson of the year' among the job candidates also competing for the job you want. Your 'advertising and sales pitch' are the best. Convince interviewers that it's the type of work you enjoy doing and are really good at it, saying "I strongly believe I can deliver the kind of successful job performance you expect throughout my career with you."

In answering each question, you must bring out all the points that make your product desirable. Showcase everything that your product (your total qualifications) has in its favor while de-emphasizing or leaving out anything less desirable.

You have a right and an obligation to yourself to present the things you have worked so hard to accomplish. You earned them—now it's time to cash in. Sell yourself as a whole person, both on and off the job—these affect each other, and both can enhance the company's image.

Our society tends to discourage 'tooting one's horn,' so when the situation finally calls for it, most of us need some encouragement and coaching. Ask your spouse and closest friends to describe how you are when you are at your best. Use that positive image as your role model in presenting yourself in your interview. Ask those closest to you to help you list your job-related strengths, skills, and accomplishments. Work these into your answers, directly and indirectly, during your interviews. Make certain that all of your most important traits come out before the interview is over. Point out how they coincide with what the company is seeking. Let interviewers know that your work style blends in well with their standards and culture; you are flexible to the ways they operate.

You should strike a balance in presenting your technical job knowledge and your people skills. They are equally important. If anything, interviewers will place more emphasis on your personality, character, emotional makeup, leadership, and people skills than on your technical capabilities—when the job you are applying for requires them.

You can describe your accomplishments without sounding boastful; it's all in the *way you say it*. Put yourself in the interviewer's place, hearing either "Bet you haven't talked to too many candidates with a 3.4 GPA, have you?" or "Although I worked 25 hours a week and was heavily involved with sports, I managed to earn a 3.4 grade point average." Relate your achievements as though you are a reporter relating an important news story. Give the facts without commentary. You're simply stating the truth.

Don't memorize what you plan to say in selling yourself. Most of us aren't excellent actors and actresses who can deliver a prepared script 'word for word' in a spontaneous manner. We would sound more like someone who has memorized words we were told to use. When you *know* the key thoughts and points you want to make, the words will come to you. You will sound 'real' (not rehearsed), spontaneous, credible, and sincere. When people unaccustomed to memorizing what they are about to say try delivering a memorized 'speech' and forget a word, phrase, or line, it throws them off and they fail to impress their listeners. Don't let that happen to you in a job interview.

People judge others by *what* they say. If they say a lot of impressive things in a believable manner, we're impressed. If they only say a few impressive things, we're not quite as impressed. If they say very little and nothing noteworthy, we're not impressed at all.

Even if you don't have a personality that makes people like you, or can't dramatically change to become more appealing, you can improve little by little by simply practicing smiling and laughing more often. Let yourself get more enthusiastic and excited about the things you're doing in your interactions with the people you work with, family members, and friends. After a while, you actually become that way and take on a more impressive air. In turn, you can apply this positive modification to your job interviews. It's not much different from continuously switching roles in your life—from parent to spouse, friend to neighbor, teacher to student, subordinate to boss, leader to follower. During a job interview, you switch to the role of 'salesperson' for an extremely important product... 'You.'

If you aren't willing to sell yourself in your interview, why should your close friends (who may be employed with the company you want to work for) go out of their way to sell you to the hiring manager? Why should the interviewer work hard to convince people 'up the line' that you should be hired? Most people will go the limit to help you even when you're not doing well as long as they know you are doing everything you possibly can to help yourself...in this case, to sell yourself in every way you can.

When you demonstrate your ability to sell yourself in an interview, there's a bonus: interviewers recognize this as a skill you can apply on the job—'selling' potential customers on the benefits of choosing their company's products and/or services. You would most likely be successful in convincing internal customers (other employees) that you can deliver 'top quality' user satisfaction when working with you.

"I believe in family involvement."

9

INTERVIEWING FOR A 'PROMOTIONAL' JOB OPPORTUNITY

Competing with Others 'Inside/Outside' the Company

You cannot assume that just because you're working within the hiring department, you have an inside track on landing the job that represents a promotion for you. It's still an open field for other employees within and outside the company. View the interview as though it were for a better job, with a better company. Don't take anything for granted. Put in as much time and effort for it as you would for 'The best job I could ever hope to get.' Decide on what you're going to say and how you're going to say it.

You don't have to spend much time convincing the hiring supervisor (who could happen to be your current boss) how much you know about the company, its products and services. He or she expects you to already be fully aware of these. You do, however, need to focus on how much you want this job, how well qualified you are for it, your past successes and accomplishments, and your ability to perform all the new job responsibilities and assignments to the hiring supervisor's complete satisfaction.

Since the hiring supervisor will most likely have full access to your HR employee personnel file, he or she will become aware of many of your attributes and job qualifications—through reviewing your educational background, training received, positions held, periodic performance appraisals, salary progression, awards received, and other evidence of your accomplishments.

Also, apply the same networking techniques that got you most of your past job interviews. This time, apply them to people around the company with whom you have a good working relationship, who are well-liked and respected, and are willing to endorse you to the hiring department supervisor.

Presenting Your Best Selling Points

During your interview preparation, think of everything you've accomplished that you consider noteworthy in every job you've ever held. Then, pick out those that are the most impressive. Integrate them into your 'sales pitch:'

- Took the initiative to speak with the person who is currently in the position, in order to get a bird's eye view of what the job involves, the job responsibilities and typical job assignments. Wanted to find out the job requisites and skills needed, whom he or she most closely interacts with, job procedures and practices, trouble spots to avoid, and so forth.
- Spoke with several other employees in your department who seem to have a good understanding of the department's strengths, capabilities, limitations, mission, plans for the future, goals, and objectives—to get a feel from their perspective. Am primarily interested though in how *you* view these.
- Put in considerable time anticipating questions you might wish to ask me and how best to address them, honestly and openly.
- Have had the chance from time to time to work directly with a few of your employees and was impressed with their friendliness, job knowledge, skills, and attitude. Got along great with them! (It would be wise to particularly point out those who were group leaders or supervisors under him or her.)
- On a few occasions, have had the opportunity to interact with you. Found you to be very competent in your position, cooperative, and personable. You also appeared to me to be realistic, understanding, tolerant, fair, and considerate. I'm not trying to 'butter you up.' I'm being sincere when I say that feedback I've gotten on you from highly respected people throughout the company supports my observations. I wouldn't be applying for this position if I felt otherwise.
- Have developed strong 'people skills' which have enabled me to work well with other employees in a variety of positions and job levels—many of whom have personalities, styles of operating, approaches and opinions which differ from mine. We interacted closely as a 'team.' (Cite examples, key players, and 'results achieved' in terms of increased department efficiency, cost-savings, innovative ideas, and increased morale.)

- Worked well with each of my supervisors and consistently built a strong working bond. I understood their job/productivity expectations and work standards. (Point out how you believe you could also build such a close bond with him or her.)
- Helped my current supervisor resolve a recent serious problem facing our department. Also helped in preventing one from occurring. (Provide details.)
- Make every effort when approaching a new job to understand the job demands, restraints, stresses and pressures. Welcome the opportunity to prove I can handle them all very well.
- Am proud of the reputation I have earned in my department of being an astute problem-solver and decision maker. (State one or two on-the-job technical and people situational examples which demonstrate your skills in this area.)
- Volunteer to take any new job assignments and projects which go beyond the scope of my job description. (Provide a recent example.)
- Have come up with new ideas which were implemented and saved the company thousands of dollars (specify the amount); improved a daily job procedure that shortened, and in some cases, even eliminated several steps.
- Place emphasis upon quality, reliability, working within time frames, follow up, and end results in everything I do.
- Establish criteria and milestones by which the progress made on every job assignment and project I'm given can be measured. (Cite examples.)
- Place great importance on flexibility and acceptability—thinking of ways to better satisfy the needs of the department, company, and customer.
- Believe in helping those around me when they could use some support in resolving a problem they're facing. Someone they can 'bounce things off of' and confide in. (Cite an example.)
- Am not a 'clock watcher.'
- Believe in being loyal to and supportive of my boss. Should I disagree with him or her on some matter, would tactfully make my case. Would never be disloyal because he or she didn't concur with me. Every supervisor needs the full support of their subordinates in order to accomplish his or her job goals and objectives.
- View this new job opportunity as the next step to fulfilling my

long-term career goals. (Point out the approach you would take if you were selected to fill the position, in performing all the new job responsibilities and assignments; the techniques you would use in handling 'tough assignments;' the kinds of short-range, intermediate, and long-range job goals you would set for yourself, in harmony with those of your boss.)

• Would like to point out the major advantages I have over my competitors for the job opening. (Provide several in a non-boastful manner.)

Should the sought-after position be a 'supervisory' one, stress your ideas on how to best motivate, manage, assess, and counsel subordinates in order to achieve the highest level of employee productivity, while still maintaining high morale.

Concluding the Interview

Before leaving, tell the hiring supervisor that now that you've gotten to know both him or her and the job better, you're more excited than ever about the job and the thought of working for them. Welcome being 'checked out' around the company and offer to return and answer any additional questions he or she may wish to ask you. Conclude with thanking them again for the opportunity to be interviewed and to express your thoughts. Give your biggest smile, shake hands firmly, and say, "I hope I'll get the opportunity to work for you."

■ ■ ■

Ask yourself each morning
"What can I do today to help someone?"

■ ■ ■

10

INTELLIGENCE, EMOTION, AND INTUITION

This could be the most important chapter in the book. When it comes to successful job interview preparation and performance, making the most of your intelligence, emotional maturity, and intuition can be as important as—if not more important than—your job experience, training and education. Your understanding and use of these assets can tip the balance in your favor when the interviewers decide whom they will hire.

Defining Intelligence

What exactly is intelligence? Answers vary. Some say it is what a person knows, measurable by written tests. Others say it is the ability to grasp new knowledge and information. Some think it reflects the level of achievement a person has reached in many different areas of life.

If intelligence could be ultimately defined and accurately measured, we could predict how everyone would perform if challenged to achieve a particular goal. Those who are considered highly intelligent ought to excel in everything they attempt, shouldn't they? Well, it just doesn't work that way.

You probably know a highly intelligent person who longs to master a musical instrument yet, despite many lessons and diligent practice, can never progress beyond a beginner's skill. Others who appear less intelligent quickly learn to play an instrument 'by ear,' without lessons and with little practice.

So let's come up with a more practical definition of intelligence, one that most people can relate to. I propose that intelligence is the ability to "successfully apply" what you know—in any situation—on or off the job.

This ability to 'successfully apply' can relate to every aspect of building your job qualifications (and, of course, every aspect of your personal life as well). Certainly you can use it in preparing good answers in preparation for your interview.

Some people gain more knowledge than others but *apply it less successfully.* How well can you apply what you know to impressively present yourself in a job interview? You don't have to know more than the other candidates competing with you to succeed in being hired. All you have to do is effectively apply 90 to 100 percent of the knowledge you already have to preparing for the interview. Present every positive aspect of yourself during the interview and answer every question to the very best of your ability. Each interviewer will decide just how well you are accomplishing this by the answers you give. Do you seem to absorb the significance of the question quickly and come up with an impressive answer, despite the limited knowledge you have in that area?

The Role Emotion Plays

Many scholars and psychologists believe that in addition to measuring mental intelligence, we should also measure a person's emotional maturity, otherwise known as emotional quotient, or EQ. You can observe the role it plays in many areas of importance in the workplace:

- Perception of and reaction to surrounding situations and events
- Emotional stability and resiliency
- Ability to successfully cope with or prevent different levels of stress
- Compassion and concern for others
- Ability to control impulses, moods, and feelings
- Patience with progress being made
- Perseverance in pursuing goals and objectives
- Persistence in follow-up until success is achieved
- Determination to succeed despite great obstacles

Many job candidates find it difficult to convince HR and hiring department interviewers that their level of emotional maturity is parallel to their level of mental comprehension and application. IQ, it seems, is easier to sell than EQ. Although you can't do too much beyond a certain age to noticeably raise your IQ, you can raise your EQ. Employers want to hire a job candidate with emotional control, and someone who has developed and strengthened the traits just mentioned. In the work force, emotional maturity is a tremendous asset in relations with supervisors, peers, and customers. It's something that impacts every aspect of your life, both in and outside your job world.

It is impossible to have 100% control over your emotions—sometimes, chemistry takes its own course. However, you can slow down the process by not immediately reacting verbally. Time, as it is in so many other situations, is your friend. It can soften most 'emotional blows' thrown your way.

For example, when you're under stress at work and your boss or co-worker makes a critical comment directed to you, it can help tremendously to simply wait five seconds before reacting. This brief pause can cool you off and prevent a breakdown in your relationship with that person.

Your Brain and Mind at Work

Your brain and your mind together create your intelligence. They are inseparable and interdependent.

Your brain stores your every thought, idea, experience, emotion, feeling, insight, value, and belief. It's been doing this throughout your entire life. It's all there. Some of these fade over time but are never completely lost unless there is damage to the brain.

This accumulation forms what is considered to be 'your mind,' your unique personality, character, value system, insights, perceptions, talents, knowledge, ideas, opinions, actions, style, attitude, emotions, and reactions to everything that is happening around you. It is *what* and *who* you are.

In preparing for your job interview, managing your mind is crucial. You must use all this great stuff your brain has stored to decide, in advance, the best approach to preparing yourself for your interview(s).

Interviewers can—and will—ask you to recall and explain certain experiences and actions. To do this successfully without preparation is very difficult and risky. You have only three or four seconds before beginning your answer—not enough time for even the nimblest mind to scan all the possibilities and pick out the most appropriate examples. You can't call 'Time out!' to access your information and compose the perfect answer. You need to take time *beforehand* to sort through, pick out 'the best,' and provide well-organized explanations.

The Power of Your Subconscious Mind

Let's examine an example of how the mind operates that we can all relate to. Let's say you try to remember something that happened quite a while ago. The harder you try, the more difficult it is to remember it. You finally give up and go back to doing other things. Then later, when you are more relaxed and refreshed, you think about it again and pow!—you remember it.

Here's how it works. Your mind consists of the conscious and the subconscious. The conscious portion represents all that you readily know, feel, and can recall quickly or within a reasonable period of time. It's like the surface crust of the earth. It enables you to live your life with other people, make decisions, take actions, resolve situations, and so on. You call upon it continuously to help you cope with every daily challenge you face. You could not function without it. It is through the conscious mind that you can remember things that you need to readily recall. It's the 'at-your-fingertips' portion of your knowledge and self-image—your conscious being. When you use your conscious mind, it's 'hands on' thinking.

The subconscious part of your mind stores what *used to be in the conscious part*—thoughts and feelings that once were strong and instantly accessible because they had recently happened. Now, in the subconscious, they are very faint, nearly forgotten, seemingly out of reach. Your subconscious is like the core of the earth.

However, you can and do recall many of those buried thoughts, feelings and experiences from time to time, by association with other things. For example:

• You smell food cooking that you haven't smelled in years. Suddenly, vivid memories of the times you smelled those foods in earlier years come flooding back to you.
• You meet someone who you knew years ago that you worked with but cannot recall his name, but he remembers yours. You begin thinking about the things you did in the job you held back then. One particular job assignment suddenly brings to mind the name of that person, and other things about him suddenly surface.
• A face, a voice or sound you haven't recalled in years will trigger experiences and feelings that you thought were long forgotten but have now returned. If you think back to your childhood and what

you did after school, *feelings* you had at the time start coming back to you as though they just happened. These associations are formed with both singular and recurrent events.

THE MIND

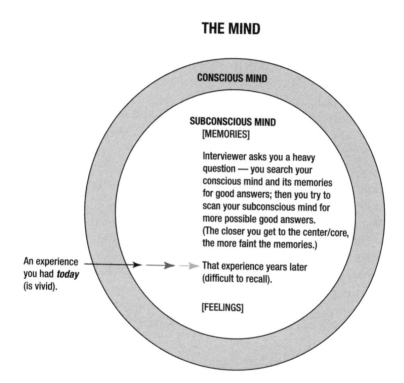

When you find and recall important experiences, thoughts, ideas, and feelings in the subconscious, they will *instantly* return to the conscious.

In preparing for a job interview, you must come up with the best points and examples you need in order to be very successful in answering each question. To do this, you often must rely on not only the conscious part of your mind, but the subconscious as well. If you don't, you'll be like the many job candidates who have told me the same frustrating story: On their way home from an interview they suddenly thought of something very important that they should have said—something they should have thought of while preparing for the interview, not on the way home from it.

When you understand the roles played by your conscious and subconscious minds, you gain two powerful tools. First, you can more readily tap into buried memories of long-ago experiences—ideally, as a purposeful exercise well before you are in the interview and being asked about them. Second, you can avoid setting off negative thought-feeling chain reactions, and learn how to create positive ones.

Thought-Feeling Chain Reactions

Your mind associates thoughts and feelings, which in turn can produce additional thoughts, accompanied by various different feelings, in a chain reaction. If you begin thinking that you could 'blow the interview' when you walk into the interviewer's office, thinking that can produce negative feelings which could cause you to actually blow the interview. This could significantly hamper the way you planned to handle yourself and present your responses to their questions. It can show up in your facial expressions, body language, and voice as you deliver your answers.

Sound like your worst fears come true? How can you not worry about blowing something as critical as a job interview? It is possible! You can control the thoughts that produce the feelings. The secret is to *recognize* negative thoughts as soon as they arise. Stop them dead in their tracks. *Focus on positive images!* These lead to positive thoughts and positive feelings follow. You look, act, and behave with greater self-assurance. You *are* more self-confident. *Control your thoughts and you'll control the emotions you experience in every area of your life.*

You can apply this approach throughout your interview. Whenever you begin thinking negatively about anything, take note, stop, and start thinking about something positive. In no time, positive feelings will begin to flow. If you catch yourself worrying, immediately bring your thoughts back to what you plan to do that will help you do well.

We all associate experiences with feelings; one impacts the other. If you are in an especially good mood when facing a particular situation, you are more likely to take a positive course of action such as trying something new or helping someone out. If you're in an especially bad mood, you're more likely to take a negative course of action such as withdrawing, declining to help, or discouraging others. Yet, if someone asked you why you made that choice, your first response would probably not be, "Because

I felt so good/so crummy." You would instead *rationalize,* coming up with some seemingly practical, logical reason. It's hard for us to recognize, let alone admit, how much our moods and feelings influence our actions. We come up with a justification which seems reasonable, not the actual reasons for our behavior. In many cases, we may not fully understand why we acted the way we did.

Associations are powerful. When you meet someone who strongly resembles a close friend or family member, you can't help but instantly feel good about this stranger, though you may not realize why. It works the other way, too. Have you ever taken an immediate dislike to a new acquaintance? Perhaps a friend asked you why, and you struggled to rationalize your response—or, if you felt you could confide in your friend, you admitted "I don't know why; I just don't like her." That's your *subconscious* calling the shots. It may or may not be right.

You'll find that really astute interviewers can spot the rationalizations which candidates offer to disguise their emotional responses. They won't be impressed with the first line of defense rationalizations offered by a candidate who didn't prepare.

Interviewers also bring their own thought-feeling associations to the table. Like all of us, they react to facts based upon their particular background and the feelings associated with everything they have experienced. One interviewer may feel turned off by a candidate's low college GPA. Perhaps when she was in college, she worked hard to make good grades, earning an impressive GPA while holding down a full-time job to pay for her education. Another interviewer whose GPA was just average, but who's done well in his career, may feel that grades aren't that important to success in job performance, and focuses on the candidate's other credentials.

You could encounter similar divergent reactions with interviewers weighing the relative worth of military experience versus civilian experience. One interviewer may have heavy military background; the other may come from the civilian world. As hard as they may try to be objective, their experiences and associated feelings will color their judgments.

Having trained and developed many interviewers, I feel strongly that any interviewer who can't overcome an obvious personal bias when interviewing a candidate should withdraw from the interview and let a replacement take over. Anyone making an important decision must take the time to weigh and gather the minimum information necessary to reach a valid decision. If the interviewer frequently fails to do this, he or she should not be an interviewer. Most interviewers work hard to keep their bias to a minimum. They understand their limitations, as well as their capabilities, and give job candidates a 'fair shake.'

In order to build good answers to heavy interview questions, you must go back to your earlier education, training, and work situations that may be buried in your subconscious. Remember, your mind is a super database of everything that has ever happened to you since birth (some psychologists say even while in the womb). You need to think back to your earliest career interests, the education and training your received, each position you held, the people you worked for and with, your job assignments, the companies you worked for, job successes and failures, people that were important to you, how you coped with stress and criticism, and so on. Then you will be prepared to bring out the most appropriate and impressive facts about yourself for discussion during a job interview. From the interviewer's viewpoint, if you don't tell him or her about it, it never happened.

Intuition

Let's talk about this intangible faculty that we call intuition. Merriam-Webster defines it as "the act or process of coming to direct knowledge or certainty without reasoning or inferring: immediate cognizance or conviction without rational thought: revelation by insight or innate knowledge." Quite a mouthful to think about.

Intuition is a reflection of your *subconscious* mind. When you confront a situation or problem, whether in your job or in your personal life, long-forgotten thoughts and feelings come to the conscious portion of your mind as instinctive inclinations or 'gut feelings.' It's an automatic, subliminal, spontaneous process—somewhat like driving an automobile. As you drive along, talking to a passenger seated next to you, or conversing with someone on your cell phone, listening to the radio, a CD or tape, your subconscious knowledge and experience of driving takes over. Seemingly without your conscious guidance, you check the speedometer, glance at the front and rear view mirror, and steer. You observe traffic ahead, behind, stop signs and stop lights, speed limits, street signs, buildings, children playing on the sidewalk who could run out into the street—all this without consciously thinking about it as you converse and drive. Your mind is on autopilot. (Of course, it's better to give conscious attention to your driving and stay alert to the unexpected, but it's easy to be lulled into that autopilot state.)

Some psychologists believe that most of our decisions are intuitive—based upon what our subconscious feeds to our conscious mind. The majority of all we've ever learned is stored in our subconscious mind.

What does intuition have to do with interviewing? Employers value it and look for evidence of it in each candidate. Astute employees can pick up on numerous things that are happening around them and avoid many obstacles that others fail to recognize. Many of your best answers will come from active use of your intuition. It involves tapping into the subconscious, pulling out everything there and depositing it into your conscious mind, weighing the value of each to be used in building an answer and making final selections.

Many candidates draw only from what they are presently aware of and don't dig into their subconscious in developing responses to the interviewer's questions. This severely limits the number and variety of significant points they can use as building blocks in creating impressive answers. Their answers are narrow in scope and score fewer points with the interviewers. Let's explore this area further.

Tapping into Your Subconscious

If you've ever done any relaxation or visualization exercises, you've already experienced an effective method for tapping into your subconscious. If you haven't tried this method, chances are you've read or heard about it. *Visualization* has been effectively used by athletes, business people, and artists to improve performance and achieve goals. With a little practice, it can work for you.

Visualization is best done at a time of day when your mind is freshest and clearest; at a time when you expect to have minimal distractions, such as when lying in bed at night or during the early morning hours…when it's darker and quieter.

Think about one of the tough interview questions that you anticipate—one that you are not certain how to approach. Close your eyes and breathe deeply, calming and relaxing your body and mind.

Now give this question your full attention. Block out everything else. If you are distracted by sounds, just note them and return to your question. Your goal is to do some creative thinking.

While focusing on the question you expect to be asked, let your mind wander freely, undirected. It will rapidly scan its enormous subconscious storage of past happenings that tie in with the question. Your subconscious mind speeds through these stored thoughts many times faster than your conscious mind. Memories will fly by. As they do, you can capture and recall many applicable situations that would fit in nicely with the question. While you are still in this semi-conscious state, jot down those that you want to remember immediately so that they won't slip away. However, don't focus so intently on these that you return to a fully conscious state of mind.

The memories and thoughts you obtain through this process can make your answers more complete, raise your score, and perhaps result in your being hired. They were there all the time; you just had to bring them to the conscious surface of your thoughts.

With practice you can develop this skill as a reliable tool. The key is to not press yourself but just let it happen.

You can also come up with significant ideas for good answers immediately after taking a fifteen-minute 'power nap.' This is best done in a reclining chair. If you lie down completely flat on a bed or sofa, you're more likely to fall deeply asleep and wake up groggy.

Good ideas for answering questions can come to you any time of the day, wherever you are, during various occasions, around anyone. Always carry a small pad and pen to jot them down. Too often something useful pops into our conscious mind and we say to ourselves, "I'll remember that and jot it down later." Within a few minutes, it's gone.

Make the effort to bring all the great stuff that's stored in your subconscious to the forefront of your mind. Yes, it takes patience, focus, and concentration, but so do most of the things in life that are worthwhile. Isn't an opportunity for landing a job that means so much to you worth the time and effort involved to master this technique?

■ ■ ■

Age is a great asset for learning—
if only it didn't kill the student.

■ ■ ■

11

MEASURING YOUR SITUATIONAL AWARENESS

Whenever an interviewer asks you a question, he/she is testing the breadth and depth of your situational awareness. In essence, you are being asked, "Of all the many things you've seen and experienced, what applies most to what I have just asked you? Which do you feel would be significant to tell me about?"

What is Situational Awareness?

Situational awareness is basically being aware of everything that is going on around you at all given times. It's extremely important in performing in your job assignments well. It can help you to be aware of everything that is occurring on the job which could impact (positively or negatively) the outcome of all your work efforts to perform your tasks at your best. It can help you to complete your tasks more quickly and avoid making mistakes. For instance, you may have overheard a conversation going on in the background between two co-workers. They may have discussed a problem that came up and how they resolved it. The problem may be similar to what you are now facing. By picking up consciously on what they were saying, it may have given you insight into how you could avoid such a problem.

To respond aptly to an interviewer's question, you need to tap into your situational awareness. This will allow you to uncover many more impressive points to present in your answer than you would have without using this approach. Your level of awareness of what is happening when performing job assignments becomes broader. You must remove your own self-imposed restrictions, limitations, and narrow interpretations of what you can include in your answers and 'get outside the box.'

How it Applies to Answering Questions

Let's say the interviewer asks you, "What's it like outside? I have been busy interviewing all morning." One job applicant might answer, "It's nice out." Another might reply, "It's great! Sunny, clear, and about seventy-five degrees with a slight breeze coming out of the west." Which of these answers reflects greater situational awareness? Which candidate do you think will score highest on this question?

Now apply your state of awareness to other open-ended questions: "Why do you think you were turned down?" and "Tell me about yourself" as well as "Why do you want to work for us?" And so on.

Interviewers don't want to hear about just one or two things—they would like to hear whatever you think is *important and relevant.* Some things are important to you but not to them—you must choose those that they will find meaningful. Put yourself in their place as much as possible. What do you think counts the most to that interviewer and that company?

Take, for example, a request that may be made to an applicant flying in for an interview. The interviewer asked, "Would you tell us about your trip?" Your answer can be an excellent measure of your situational awareness. Unspoken, but implied are more specific questions: "What did you observe that was important for us to know about? Did you take the initiative to interact with other passengers and cabin crew members? What did you observe, throughout the flight, that would be important to us?" The interviewer will assess, evaluate, and grade you on how many significant things you can recall and describe, from start to finish; for example, the type of aircraft you flew on, the approximate number of passengers on the flight, departure and arrival times, weather conditions, any stops en route, smoothness of takeoff and landing, overall comfort level, service provided, teamwork between the flight attendants, your speaking with crew members (even remembering their names), and previous times you've flown on that airline. You probably wouldn't want to use every one of these, but certainly you'd use many of them if you want to beat out your competition on this question.

When you leave out important observations, interviewers think that you have rather limited situational awareness and don't really pay too much attention to what is going on around you. They may think that you're in a hurry to come up with a quick response, or that you can't handle the stress and pressure of an interview and aren't able to think calmly and clearly. Situational awareness ties in closely with our discussion of the mind, emotion, intuition, and the subconscious.

The interviewer may pose a job-related problem situation in an area of work you're familiar with and ask you to resolve it. He or she will expect you to point out exactly how you approached the situation, what insights you had, how you planned to carry out each step, actions taken, your objectives, and how you were going to measure your 'progress' and 'end result.' In explaining everything you did and why you did it that way, you will point out how your situational awareness helped you each step of the way.

"Do you play 'drums'?"

12

PREPARING FOR THE INTERVIEW: AN OVERVIEW

More job candidates are either turned down or hired in the interview phase of the company's screening and selection process than in any other phase. That's why it is so important to heavily focus your time and effort on preparation for your interview. There is a greater differentiation between candidates in how appealing they are in the interview phase than in any other area of applicant assessment. Candidates are much more closely grouped together in the other areas than they are in their interview scores. *Those with the highest interview scores are most likely to be hired.*

Consider the range of interview performance assessment. In which of these categories would you like to be placed?

Poor: "I wouldn't want to work with that one."
Fair: "This one's probably okay."
Average: "Wouldn't be too bad to work with."
Good: "I'd enjoy working with this individual."
Excellent: "I'm quite impressed."
Outstanding: "Great—I would love to work with this person."

When you show up for your job interview, you should be able to say to yourself, "I'm well prepared and will do well." If you have done everything you possibly can to be ready for your interview, you will do well! Some questions that you prepared for may never come up in your interview, but you will go into the interview with greater self-confidence, knowing you gave it all you had. While other less-prepared candidates are scratching their heads, trying to think of something to say, you will be giving several good points with positive spins.

Put yourself in the interviewer's place. How would you react to a well-prepared candidate's answers to your questions? How impressed would you be, overall, in comparing her/him to other candidates you have interviewed? Wouldn't you be able to tell the difference?

Thoroughly preparing for your interview has a bonus effect: because it takes much more time and effort than the actual interview, you can be assured that the most time-consuming phase of the process is behind you.

The Preparation Strategy

Here are some important points to cover as you prepare for your interviews:

- Plan Ahead
- Prepare Your Own Answers
- Don't Memorize Your Answers
- Offer Them More than the Other Job Candidates
- Show You Sincerely Want the Job
- Present Your People Skills
- Highlight Your Decision-Making Skills
- Consider the Career Choices You've Made
- Prove You're More than Just Another Job Candidate
- Look to Your Future

Plan Ahead

Many job candidates wait too long to prepare answers to questions they expect to be asked. Begin as soon as you expect to be called in for an interview. When you actually receive an interview appointment, you should spend the remaining time fine-tuning your answers, not initiating their development. *It takes a great deal of time to do an outstanding job of preparing for each anticipated question.* There are so many other things to do—travel arrangements (if living a long distance away from the location of the interview), packing for the trip, arranging time off, buying appropriate clothes, putting together the paperwork you intend to bring, getting your haircut, and so on.

Answering an interviewer's questions during an interview is like delivering an important speech. You don't write the speech while you're delivering it; you do that long before then. Actually, answering questions and delivering the speech are finishing touches, not the initiation of this process.

You'll find an exhaustive list of possible questions you could be asked in chapter 14. There are far more than you can possibly prepare for individually, but you should review the entire list and note those which you believe are most likely to be asked—especially those which might be the most difficult for you to answer. Place a checkmark to the left of the most important ones. Focus on these and then work on the others as time allows. Clearly, you don't need to practice the 'yes' or 'no' answers; just be certain which answer you'll give.

Prepare 'Your Own' Answers

Interviewers have heard a lot of answers from a lot of job applicants over the years. Ask yourself: "Are there one or two more good points that I can bring up that others may not have covered which could make me 'stand out'? What else is out there that I'm missing?"

It's tempting to use 'sure-fire' answers provided by friends and interview briefings, but the answer that could be good for one applicant may not be good for another. Differences in education, training, job experience, and type and level of positions held require different approaches. A mistake made by a younger, less experienced candidate during an interview may be acceptable to an interviewer because of the candidate's limited job experience. The same mistake, if made very recently by a heavily experienced candidate, would be unacceptable. A less experienced job applicant might understandably have only three worthwhile points to make when asked a certain question; a heavily-experienced applicant might be expected to give five or more points. The very same good answer will score higher when a less experienced applicant gives it, than when a seasoned one gives it.

Being unique for its own sake is not the point. Some job candidates say that they have heard that answer given too many times. They say, "I'm going to tell it the way it really is and be different." It's true that the same point, worded exactly the same as many other candidates have presented it, is a canned answer and should be avoided. However, be careful. *Different isn't always better.* If those 'different' answers are obviously better, (using an equally good, fresh approach) then by all means use them. You can word them differently and sound quite spontaneous. Unfortunately, there are only so many of these terrific insights to be had. Choose wisely. You don't want to give a unique answer that is considered a poor one.

Don't Memorize Your Answers

We touched upon this earlier and it's an important point to observe: practice going over each answer until you know it and the thoughts you want to convey. Your words may vary but they convey the same ideas. If you memorize your answer, it can't help but sound memorized to an astute interviewer who has heard many, many responses to their question. He or she may feel that you are mouthing the words of others as though you had a speech writer. If you're quite nervous, it's easy to forget what you were supposed to say next or stumble over a phrase you couldn't recall. All of a sudden there may be dead silence and you want to avoid this obviously. Memorizing lacks spontaneity. Astute observers can detect whether someone is talking spontaneously or reciting words that were memorized.

Offer Them More than the Other Candidates

Keep in mind that many people are hired who have less education, training, and job experience than those who were rejected. Those who were hired prepared and presented a greater percentage of what they have going for them than did those who were not hired. When you present 90 to 100 percent of what you have to offer in any area of consideration, you will appear more impressive than someone who knows more but only utilizes 60 to 70 percent of it. You must put as much effort into selling your accomplishments in your interview as you put into building them.

Your preparation can actually become a selling point. It's common for interviewers to start or wrap up the session by asking "How did you prepare for your interview with us?" As you prepare, take note of all the individual major tasks involved; these will make a great summation in answer to this question. (You'll find an example in chapter 17 under "Impress Them with Your Preparation.")

Here's an example of how you can take advantage of every opportunity to add more. Suppose you have just finished answering a question. The interviewer catches a quick glimpse of you while he or she is looking down at your employment application and says, "You look like you were going to say something, were you?" If you've realized that you overlooked some important point, you could reply, "Yes, a little earlier you asked me about...I would like to add..." You can capitalize in the same manner anytime you're asked if you'd so care to make any comments. This strategy allows you to add points to your score that you might otherwise have lost.

Show You Sincerely Want the Job

Let the interviewer know that you would really enjoy performing all aspects of the job. It's what you want to do and look forward to every job challenge and opportunity to contribute to the department's and company's future success. You don't want to convey the image of someone who had to be talked into entering your career field and profession, or a person who didn't quite make it in college (for whatever reason) and was forced to turn to his or her second career field choice. You aren't in it only for the money, benefits, and prestige. You just enjoy the type of work you are in.

If you developed an interest in your career field and profession at a very early age, bring this out in your interview—the sooner, the better. The younger you were when you became interested, the higher you will score with the interviewer. Make it clear that you weren't talked into it by family or friends, or talked out of another profession that interested you more. Studies of people who have greatly excelled in their fields reveal two common characteristics: high intelligence and a strong interest in that profession developed at an early age, before entering college. As we are exposed to ideas about different fields and professions we might wish to pursue, we gravitate to what interests us most and the earlier your interest develops, the more strongly you'll be motivated to do whatever it takes to enter that profession and become successful.

If you are married, engaged, or have a live-in relationship with someone, point out how supportive that person has been of your efforts to get ahead in your chosen career field; their willingness to do whatever it takes to help you achieve your career goals.

Job candidates with extensive experience sometimes tend to be less enthusiastic when talking about their present and prior positions. No matter how many years you have been in your profession, you should show the same level of zest and excitement today that you displayed when you first entered it.

Point out the pride you have in being a top-quality professional in your field. Convey that the job opening you hope to fill will provide the opportunity to further build upon that reputation. Make it clear that you would be willing to work overtime, travel—do whatever it takes to get the job done—that's how much this position means to you.

Present Your People Skills

Most of the people who haven't worked out well are those who had problems interacting with people, rather than in their job skills and knowledge.

Interviewers have a wide latitude in scoring job applicants on their 'people' skills. Most candidates have solid training and experience, and will give similar answers to job-related technical questions. When interviewers ask candidates non-technical questions—how they would handle certain people problems and situations, they hear a strikingly wide range of observations, explanations, and insights. This is an area that often determines who will get hired. Having good people skills is crucial to success in getting ahead in your career—in everyday life.

Follow the suggestions in chapter 10 to tap into your memory bank of interactions with people and prepare pertinent anecdotes and lessons learned. Get into the habit of saying "we," "us," and "our" rather than "I," "my," and "me." You will be letting the interviewer know that your emphasis and perspective is on the 'team' more so than on 'individual' pursuits.

Highlight Your Decision-Making Skills

All employers emphasize the importance of sound decision-making and want to find conclusive evidence of it when assessing job candidates. They want to understand not just the good decisions you've made (which could have been lucky guesses), but the process and methods by which you make good decisions and solve problems to be effective in your job.

When you explain your major achievements, bring out the challenges you faced and the obstacles that you successfully overcame. Interviewers are impressed by a logical, thorough, systematic approach to decision-making and problem-solving.

Consider the Career Choices You've Made

Think about the path you've taken to reach this point: educational level, school and degree selection, career field chosen, training received, employers you sought to work for, positions you've held, and so on. What attracted you to them? What were your other options? Identify the compelling reasons and factors in your life that have led to these choices. What process did you follow? How tough was it to make your final selection of the career field and profession you would pursue? You may be questioned on one or more of these.

Prove You're More than Just Another Job Candidate

Interviewers want to know you as a whole, integrated person, not two separate entities of job holder and private person. Although many of the skills and experiences in each sphere of your life may seem to belong exclusively to one or the other, they are connected and affect each other.

Companies are legally prohibited from asking certain questions, both on their employment application and during their interview with you. These relate primarily to race, sex, sexual orientation, age, religion, political affiliation, nationality, ethnic background, and so on. All their questions are supposed to be job-related in some manner. You, however, are not prohibited in any way from talking about yourself in any manner you choose during your interview. Whatever you bring up should, of course, enhance your image and should be presented thoughtfully and tactfully.

Advance preparation is the key. Consider how you apply your people skills, leadership capabilities, cost-consciousness, physical fitness, and so on in every situation: whether on the job, 'after hours' with colleagues, at home, out and about with family and friends, in volunteer activities, or pursuing hobbies. Prepare to give interviewers a true, total picture of who you are: well balanced, mature, flexible and enjoyable to be around under every circumstance and situation that may arise.

Look to Your Future

Most job candidates talk to interviewers about their accomplishments, but few think to point out their potential for future growth or their plans to enhance themselves in their profession; to continue growing through greater exposure to more advanced training, education, and varied experience. You need to also point out your plans for growth as an individual, through more interests, hobbies, sports, new friends, or community participation. Think ahead and prepare to talk about your future career, personal goals, and things that will make you a better employee, professional, leader, and person. Spell out your plans to keep growing, learning, and, if hired, finding new ways to contribute to the company's success.

■ ■ ■

A pilot has an office with three windows and a terrific view.

■ ■ ■

13

QUESTIONS YOU SHOULD ASK YOURSELF

I n planning your interview approach and strategy, begin first with understanding yourself. What have you achieved to date that is important to relate to the interviewer? How have you handled yourself in past interviews (especially if you didn't get the job—these are great learning opportunities). You can accomplish a great deal by asking yourself questions like these:

This Particular Company

- How well do I know this company? Where do I obtain my knowledge? What and who are my sources? How reliable and comprehensive are they in their data collection?
- Are my career and job goals compatible with those of this company, its philosophy, culture, structure, people, job progressions, and ways of operating?
- Do I sound enthusiastic about wanting to work for this particular company? Do I seem pleased and excited (to the interviewer) to be given the opportunity to interview with them?

My Career

- Can I impressively explain how, why, and when I became interested in this particular career field, and why I decided to become a professional in it? How can I compellingly describe how much I enjoy doing what I do?
- Do I have good explanations as to why I waited so long to decide to enter this profession?
- Considering my particular background, what sort of questions should I be prepared to answer? Do I have impressive answers for

each one? How shall I prepare great answers well in advance of my interview date? Am I prepared for follow-up questions?

- What are my most important accomplishments and achievements? Have I covered all areas pertaining to job performance, training, education, people interaction, decision-making, problem-solving, new ideas, saving time and money, and improving efficiency?
- What are my most memorable job experiences? Which would be the most impressive in reflecting strong performance under pressure?
- What are all the leadership roles I have held? How long? Am I bringing out my leadership experience and skills as strongly as my technical skills? Have I figured out the safest examples to give if asked to relate mistakes and failures I have made as a leader and professional? What are the things that I have learned from them?
- What's impressive and/or unimpressive about my training, education and job experience? Do I hold degrees, certificates, licenses and awards that most candidates for the job openings don't have? Do they reflect a strong quality image of what I have accomplished?
- Do I have good explanations for having left jobs, been laid off, taken lesser positions or changing career fields?
- Will I leave out important positions I held? Will I point out my steady job progression? Do I have a good explanation as to why I was passed over for promotion?
- Do I have good explanations for any failures on the job and what I learned from those experiences?
- Have I thoroughly gone over my employment application and resume? Any red flags or alerts? How do I handle them?
- Have I covered my most important job skills, interactions with other employees and customers, and my expertise in leading and managing people?
- Have I chosen the best example I can recall of my most challenging job assignment—one that shows how well I handled the situation?
- Am I planning to point out the strong reputation I have worked so hard to earn among my supervisors, peers, and subordinates?
- Have I shown that I work just as well with people outside our department as I do with those within the immediate group?

- Does my explanation for not pursuing a military career sound reasonable and tactful to an ex-military interviewer who might be interviewing me?
- If I just left the military, do I offer good reasons why I didn't pursue a 20 to 30 year career with them?
- Is my ratio of job level to time in position(s) impressive? (The higher the job level and the lower your time in position(s), the higher your score.)
- Can I offer examples of my positive attitude, people skills, and willingness to take on any assignment given? Which of these would best reflect my strong reputation?
- What are my strengths, weaknesses, and limitations? Which strengths are the most impressive? Which weaknesses are the most damaging to my image? What are the most tactful ways to discuss them without killing my chances of getting hired?

Interview-Specific Skills

- Am I continuously working on reducing my level of nervousness to a point where I will remain relatively calm after the first five minutes of my interview, to avoid making mistakes that come with being highly nervous?
- Have I practiced giving my answers 'out loud' enough times that they come out sounding natural and spontaneous? Do I avoid appearing irritated by interruptions?
- Can I easily describe who I am in a positive yet realistic manner?
- Do I have a game plan to bring to the interviewer's attention all the most important things I want him or her to know about me? Have I forgotten something significant?
- What are the key aspects of the job opening I like most? Least?
- Overall, am I projecting a strong, positive image of myself at all times throughout the interview?
- How do I 'stand out' from other people applying for the same position? In what ways do I go beyond what is expected of me? For example, am I more thorough, quicker to catch on, a faster worker or have higher standards and objectives?
- Am I listening closely to each of the interviewer's questions? Do I fully understand what I'm expected to cover? How are they different (in any way) from what my friends who applied for the same or

similar positions were asked in their interviews? In what ways are they another version of the same questions?

- Do I pause long enough before my answer to show that I'm not giving a rehearsed answer, or do I blurt out what I planned to say, sometimes even before the interviewer completes his or her question?
- Are my answers unique enough and fresh enough so as to not sound canned?
- At what time in the interview should I bring up each point I plan to make? Will I work them all in before the interview is over? How should I word them?
- Do I appear frightened that I will say or do something wrong?
- Are the length of my answers proportionate to the weight of the questions? Am I giving too short an answer to an open-ended question and too long an answer to a closed-ended question?
- Do I need to get to key points more quickly?
- What don't I have going for me? Can I somehow explain these if asked and make them sound less negative, yet still believable?
- Should I smile more? Am I too straight-faced? Do any of my facial expressions convey the wrong message?
- Am I leaving out anything else that is important? Have I taken out everything that is negative?
- Am I giving only average answers when I should be giving impressive ones?
- Am I milking each answer I present with too many small details when I should be making more good points and providing only the most important details.
- Am I repeating myself at times?
- Am I stressing the importance of quality in everything I have achieved?
- When asked for examples to support an answer, have I chosen ones that make me look at my best? Which examples of weaknesses are the least damaging to my reputation?
- How can I appear self-confident and assertive without appearing cocky and overly aggressive? How do I appear humble and combine friendliness with professionalism?
- Am I going to feel comfortable with the personalities, style, and approaches of the people I meet, especially my future boss? Will I look forward to working with them?

General Communication Skills

- What's my style in communicating with people in general and in handling people who are difficult to get along with?
- Am I pacing myself well? Am I talking too fast or too slow?
- Do I speak too loudly or too softly?
- How clear is my diction? Do people ask me to repeat things?
- Am I too restrictive in the use of my vocabulary?
- Do I need to express my thoughts more concisely?

My Background and Personal Life

- Should I volunteer any information on my life off the job?
- Is my personal life stable? If not, do I have explanations that would satisfy the interviewer's concerns that I might be unstable and a job hopper?
- Am I explaining to the best of my ability why I chose the college/university I attended and the program I majored in? Am I able to point out how it ties in with the career field I'm in? Will I also point out how competent the instructors and professors were? How solid the program was?
- Am I prepared to explain my lower grade average, especially the D and F grades, the incompletes and withdrawals?
- What's most important for the interviewer to know about me as a total person? How can I best describe myself in terms of my personality, character, values, beliefs, temperament, disposition, and so on, without sounding egotistical?
- What's most important in my life?
- What can I say about my community involvement and memberships?
- Have I worked into my answers some of the skills I have displayed in sports, hobbies, and in my other interests that could possibly reflect positively upon my career achievements? Am I prepared to show successful applications of them?

"Were they most impressed with my new blog
or my Dad owning the company?"

14

QUESTIONS INTERVIEWERS ASK

The questions listed in this chapter represent a thorough cross section of those asked in job interviews by large and small companies across the country. Questions can vary from one company to another, one area of the country to another, and from country to country. Since this book was written to cover a multitude of professions, at numerous job levels, in all career fields, the questions relate to many subject areas.

The hiring department and HR ask some questions that are the same—others differ greatly. You may be asked only five or six questions, or as many as twelve to fifteen (by each interviewer), depending on the type and level of position for which you are being considered. Interviewers are considering your potential for advancement as well, so there may be many follow-up questions.

Most large companies rotate and revise their questions periodically to keep pace with 'changing times' and legal restrictions on what can and cannot be asked in interviews. Other companies modify their questions with changes in people, conditions, and standards in the company. Companies want to avoid continuous use of the same questions. If used over and over, they become common knowledge among the majority of job applicants applying for the same position.

Some questions border on being illegal to ask; some may become illegal in the future. In general, questions asked during a job interview must be *job related*. It's a tough line to identify and interviewers may cross it periodically. However, it is best to answer them willingly and without displaying animosity. Demonstrate that you have nothing to hide or fear. Don't act uncomfortable addressing such questions. If a question covers a very personal, non job-related area (in your opinion) that you do not wish to discuss, you can respond, "I prefer not to discuss that area but would be happy to answer any questions you have pertaining directly to my job qualifications for the position you have available." It could be the interviewer didn't realize the question was an illegal one or how sensitive you would be about answering it.

In small organizations, interviewers may not be familiar with laws prohibiting certain questions from being asked. They may ask an illegal question or one deemed inappropriate unknowingly . In such a case, don't act offended. When you make a critical remark and embarrass the interviewer with your reply, you won't be hired. Avoid being confrontational. Turn the conversation in another subject-related direction in which you can make a favorable point about yourself.

Certain employers gear their questions to the specific background of each job candidate applying for that particular position. They may ask several variations of the same questions, each variation worded differently. They may ask for a main reason or all significant reasons. Questions may pertain to your present job involvements and/or your personal and safety concerns for all the company's employees, facilities, and vital equipment. Interpret the questions broadly—don't focus so narrowly that you eliminate a good point you could have made. Unless it's clearly a 'yes or no' question, the interviewer expects to hear more. Those interviewing want explanations and examples of what you have told them. They often like to throw in extra job-related problem scenarios, such as, "What if the following happened to you ...?"

Each employer asks certain questions that relate to its primary areas of concern. Some are tailored to the specific strengths and weaknesses of a candidate's technical credentials. The interviewer wants to gain insight into your understanding of the depth and scope of the question asked. He or she wants to know how you can help their company grow, become more profitable, increase the quality of its products and services, and resolve significant problems as they occur. It's not whether or not you can answer each question asked, it's *how well* you can answer each one.

Should the area of concern relate to periods of unemployment, your explanations could cover taking courses, lots of work-related activities and reading, doing community and/or church work, helping family members 'in time of great need' (illnesses and other crises), unpaid work for others, involvement in sports, hobbies, and special interests, and travel to visit friends and relatives. You want to show you were using your time *constructively*—not brooding about being unemployed.

Interviewers will sometimes deliberately ask you a question about something that they know you don't have the qualifications to be able to answer, just to find out whether or not you will try to bluff your way through it. Don't go there! You may think that they expect you to have all the answers—they don't. Simply say, "I don't have the education, training or job experience necessary to answer that question." Interviewers feel you should be trusted by everyone around you. This is one way they can sample your honesty and trustworthiness.

Interviewers may ask you your opinion on something you know very little about. Be careful what you say. Unless you have some idea of what their position may be on that matter, it would be best to say, "I have never thought enough on that matter to form an opinion. I would have to give it a lot of thought and want to be as objective as I can."

If the interviewer doesn't ask any (or very few) future-oriented questions, it generally means he or she has already decided not to hire you. You're not someone who will be part of the company's future.

The questions I have listed are organized into areas of topic coverage. Read through all the questions, but don't expect to become an expert in anticipating and addressing every one of them; that's just not possible! Be prepared for the tough questions you could be asked. You don't want to blow an interview because you were thrown questions you hadn't thought of nor prepared a well thought out answer in advance. Interviewers' questions can stimulate ideas on bringing out more of your strong points and examples of situations you were in to support them. Do your best in the time you can spare, in preparing for those questions you believe you will most likely be asked; every minute you devote to preparation will pay off. As I've stressed, you are better off preparing many good answers in advance, almost to the point of overkill (see chapter 16). You're bound to forget some points you planned to make through interview nervousness and will come up short if you don't have a full reserve tank.

Many job candidates find it helpful to make a photocopy of these pages for annotation, placing a checkmark to the left of those questions that they are most concerned with, highlighting 'hot' questions that deserve extra focus.

Establishing Rapport

- How do you pronounce your last name? Do you go by your full first name? What do most people call you?
- How was your flight/long drive? Tell me about it. Did you have

any difficulty finding our facilities? By the way, would you like something to drink?

- I understand that you know [name of employee]. Did you work with him or her? How long have you known him or her? Know any of our other employees? How well do you know them?
- What are the three most important things you want people meeting you for the first time, to know about you?
- What would *you* like to talk about? How about telling me about yourself and how you've built your career [in three minutes]. Tell me out something I can't find out about you from reading your resume and employment application.
- Tell me, in just one sentence, why you are here today.
- Wasn't that something about [breaking news story of significance]?
- What did you do to arrange for time off to attend this interview?

Other Companies

- What other companies have you applied with? Why did you choose those in particular? Why haven't you applied with others? How much do you know about our competition? In what areas do you think we're not as competitive as we could be with our competition? Which five companies would you most want to work for? In what order? For what reasons?
- Have you had any interviews? With whom? When? What was the outcome of each? Why do you think you weren't hired? What's your best guess? Do you have any job offers pending? With whom? If you receive a job offer from one of them while we're still debating on our final decision, what will you do?
- How would you differentiate an average company from an exceptional one? Why do you think some companies 'fail' even though they seem to have good products and services to offer their customers? What do you look for in an employer? What do you think are the biggest problems our industry faces today? In five years?

The Interviewing Company

- Why do you want to work for us? What would you enjoy most and least about working for us and in this job? What do you know/hear about us? What's our company's history? When did we start operations? What are some of our major achievements? Anything else?

- Who is our CEO, president, head of our department? Who is the most important person in our company? Why? How many employees do we have? What is our main product line? What services do we offer our customers? Where are our locations? Are you aware of recent planned expansions/mergers/takeovers? Do you own any of our stock? What's our management style? What do you think will be our biggest challenge in the next ten years? Describe our image. What's the word out there among job applicants about working for us? What problems do you think 'team-oriented' companies might face? Why do you think that?
- Why did you wait so long to apply? Did you apply in the past? Were you interviewed? When? Why do you think we didn't hire you then? Give it your best guess.
- What do you think our customers expect from us?
- If you couldn't work for us, which company would be your second choice? Why?
- How do you compare our company with our closest competitor? What negative and positive things have you heard about us? By what *criteria* do you judge the success of an organization?
- If you were one of our interviewers, what attributes would you look for in job applicants? What questions would you ask? Why those?
- Do you have a mentor at our company? Who? For how long?
- What do you expect of us? What do we owe our employees? What can we expect from you? How long can we expect you to stay with us? In what ways can we keep you satisfied working for us?
- Do you think you will make some mistakes while working for us?
- What do you believe will be the biggest problems facing our company in the next ten years? Any thoughts on how we should address them?
- What do you believe will be the biggest challenge you will face working for us? Why? Any others?
- Are you open to frequent travel if it became necessary?
- How long do you think it will take to get promoted?
- How will you balance serving in the Reserves/Guard and working for us?
- What are your thoughts on what you've observed and heard up to this point in your interview with us?

Diversified Hiring

- What does 'diversity' mean to you in working and in hiring? Do you know whether or not we have a diversified hiring or affirmative action policy/program at our company? How do you feel about that?
- What adjustments have you made in working with female, minority, and senior-aged co-workers?
- Have you ever had or been involved with any racial or sex discrimination matters? Tell me about it. Do you have any problems with supervising or instructing women and minorities? How would you feel being supervised by a female, minority, or someone much younger than you?

Work Locations

- Are you willing to relocate to another area of the country? At what location would you prefer working? Why? What would be your least desirable location? Why? Would you plan to commute? How would you cope with problems many commuters face?
- What are the reasons why you and your family would be satisfied living here in [city]? What do you know about our area? Are you aware of our housing costs and conditions, cost of living, schools, recreational facilities, etc.? How well do you think you will be able to adjust to our climate (cold winters and hot, humid summers)?

Salary

- What is your current salary? Why aren't you earning more? How long have you been at that salary level? What is your next expected salary increase? How often do you receive a salary review? Were you ever passed over at a salary review? Why do you think you weren't given a salary increase? What is the typical salary increase for people in your position? Give me a quick rundown on your salary progression for the past five years (amount, percentage, and frequency). How did you feel about receiving the amount of your last salary increase? How did your supervisor describe your job performance in the review appraisal that supported the salary increase?
- How close are you to the top of your job's salary range?
- How do you know when you are doing a good job to justify receiving a salary increase?

- Do you know what our starting salary and salary range is for this position? How will you be able to support yourself and your family on that amount of income?
- What figure did you have in mind for a starting salary, considering the degree to which you meet our job requirements? What salary do you expect to be earning five years from now? How did you come up with these figures? What do you base them on?
- Were there any jobs you held where salary played a factor in what caused you to leave? Did you ever receive a below average salary increase? Were you ever skipped over at salary review time?
- What financial sacrifices have you made pursuing your career?
- What are the most important things to you regarding your compensation? What would be an ideal compensation package? How do you feel about profit sharing programs? Stock options?
- What if one of your respected friends said that people in your profession are overpaid and underworked? Why do you think he or she would say that? How would you respond to him or her?

How You Got Started In Your Profession

- How old were you when you first became interested in your job field and profession? How did it happen? Why not some other field or profession? How is yours more rewarding? Was there anyone in your family in this profession? Why did it take you so long to decide to enter this job field?
- When did you begin to develop a career plan? How, when, and where did you actually begin implementing your plan?
- What steps have you taken to date toward fulfilling your early career dreams?
- What do you enjoy most about your present job? Least? Dislike?
- If you were not in your profession, what would you be doing? Why?
- Convince me of your commitment to continue working in your profession when things get really tough.

Civilian Work Background

- Why didn't you choose the military to acquire your training and job experience? If you had to do it over again, would you go the civilian or military route? Why?
- What have you done at your company that would make you stand

out from others in your position? Did you ever save time or money, or improve things in other ways? Were you involved in any special projects and assignments? Tell me about them.

- What changes would you make in the way your company operates and treats its employees? What are your company's current and future goals in this respect?
- What do you think of your immediate supervisor? Department head? Caliber of the people you work with?
- Were you ever unfairly treated by your supervisor? When? For what? What was the outcome? Was a supervisor or co-worker ever hostile to you? When? Why?
- How do you handle a boss who is too quiet, too talkative, or gets too personal? Why those approaches?
- When did you not accept another employee's input? Why not? When have you caused another employee a problem? Did you have any difficulties dealing with the situation?
- Have you ever been laid off? Fired? When? Your reaction?
- Tell me about a time your company pressured you to 'press the limits' or bend the rules. Did you? Why?
- If you leave your company to join us, what will you miss most?
- Who is the best employer you ever worked for? The best employee you ever worked with? Why did you choose him or her?

Military Background

- Why did you decide to go the military route to obtain your training and experience? How did you happen to choose the [military branch]?
- Describe key jobs you held. What were the most important job responsibilities and assignments? How were you assigned to each? Tell me about a project you didn't plan well. Why didn't you?
- Describe your last three assignments and commanding officers. What did you like most about each? Least?
- What's the largest group you have commanded?
- Have you ever been passed over for promotion? Why? Describe your last two performance evaluations.
- Who was the most impressive person you have worked with? Why?
- Did you ever disobey or refuse to follow a direct order? Why? Under what circumstances would you disobey one?

- What did you enjoy most about your military career? Least? What were the highlights? Why didn't you stay until retirement? What things will you miss most?
- In transitioning from military to civilian, what do you think will be the biggest adjustment you will need to make? Why? What will you do differently to be a better professional than you were in the military? Won't starting out in a position lower than you previously held be a letdown?

Education and Training

- How much importance do you place on having a college degree? Why didn't you complete college? Do you plan to? Why not?
- Why did you select that particular college, major and minor? If you had to do it over again, would you change them? Why? Why not? Would you change the college you attended? What other colleges did you attend? Why did you leave them? Did you receive any scholarships? Describe your best and worst professors.
- What was your overall GPA, both in your major and your minor? Why was it so low? Do you recall any Ds or Fs? How could you have improved those grades? To what do you attribute your impressive grades? How important do you think grades are? Does your grade average reflect your learning ability?
- Which courses did you enjoy most and least? Which courses later helped you the most? In what ways? Which courses were the most difficult for you? Were there any you began and didn't finish? Why did you drop out? Which were relative to your chosen career field? Did you write any term papers or complete any projects that were related to your profession? In what ways has your degree helped you in the jobs you've held?
- Compare your writing and speaking skills. In which are you strongest? How do you plan to further develop them?
- Tell me the essence of the last three books you have read. What magazines do you read? Why those?
- What books have you read that has influenced you the most in your thinking? In what ways?
- Give me an example of a time when you helped a fellow student overcome a problem he or she was having.
- What was the biggest problem you faced in college? How did you

handle it? What was the outcome? What did you learn from it?
- What percentage of your college education and training did you pay for? Who helped you financially? To what extent? Were you employed throughout college? What summer and part-time jobs did you hold? How many hours per week? How did you obtain them? What do you think of them? Which did you like most and which the least? Why?
- Were you involved in any sports, clubs, fraternities, sororities, volunteer projects, and extracurricular activities? How did you get involved with them? Why haven't you been more involved?
- What did you gain from your college education? What did you like most? Least? What were your most noteworthy achievements in college/high school? If you were to do it over again, what changes would you make? Why?
- Why did you choose [major field of study] for your master's degree? Why that university? What was your thesis? What was your GPA?
- What do you think about online degrees? Do you think they are equal to a four-year, full time, on campus degree? Why?
- What are your goals for furthering your education in the future?
- What career field do you plan to enter? Why?

Legal Offenses and Convictions
- Have you had any convictions other than minor traffic violations? When? Where? For what? Under what circumstances? What was the outcome?
- Any reckless driving or DUI convictions? How many? When? Give me the details. How many speeding tickets have you had in the past five years? Ten years?
- Is there anything else we should know about, that is directly or indirectly related to your convictions, before we begin checking your records?

Medical
- Describe your health history and current health condition. Any problems? Recent concerns? How do you stay in good health? Do you or did you smoke? Over what period of time? How many packs did/do you smoke each day? Were you a chain smoker?

- Tell me about your energy level. Does it fluctuate throughout the day? Why? Any food allergies?
- Approximately how many times have you been hospitalized or treated by a physician or psychologist? When? For what reasons and how long? What was the outcome?
- How much lost time have you had in the past five years? For what reasons?
- Have you ever taken any illegal drugs? When? For what reasons and how long? What was the outcome? Would there be a problem if we were to drug test you today?
- Have you ever had any problems working nights and sleeping days?

Technical Expertise

- Give me an overview of your major areas of technical job expertise. Which are your strongest areas? How did you develop them?
- What are you doing to raise your level of professional expertise? How would you compare it to that of your peers?
- What areas of your technical expertise do you plan to work on most? What are your goals and timelines?
- What do you do to keep your technical skills current? Which are crucial?
- How do you keep up-to-date on new innovations in your profession?
- How much do you know about [area of expertise]?

The Available Position

- Are you looking for a temporary job?
- Why do you want this job? What will it provide to you that your present job doesn't? Describe your 'dream job.' Why is it taking you so long to find the right job?
- What excites you about the position? What concerns you? Will it be a 'step up' or a 'step down' for you?
- What is your next step in your current position? How long do you estimate it will be before you reach this level?
- Why do you think you would be proficient in performing the job responsibilities of the position we have open? How would you approach them?
- How much do you know about this position? How did you hear about it? What are the most important job responsibilities and

requirements? What job skills are most important to performing this job impressively? What will be expected of you? What more do you want to know about it? Any concerns or reservations?

- Where do you think this job can lead you in advancing your career? How do you envision this job impacting our company? What do you think will determine how quickly you will get ahead in our company?
- What starting salary do you have in mind?
- How long do you think it would take for you to begin making a significant contribution to your department and our company?
- Are you open to frequent travel and/or relocation to another city/state? Can you work overtime? Would you work weekends or evenings if necessary?
- Will your performance in this position be compatible with your personal goals?
- Considering that you recently retired, why do you want to return to the workplace? How long do you plan to work? Why this job in particular?
- What is something 'extra' you can bring to this job?

Job Responsibilities

- What are the most important aspects of a [position open] regarding job responsibilities? What's a good [position open]? Which do you think is more important—individual or team job performance? Why? Give me example in both areas.
- What are the most important qualities necessary to be successful in a job? What key roles do they play? How do you measure their effectiveness? What can you do in performing your job to help make your boss's job performance more successful? In what ways can you interact effectively with your peers and co-workers? How do you prepare for an important job assignment?
- How do you develop a plan for a project you have been assigned? What are the key criteria? Tell me about a project you were late in completing and one you completed ahead of time. What were the reasons?
- How do you delegate responsibility to your subordinates?
- What impresses you most when thinking of someone who performs their job responsibilities in an outstanding manner? Why these?

- Tell me about the time your job responsibilities required that you interact with supervisors, managers, and others within and outside your department at higher job levels. What was the involvement? How did each go? Why?
- Tell me about an important job assignment you were given with very little knowledge as to what was involved, no existing procedures or time deadlines, nor other significant information. How did you handle it? What steps did you take? With whom? Did you complete it on time? What was the outcome? Was your boss satisfied? Did you have any regrets?
- What are the more complex and challenging aspects of your current job? How long did it take to learn them? Which do you perform best? What distracts you from performing your job? When you have a tight time schedule with several involved tasks to accomplish, how do you achieve them all successfully? How do situational awareness and team effort come into play? How do you feel about standardized job methods and processes? Why?
- What type of job assignments do you enjoy most and which do you enjoy least? Why? What was your most innovative and challenging job assignment? What creative ideas did you use? Tell me more.
- What could you do to help expedite a pressing job project for completion? Anything else?
- Finish this sentence: "I enjoy performing my job assignments because..."

Positions Held

- Tell me more about the job responsibilities and job assignments of your current position. Which are the most important? Why? Which do you enjoy most? What has been your biggest challenge? Most difficult assignment? What are you most proud of? What was your best job? What was your worst job? Most boring job? Why? Least important? Why?
- How did you obtain each of your jobs? How do you feel about your progress and progression in job assignments and positions held? What are the key reasons for your job successes?
- What do you think of the supervision you received in your last three jobs? Who was your best supervisor? Worst supervisor? Why? How would you describe your working relationships with

them? Which supervisor did you enjoy working for most? Least?
Why with them? What qualities do you look for in a boss? What
did you do when you had a problem with him or her? When has a
supervisor done something you disliked or felt was wrong? Did
you make your opinion known to him or her?

- Which company have you most enjoyed working for? Why? What
do you like most about your current employer? Least? Why? What
turns you off when considering taking a new job?

- When do you feel as if you are beginning to feel stale in what
you're doing? How do you get out of this mood?

- In what areas of 'getting the job done' do you and your current
boss view differently? Why? How often?

- Describe a 'close-knit team.' What's most important on a team?
How do you mesh individual recognition with team effort? Tell me
how your department employees interact as a team.

- Who do you most trust? Why?

- What do you dislike about your current job, supervisor, department,
and company? Why? What have you done to change things? What
else? How has your job changed since entering it?

- What's the dumbest/most regrettable thing you ever did? Why?
How did you resolve the situation? What's the smartest thing you
did? When were you last criticized? Why

- What's the biggest job obstacle you had to overcome? What's the
biggest problem? What did you do to resolve them? Were there any
repercussions? When did you fail to resolve them? Why?

- What on-the-job surprises have you had? Why weren't you expecting them to happen? Outcome?

- Why did you leave each of your previous jobs? In what ways were
these changes beneficial? What are all the reasons that you want to
leave your present job?

- What was the most difficult job/assignment you ever had to adjust
to in a short period of time?

- Tell me about the time you played a major role in one of your
team's accomplishments. What specifically did you do? Was your
contribution acknowledged? By whom?

- What are several things you do to stay current in your job?

- Describe your typical day in your present position. On which activities do you spend the most time? Which are the most important?

How many hours a week do you typically work? Why so many?
- Do you hold any other jobs outside your present job? What type? Where? Why?
- Define and describe a successful job/assignment/project completion. What are the reasons for your success?
- What are the greatest distractions to performing your job that occur on a daily basis? Why do they distract you? How do you cope with them?
- How do you determine your priorities for each approaching work day?
- What are the highlights of your career to date? Talk about your most important job accomplishments in the past five years.
- What important oral presentations have you made? How do you compare your oral skills with your writing skills?
- Who were the best and worst supervisors and peers you have known? How would you describe the most impressive one? Least impressive? What differentiates an outstanding employee from a good one? When did you have to correct someone? Describe the circumstances and outcome. Have you ever had a conflict with one of your supervisors? Why? How did you handle it? How was it resolved? Who was the most difficult person you had to deal with? How did you smooth things out?
- What aspects of your management style would you like to change? Why? How? Describe how your style has changed during your career.
- What was the last disagreement you had with someone? When was the last time you 'lost your cool?' Why? How was it resolved?
- What types of people do you most enjoy working with? Least enjoy working with? Why?
- How would your last two bosses describe you? Is there a particular employee you would prefer not to work with? Why? Any others? What type of individual do you most enjoy working with? Describe your approach and style in handling people. Has it ever backfired on you? Has anything ever happened to you that was untimely?
- Tell me about a time when a project you were working on wasn't going very well and you had to take another course of action. Why wasn't it going well? How did your new approach work?
- What was your most embarrassing moment interacting with a

co-worker or customer? Why did it happen? What was the outcome?

- How many days of work have you missed in the last two years? Why? Before that? Have you ever taken a leave of absence? For how long? For what reasons?

- What is the most challenging part of your present job? Why? What was the most difficult job assignment you have ever handled? When is the last time you didn't perform up to your own standards? What was your most important learning experience? What have you done in your job that was beyond what was expected of you? When have you displayed 'job initiative'? Under what conditions do you perform at your best? Worst?

- When have you been distracted from what you were doing? Reasons? Outcome? What preventive techniques do you use?

- How do you prepare for a presentation or speech you have to give? What steps do you take? How do you decide what to cover and how long it should be? How do you begin and end it? How do you know if it's 'good.?' Who do you test it out with?

- What were your most satisfying work experiences? Were there any unpleasant ones? Were there any disappointments? How do you turn negative experiences into positive spin-offs?

- Have you ever worked with someone who you thought didn't perform well? What did you do? How did it turn out?

- Have you ever been passed over for promotion? When? Where? Why? Have you ever been fired or asked to resign?

- What do you think your supervisor should base his or her job performance appraisals and salary reviews on when assessing you? Why those criteria?

- Were you ever demoted? Why?

- What new job skills have you developed in the last two years? Any new ideas?

- When have you not lived up to your own job performance expectations? For what reasons? What are you least proud of doing?

- In what ways have you displayed creativity in performing your job responsibilities successfully?

- Since assuming your present job, in what areas have you most improved your job proficiency? How do you plan to further improve your job skills and expertise? How do you motivate yourself to keep your job interest fresh?

- What was the biggest thrill in your career? Who was the most memorable person to work with? Why? What was your worst day?
- When have you had to strongly assert yourself with someone? Why? Outcome?
- What was the most difficult decision you ever had to make? What was the outcome?
- Have you ever had to take control of a situation unexpectedly? When are you justified in doing so? Under what circumstances?
- What is your favorite subject? What books have you read on it?
- When have you had to switch styles because the one you were using wasn't working well? What was the outcome?
- Who do you most admire in your profession? Why?
- Did you ever have to fire anyone? Why? What was the person's reaction?
- Which do you enjoy more, performing your job or teaching someone how to perform it? Why?
- Talk about when you persuaded someone to help you in getting an important job assignment completed. How did you do it? Tell me about a time you were able to win over someone to your way of thinking. What techniques and insights did you use?
- Have you ever broken a company rule? Explain. You mean to tell me you have never broken even one?
- Have you ever had to take yourself off a job assignment because of an emotional situation you were facing?
- Tell me about a time when you had to change your approach, strategy, or actions in order to meet a critical deadline.
- Talk about how you practiced 'time management' and management by objectives (MBO). Biggest successes? Failures? Discuss the times you did more than what was expected of you. What were the bottom-line results? How did you increase sales and/or business for your employer? In what ways did your job performance contribute to the success of your department and the company. Tell me a time that resulted in a questionable outcome?
- Describe times when you have worked without any supervision? Did you make significant decisions on your own? Why and how did you do this?
- What were the biggest problems you had to resolve in your current position? How did you approach and handle each one? How

successful were you?

- Describe your working relationship with your supervisor when you first started working for him or her. What is it like at this time? How has it changed? Why has it changed?
- Have you ever had a run-in with a customer? Why? What was the outcome? Have you ever had to intervene between a customer and an employee who were in disagreement?
- When have you given a supervisor a 'heads up' on something you did, both favorable and unfavorable. What was his or her reaction? When is the last time you admitted you did something wrong? Describe. Have you ever taken the blame for something someone else did wrong? When and why?
- Have you ever been given bad information on a job assignment? Describe the outcome.
- What project sticks out in your mind most when you think about a time when you worked the hardest and felt the most satisfaction in the outcome? How did you plan and organize for it?
- What irritates you? What elates you?
- Were you ever in a situation that was getting out of control? How did it turn out?
- Describe an important project you completed within the past year. Did you need help? Were the results favorable? What's the most critical decision you've had to make in the last six months? What were your options? What actions did you take? What was the outcome?
- When you're not in charge, how do you get your team motivated to complete a project on time?
- Tell me about a time your supervisor confronted you unjustly (in your opinion).

Periods of Unemployment

- How many times have you been unemployed? How long were you unemployed each time? Why so long?
- Why couldn't you find employment? What did you do to try to find a job? Did you try to find employment in another job field?
- How many jobs did you apply for and at what locations? Did you receive any job offers?
- How did you support yourself during your unemployment? What did you do during this period? How did you spend your time?

Overall Qualifications/Employment

- Do you feel you're qualified to assume your boss's job? Why?
- Is there anything you can think of that could possibly prevent our being able to obtain a government security clearance on you?
- If you were hiring someone to fill this job opening, what qualifications would be most important to you? What would you look for? In what order of importance? Why?
- What do you think we are looking for? What qualities do you assume would be most important to us?
- What prompted you to go in your chosen direction in acquiring your job credentials? What setbacks have you experienced along the way?
- What motivates you? What can you do to further increase your technical and people skills? Any plans? What are they?
- On a scale of one (lowest) to ten (highest), where would you rate yourself as a professional in your job category? Why? How would you rate yourself among your peers? Among all professionals in your career field? What's the most important quality in a good professional? What particular, specific experience contributes most to your professional capability? Why? In what ways?
- How do you define a 'job well done?'
- What makes you stand out from others in your department? Why was your job and salary progression slow?
- How do you read and size up people? How do you get people or groups to accomplish something important? What techniques do you use to sell them on your ideas?
- What was the biggest conflict/disagreement you ever had with a boss? What was his or her job title? Where and when did this happen? Was anyone else involved? Exactly how did it start and progress? How did you decide to handle it? How did it end? If you had it to do over again, would you do the same thing? Why? What did you learn from this experience? How was your relationship with that person after that?
- Define integrity. Has yours ever been questioned? When? By whom? Why? Outcome?
- Would you share your thoughts with us on job complacency? Have you ever experienced it? When? Why? What were the results? How do you cope with adversity?

- Complete this statement: "I would like to be a professional who..."
- Tell me something that you think I haven't already heard from other job candidates in answer to my last three questions. Don't remember all three?

Conflicts/Disagreements

- In general, how do you resolve conflicts with others?
- What conflicts and/or disagreements have you had with supervisors and other employees in your department? In your company?
- Ever been involved in or witnessed an argument or personality conflict in your work area? What did it concern? Who was involved? Did you play mediator?
- How do you avoid arguments and personality conflicts?
- How many times have you lost your temper in the last two years? Over what? How did you deal with it? Outcome?
- Ever had a strong disagreement with your immediate supervisor or department manager? How was it resolved?
- When have you failed to resolve a conflict? Why? Did you learn from it?
- Have you had any conflicts with internal or outside customers? What were the issues? How were they settled?

Constructive Criticism

- How do you give constructive criticism to someone? What techniques do you use?
- Have you ever been criticized for a new idea you came up with? Why? Any regrets of your own?
- What constructive criticism have you received in the last six months? Past two years? Was it justified or unjustified? How did you respond to it? End results? Have you ever been treated unfairly? When? Why? In general, how do you handle constructive criticism? How did you gain this insight?
- Have you ever been addressed for insubordination or had to address someone for it? Explain.
- When were you dissatisfied with your performance? Why? What did you do to improve? What were the results? What did you learn? What did you do to make certain it didn't happen again?

Accomplishments and Disappointments

- What has been your biggest, proudest accomplishment considering all the jobs you have held? What about in your present job? The last year? The previous job?
- How do you think you're doing so far, in this interview? Really?
- What obstacles have you had to overcome in getting to where you are today in your career? How did you do it? How often have you gotten frustrated in performing your job tasks? What made you frustrated? How were those frustrations resolved? What are the highest and lowest points in your career? What is something you did in the past and failed, that you would never do again? What mistakes have you made in planning your career? How did you overcome them? When were you disappointed at the outcome of your effort to resolve a conflict?
- Have you ever been fired or asked to resign from a job? Why? When? Where? By whom?
- What regrets do you have regarding your career? Why? Describe a situation that you wished you had handled better.
- What is something you would never do again as a supervisor? Why? What are your biggest failures in handling employee complaints? How did you overcome them?
- How have you improved in the past year? What brought it about? When were you last praised on your performance? For what? What new ideas or suggestions have you provided to your employers over recent years in the areas of cost and time savings? What about efficiency improvements? What were the most important new ideas you ever came up with and how did you sell them to your boss and peers? Ever had an idea rejected? Why?
- What have you done or accomplished in your community? How were you involved? Why haven't you been more active?
- What does 'success' mean to you in your career and personal life? Are you successful? What are your three major accomplishments in life? Why those? Any others? What have been your most significant failures? How did you handle them? What did you learn from them? How were you able to turn them into successes?
- What do you think has been the biggest accomplishment made in your career field over the last twenty years?

Strengths and Weaknesses

- If we were to ask your last three supervisors to describe you, what would they say? What strengths, attributes, and other qualities would they attribute to you? What do you think are your strong points? What are your key job skills? What do you have going for yourself? What are your best assets? What can you bring to us?
- What comes 'naturally' to you? What is difficult for you to become 'good at?'
- What are your computer skills? What computer software and systems are you familiar with?
- What would these same supervisors say are your weaknesses/areas for improvement? What do you think they are? Why? No others? (You're more perfect than we are!) What are your greatest liabilities? Limitations? What is your worst quality?
- Rank (in order) your strengths and weaknesses. Explain your reasons for that order. Which three strengths would be at the top of your list? Which helped you most to succeed? Which would be your greatest weaknesses? Which hindered you most from succeeding? Would your present supervisor agree with you? Why? What would your spouse and closest friends say is your biggest weakness? Strength? How would they describe you in general?
- What is your strongest personality trait? What is your weakest? How have you improved yourself over the past year?
- As a professional in your particular field, what are your strongest skills? What are your weakest? What do you do to improve yourself in general?
- What awards, citations, commendations, medals, recommendations, and other forms of recognition have you received?

Handling Stress

- Overall, how do you cope with stress? How well can you think and perform under pressure? In what specific ways? In your current position, what kinds of pressure and stress do you have to deal with? What is creating it? How do you handle it? What is the most stressful period in performing a new job assignment? Why? Walk me through your most stressful job and 'people experience.' How did they happen? How intense was the pressure? How did you handle them? How did they turn out?

- Looking back over your entire career, what was the most stressful period? Why? Describe your most stressful experience.
- What are the signs that let you know that you are experiencing stress? How could you have prevented them from occurring? What frustrates you? Describe conditions and situations that can cause a great deal of stress on the job.
- How do you deal with someone who lied to you on an important job-related matter?
- What has a supervisor done that was very irritating to you and put you under a lot of stress?
- Have you ever lost your temper in dealing with your supervisor or other employees? Why? How was the situation resolved?

Professionalism/Situational Awareness

- What is professionalism? In what ways do you consider yourself professional? How can you become more professional? Describe how a very professional person in your job classification operates. What image should be projected to others within your company, customers, and the public? In what ways? What image do you project to your superiors, peers, subordinates, and employees in general?
- What is situational awareness? How does a person develop this skill? In what ways? How does it apply to job performance? How can it be measured? Why is it so important?
- In supervising others, when have you acted in an unprofessional manner? Why?
- What is the difference between a good performer and an outstanding one in your profession? What is the relationship between attitude and performance?
- Who is your role model for building your professional approach to work excellence? What person in your profession and/or career field has impressed you the most? For what reasons? What quality do you most value?
- What was the most challenging situation you faced in selling an idea, concept, or new approach to performing an assignment? What techniques did you use? To what extent were you successful? Did you ever need cooperation from groups that did not report to you? How did you gain their support? What was the outcome? Why did you use that approach?

- How have you helped another professional improve their job skills?
- What's the difference between assertiveness and aggressiveness? Which approach to people do you typically use? Why?
- What have you done to improve your professional image over the last five years?
- Give me several examples of strong and weak situational awareness. What was your best display of its use? Worst? Did you ever have to counsel someone in this area?
- If your boss said or did something that you questioned, what would you do? Why that?

Decision-Making and Problem-Solving

- What is your decision-making and problem-solving process? What steps do you follow? How did you develop this process? Give me an example of how you applied it to a job assignment. What was the most difficult decision you had to make? Tell me about your most time-critical decision.
- Let's say a serious work-related problem came up and there were no company policies, practices, procedures or guidelines pertaining to it. How would you handle it? What would you do? Who would you talk to about resolving it?
- What is the most important decision you have ever made? What made it so important? What made it the toughest and most difficult? What is the most important decision you have made in the past year? What was your best decision? Quickest? Worst? Most unpopular with those impacted by it? How did you handle them? Why in that manner? What was your biggest 'surprise' problem? Why was it a surprise?
- Describe an important project/job assignment that best reflects how you used your skills, talents, knowledge, and analytical ability to resolve it.
- Describe how you went about building your career. What were the most difficult decisions to make? Why? Have you ever misjudged something? Why? How did you resolve the situation? How did you prevent the same thing from happening again? What do you wish you could change? Why?
- When have you tried but failed to make the right decision? What happened? Which decision do you most regret having made? Why?

How could you have handled it differently? Have you ever failed to make a decision you were expected to make? Why? When have you had to reverse a decision you made? Why?

- Can decisions be 'flexible?' How? When? Why?
- Do you make decisions logically or intuitively?
- Have you ever made a snap decision without thinking about it?
- When have you recognized a problem developing before anyone else did?
- Have you ever had to change strategies to accomplish the job?
- Have you ever had a decision you made questioned by someone above you? Have you ever made a decision in error? What were the consequences?
- When have you done extensive research on a problem before tackling it? Describe a decision you made when you didn't have all the facts. What was the outcome?
- What risks have you taken in your job? Why? How did they turn out?
- Rank the following according to the value of their importance to you: industry, company, job, boss, job advancements, work environment, family, close friends, salary, benefits, job security, education, and training. Why that order? Explain further.
- What is the biggest problem you have ever had to resolve? In the last year? In the last six months?
- Describe a time when you were on a team that failed to get the job done.
- What was the most recent important work-related decision you made? What were the results?
- What is the most serious emergency problem you've had to resolve quickly? What did you do? What were the results? Tell us about an emergency you would have handled differently today. What things must you do in handling an emergency?
- If you received two job offers, what factors would you consider before making your decision? Why those? What else would you do?
- Tell me about a time you decided to speak up/assert yourself in order to correct your boss. How did it turn out? Tell me about a time when you disagreed with a decision he or she made? As a supervisor, have you ever had a decision you made or your authority questioned by a subordinate? Explain.

- When have you had to make a split-second decision? What were the results? Have you ever had to make a delayed decision to give yourself more time to think? Why?
- When has a 'higher up' disagreed with a decision you made? Why? Outcome?
- Have you ever experienced a 'bad judgment day?' When? What happened? Why? What were the results?
- Have you ever helped another team member solve a problem? Discuss. When were you part of the problem?
- When have you had second thoughts on changing jobs? Why?
- How do you decide your priorities? What are they?
- Why do you think interviewers turn down the majority of job applicants applying for a position? They're qualified; we wouldn't call them in if they weren't. Any ideas or guesses?

Leadership

- What leaders have most inspired you throughout your career? In what ways? Who was your key role model? Describe their leadership style.
- Why did you decide to go into 'supervision?'
- What are the qualities of a very good leader? What's the difference between a good leader and a good manager? What are the qualities of an impressive/outstanding supervisor/manager. What would you like to change about the leadership style your supervisor uses in dealing with you? Why? In what ways? What leadership roles have you held? Of which are you the proudest? Which was the most significant to you? Why?
- What's the largest group of people you have ever had to lead? Doing what? What made you successful? What is your leadership philosophy? What is your leadership style? Give me examples of situations that best reflect your leadership style. How has your style changed over the years? How did you develop your particular philosophy and style?
- As a supervisor/manager, how do you prepare and conduct a salary review and performance appraisal? How do you motivate your subordinates? What methods and techniques do you use? Do you use the same ones on all your employees? On what factors do you judge their performance? Which do you think are most important?

- How many people have you interviewed and hired for your department? How many have you promoted, counseled, and terminated?
- How do you delegate work assignments? What approaches and techniques do you use? How do you determine how much work should be delegated and to whom? How do you determine when you're overloading someone?
- Have you ever have a situation get out of control? What happened? Why? How did you get it back under control?
- What have you done in the last three years to improve your leadership skills? When did you first recognize that you possessed leadership potential?
- Have you ever been in a leadership role in which you felt uncomfortable? Why? How did it turn out? Have you ever refused a leadership role? Why? When did people not respond well to your leadership style? When have you failed as a leader? How did you bounce back? What's the most difficult part of being a leader? What leadership qualities are you weak or lacking in? How do you plan to improve them?
- When were you unexpectedly placed in a leadership role? What did you do? How did it turn out? Have you ever turned down a leadership position? Why?
- Why do you think some leaders are more effective than others?
- What are the different styles of teaching? Which do you use? As an instructor, what do you think would make it difficult for a person to learn? How do you teach very complex concepts? What problems have you had in instructing others? How do you deal with slow learners? What are the characteristics of an impressive evaluator? How do you motivate those you are teaching? What are the advantages and disadvantages of being an instructor/leader? Do you learn more by giving or receiving instruction? How do you handle someone who isn't responding well to your instruction or is indifferent?
- Who is the best leader you've known? For what reasons? How have you learned from him or her? What do you think is over-supervising and under-supervising your employees? How does an effective leader set the right tone in the workplace? What is the most important characteristic a good leader should possess? Why?
- How would your subordinates and peers describe you?
- What have you done to set a good example for your subordinates?

How do you brief a new employee joining your department? What do you cover? How do you size up people you've just met? How good are you at doing this?

- How do you get better performance out of a subordinate who is not performing up to your expectations? How do you approach him or her? Tell me about the most serious problem you've had with a subordinate. How did you resolve it? What is the most serious problem that your boss has brought to your attention? How did you handle it? Who was the most difficult employee you've had to handle? What was the most recent incident? What did you do?
- When is the last time you have had to counsel a subordinate? For what reasons? What was the outcome? What would you do if the employee took your constructive criticism too lightly? What techniques do you use to motivate your team? How do they differ from those you use to motivate individuals? In general, what's your philosophy of how to best manage people?
- For what reasons would you need to fire an employee?
- What do you dislike about being a leader/supervisor/manager? Why? What are the drawbacks to being a supervisor?
- How would you compare the importance and level of your technical expertise with that of your supervisory effectiveness?
- Have you ever supervised a group of subordinates who didn't click as a team? Why didn't they click? What did you do? What was the outcome?
- How do you get people who don't report to you to support/help you? When have you had a strong, positive influence over such groups? What techniques did you use? How would you go about forming a group to resolve an important problem? Explain, step by step.
- How do you compare the roles you have played as a leader with those of a follower? Are you a better leader or follower? Why? When? In what areas? Give examples. In which role are you the most comfortable? Why?
- When were you the first on your team to come up with a good solution to a problem? How did your team/group resolve problems among its members? Where there any 'whiners?' How were they handled?
- Describe the most important recent project you headed. How did it turn out? Describe an important project that you *initiated* and were

responsible for its completion. What was the outcome?

- What innovations have the 'leaders in your profession' implemented over the past fifteen years?

Hypothetical Role-Playing Scenarios

- You're still new on the job and on probation. Your boss does something that is questionable and begins acting erratically. What would you do? Why?
- Your boss shows up with what seems to be the smell of liquor on his breath. What would you do? Why? Are there any other options?
- Your supervisor asks you questions concerning a sensitive area of your personal life? He or she began going into great detail about sensitive areas of his or her personal life? What would you do? Why?
- You and your supervisor just completed a long, difficult day together resolving a big problem. What could you say to him or her that was uplifting? Anything else?
- You're given several complex tasks to perform. How would you approach accomplishing all of them in a reasonable period of time?
- The group of employees you're with starts talking negatively about the company. What would you say? Why?
- Your boss tells you he or she needs something very important done in the next two hours. His or her boss phones you with an equally important assignment that needs to be completed within the same time period. What do you do? Why? Any other options?
- You're in a meeting and your supervisor disagrees with his boss over how to best manage a problem your department is faced with. Both turn to you and ask for your input on the controversy. How would you handle the situation? What would you say?
- You approach a peer, whom you were assigned to work with, on an important project. This peer had a reputation of being a 'weak performer.' How would you handle the situation? Why in that manner?
- You found out that a co-worker lied to your supervisor on an important matter? What would you do? Why?
- Your supervisor showed up for work in a very bad mood. What would you do? Why?

Job Situations Faced

- Describe a time when a situation was getting out of hand and you had to act quickly. What did you do? Why? Anything else?

- Have you ever told your supervisor you did something wrong so that he or she heard about it first from you? What was the supervisor's reaction?

- Have you ever been in a situation where you felt strongly that the person you were talking to was deceiving you? What made you think this? How did you handle it? Why that way? What was the outcome?

- How do you prevent yourself from getting bored when performing routine or repeated tasks?

- Tell me about a time when you had to be very persuasive in order to get the job done well. What techniques did you use? How did it turn out? Tell me about another time you overcame adversity to achieve an important goal?

- Tell me about a time when you had to deal with an especially sensitive or difficult co-worker or customer. How did you handle it? What was the outcome?

- Have you ever intervened in a situation where two individuals were getting into a very heated discussion? When? What did you do? What was the outcome?

- Have you ever experienced a situation that involved office politics? Describe what happened, your involvement, and the outcome. Looking back, what are your thoughts on it?

- What have you done recently that was considered 'taking a risk?' When is the last time you became upset with a situation that developed in your department? What happened? Why? What was the outcome?

- Describe a work situation when you were directly responsible for preventing a serious problem from occurring. Also tell me about the most impacting work decision you ever made.

- Describe a time that you had to use a great deal of resourcefulness, persuasion, and initiative to get the job done.

- What was your biggest 'people problem?' What happened? How? Why? Who became involved? How was it resolved?

- What was the most difficult time you had in establishing rapport with another employee? Why? What was the outcome?

- Tell me about a time you were asked to do something but refused to do it. Why?

- In a group, which role do you most enjoy playing: spokesperson, leader, or devil's advocate? Why? What is an employee's role in public relations (PR)?
- What factors would you consider when tackling a new job? Any others?
- Walk me through your typical workday.

Employee/Management Relations

- What do you think is a healthy employee/management relationship? To what extent does it exist in your present company/organization? How do employee needs and concerns come to management's attention? How should they? How are management's needs and concerns brought to the attention of employees? How should they be addressed and resolved, in your opinion? By whom? In what manner? Are you aware that many of our employees have representation through [name of national or in-house association]?
- What roles do you think job performance, job seniority, and length of company service should play in making major decisions impacting all employees?
- What do you think of what is happening at [name of another prominent competitor]?
- What kinds of employee issues do you think should be brought to management's attention? By whom? Which issues should not be? Why? When have you registered a complaint to your boss or someone else that you feel was justified? Concerning what? What were the results?
- How would you describe the perfect job/work atmosphere? What would be the type of company management style? When would you feel justified in going over the head of someone? Have you ever done so? When? Where? Why?
- What does value added and total quality management (TQM) mean to you? Give me an example of a time when you've observed it or participated in its success.
- Have you ever been responsible for or involved in setting new standard operating procedures (SOP) or changing existing ones? When? Where? Which ones? Outcome?
- Have you ever disagreed with management policies, practices, procedures, or rules? Ever deviated from or bent them to meet a dead-

line, resolve a crisis, or get the job done? When? Why? What would you do if you observed someone breaking a company rule? Ever been asked or pressured into doing something that would be illegal or break a rule? Explain.

- Have you submitted any recommendations to management (up the line) for changes that were accepted and implemented? What were they? Any of them save time or money? How do you feel about 'cutting corners' to reduce costs?
- Tell me about some management policies that you thought were unfair to you. Why? In what ways? Did you speak up? What happened?
- Describe a time when you followed and supported management directives even when you personally disagreed with them.
- What problems, if any, do you think you could have leaving the military and entering a profit and customer-oriented, highly cost-conscious business/industrial atmosphere?
- What are the various roles of your work team members? Whose opinions are the most important to you? Least? Why?
- How much lost time have you had in the past five years? What was it for?
- What would be justifiable reasons to terminate an employee? Any others?
- What are the toughest groups you had to seek cooperation from? Why was it difficult? How successful were you?
- Tell me about a time when you had to sacrifice your family obligations for your job responsibilities, during a department/company crisis.
- What significant projects, programs, committees, studies, and research have you worked on? Did you volunteer?

Customer Concerns/Needs
- What are the concerns of customers when choosing a product and a brand.
- If you had to choose a product and brand, what factors would be most important to consider? Rank them. Why in that order?
- What specific roles do employees play in satisfying the needs of their employer's customers? Any others? Give your best example of a time you played an important role in resolving a customer's concerns or handling an irate customer.

- Do you happen to know who our biggest customers are?
- In what ways can a company attract new customers? What should a company avoid doing?
- How do you measure customer satisfaction? What role can employees play in measuring it?
- What was the biggest problem you've had in dealing with a customer? How was it resolved?

Career Goals and Progression

- What career goals, targets, and timelines have you set for yourself? How many have you achieved? Which ones do you have left to achieve? When do you expect to achieve them? Which have you failed to achieve? Which have you changed? For what reasons? How have you dealt with unexpected problems that have come up?
- In what areas and in what ways have you grown in your profession over the last five years?
- What job challenges are you most looking forward to tackling?
- To what do you contribute your success in getting this far in your career? What is the biggest obstacle you had to overcome?
- What has been the apex of your career so far? Where do you see yourself five years from today? Ten years?
- What did you do to speed up your job progression?
- What would be your fantasy job if you could be anything you wanted to be or could have any job you wanted?
- What are the most important reasons why you want this job? How long do you think it will take for you to get promoted? What factors will determine that length of time? When did you receive your last promotion? What was the new job?
- How does your spouse/special person feel about your changing jobs, companies, relocation, and your traveling more?
- What things are the least important to you as far as goal-setting is concerned? Why?
- What do you look for in a company, department, boss, and job?
- Walk me through your entire career in three minutes.

Personality and Character

- Describe yourself. How would you describe your personality? How has it changed over the years? What is character? How can you measure it? How would your supervisor, spouse, and closest friends describe you professionally and personally? How have your personality and character helped you to be effective in performing your job assignments.

- What are your best qualities? Biggest disappointment? Greatest challenge? How did these impact you?
- Tell me one word that best describes you. What three adjectives would best describe you? When are you most at ease? Least at ease? Have you ever worked with someone you couldn't stand?
- What do you do to get someone you're working with who isn't very communicative to 'open up' to you?
- What are your pet peeves? What irritates you? What causes you to lose your temper or get angry? Why? When is the last time you lost your temper? Why? When? Where?
- What habits do you have that annoy others?
- What was the last argument or disagreement you had with someone at work? Describe them. What caused them? How did they end?
- How do you relax? What techniques/approaches do you use?
- Tell me about a time you 'put your foot in your mouth?' How come? How did it turn out?
- Who do you most admire? Who do you most dislike? Why?
- What's the most interesting job-related thing that has happened to you in the last year?
- What do you most like to talk about? Why?
- Has anyone ever treated you in a hostile manner? When? Why? When were you unable to resolve a conflict with another employee? Describe. When is the last time you became angry with someone? Describe. What conflicts have you experienced while handling your present job assignments? What was the resolution? When do you become impatient with someone or something that's going on? What one thing frustrates you the most? Why?
- What type of person do you get along well with? Why? What type of person do you have the most difficulty getting along with? Why? Describe your best friend. What's your best personality trait? What's your worst? Ever dealt with a proficient but irritating co-worker or other employee? How did you handle it? Describe your worst enemy. How do you deal with very sensitive people?
- In what ways have you benefited from your disappointments?

- What motivates you? What turns you off? What do you like about yourself? What do you dislike? Why? What makes you happy? What makes you sad? Why? When do you feel indifferent?
- Do you believe that past experiences, decisions, and actions can predict someone's future behavior? Why? Why not? To what extent? In what areas? What event in your life has impacted you the most? One that was the most challenging?
- What do you do to raise your spirits when you're feeling blah? Is this approach always successful? What do you worry about? How do you cope with rejection?
- If you could change your life instantly, what would you change? Why would you want to change it?
- How do you *measure* success? In what ways and by what criteria?
- What's the difference between attitude and performance? What's the difference between being aggressive and being assertive?
- How personal do you think employees should become with one another? Really? Why? Who are your closest friends? Why are you so close to them? Describe them.
- How do you avoid arguments and personality conflicts? What approaches and techniques do you use? Has anyone ever referred to you as being hard-headed? Why? Have you ever had a problem establishing rapport with someone? Describe. When is the last time you apologized to someone? Over what?
- What's your favorite work place story? Describe your sense of humor. What role does it play in working with others? How do you know when someone is being plain funny and when they're using sarcastic humor?
- Is there anything about yourself you would like to 'go back' and change, or change today? If there was one thing, what might it be? When have you said something to someone and later regretted saying it?
- Have you ever helped another employee overcome an attitude problem? What tactics did you use. Have you, yourself, ever had an attitude problem? How did you overcome it?

Free Time

- How do you manage your free time away from the job? How do you prioritize what's most important to you? What are your hobbies and interests? Are you involved in any sports? Which do you enjoy most? Are you into any creative activities? Which of these do you enjoy most? What are your interests in music? Do you play any musical instruments? Do any song writing? Do you have any interest or involvement in other art fields? Describe them.

- What social, community, professional clubs and organizations do you belong to? Do you perform any volunteer work? Have you done any counseling? Have you managed youth groups? Why haven't you participated more?
- What type of non-fiction reading do you do? Does any of what you learn benefit you in your job, professional and personal development? What are you reading now?
- What job-related seminars and programs have you attended in the last two years?
- Are you taking any job-related courses? Are you working on a certificate or advanced degree? In what areas of study? When will you complete them?
- If you could have dinner with anyone, who would it be? Why that person? What would you want to discuss?

The Future

- Where do you expect to be in your career and what do you expect to be doing five years from now? Ten? How do you expect to get there? What do you need to do?
- What do you expect to contribute to our company? In what areas? What do you expect to receive from us?
- Are you planning to join the guard or reserves?
- What job-related changes do you see yourself going through in the next two years? How will you be different from what you are today? How will you have improved to become more productive in your position and profession?
- What problems do you think our industry will face in the next decade?
- What would you do if you were laid off?

Questions for Them

- Do you have any questions you would like to ask me/us? We have time for one or two, maybe three at the most. You don't have any?

- Have you heard any rumors about us and want to know if they are true or not?
- Would you care to ask our opinion on what more you can do to improve your job qualifications?

Wrapping Up

- Is there anything else we should know about you, or anything more you would like to add to what you have told us, before we wrap up our interview? Would you like to further clarify what you have said before we contact your past employers? Are there any problems that have slipped your mind? Can we contact your present employer and inquire about you? Are they aware that you are interviewing with us?
- Why should we hire you over all the other fine job candidates we are interviewing? If we can get someone with more job experience, more education, and more training, why should we give you preference? What is better about you than them? What sets you apart from them?
- What did you do to prepare for your interview with us? Did anyone help you prepare? Did any of our employees help you?
- When would you be available for employment with us?
- What if we don't hire you? What will you do?
- Do you have any last words? What one thing about you would you most like to leave in our minds before we conclude our interview?

"Hi! I'm Captain Meyers. How are you?"

"This is one of those trick questions, right?"

15

THE PSYCHOLOGIST'S EVALUATION

Some companies have job candidates evaluated by a psychologist or psychiatrist. If you are scheduled to be interviewed by one of them, be prepared—understand what to expect.

A psychologist (or psychiatrist) will spend anywhere from 30 minutes to an hour (sometimes more) with you. This expert will examine and assess your attitudes, personality, character, ability to cope with various stress situations and conflicts, emotional stability, and social extroversion. He or she will also want to examine your truthfulness, self-confidence, ideas, opinions, perceptions, insights, values, traits, motivation, and overall attitude toward yourself and your treatment of others. Questions will relate to your jobs, career progression, work experiences, educational background, training, leadership, professional skills, people skills, personal life, family background, early childhood, strong beliefs, outside interests, career aspirations, and hidden problem areas. Because of their extensive psychological training and experience, psychologists can legally ask you questions that HR and the hiring department cannot—questions regarding separations, divorces, family breakups, marriages, deaths, mental health problems, childhood traumatic experiences, and so on.

Questions Asked

Be prepared to give open, honest, yet tactful answers to questions such as these:

- Have you ever been treated by a psychologist, therapist, or counselor? When? For what? Do you take any medications? For what?
- What do you worry about? What problems do you have?

- Tell me about your family. Are your grandparents living? Are your parents living? How long have they been married? Are they divorced? How long have you been married, engaged, or living with someone? Who? For how long? Describe your relationship and interaction. Do you have any children? What are their ages? How do they differ in personalities? How do you motivate them? Discipline them differently? What do your parents, brothers, sisters and spouse do for a living? Describe each of them. Are any of them in your profession or career field? What makes a good parent and a good spouse?
- How does your spouse feel about your type of work and being away from home often? How much time do you spend with your spouse and your children? How old are your children? Describe each of them.
- Describe growing up. What was the atmosphere like? Who disciplined you? How? Who did you feel closest to, your mother or your father? What did you worry about? Do you think you had a happy childhood? Why do you feel that way? Were you ever abused? What happened? How often? Tell anyone about it? Why not? Ever bully anyone? How often? Why? Where you ever bullied? What were your feelings?
- How do you and your spouse/live-in resolve conflicts? What do you do that bothers him/her? What does he or she do that bothers you? What does your spouse/significant other like most about you? What do they like the least? Why?
- What makes you content with life? What's your philosophy of life? What are your likes and dislikes? Why have you made so many/few changes in your life?
- What makes you happy? Sad? Mad? What's most important to you? Why? Tell me more about that area.
- Are you a loner or a joiner? Why do you feel that way?
- How many very close friends do you have? For how long? Describe them to me. How often do you see them? What makes a good friend? Are you a close friend to others? How many?
- What secrets did you keep to yourself as you were growing up? What secrets do you have today? Any others?
- What was the proudest moment of your life? What was your most embarrassing moment? What things excite you? What things bother you? What things frighten you? What things motivate you? What do you daydream about?

- Were you married before? For how long? When did you divorce/split? What led to your divorce/split? What are you feelings about divorce? Do you still have some contact with your ex-spouse? How would you describe that relationship?
- How easily do you become defensive or upset? Over what? Why do you feel the way you do?
- How do you control anger? Give me an example. How often do you get angry? Over what? How do you manage your anger? Did you ever receive treatment for controlling it?
- When did you mature? What things happened in your life that matured you more quickly? What don't you like about yourself? Why? What is your worst attribute? What wouldn't you like me to know about you? Surely there must be something.
- Have you ever stolen anything? Really? Never?
- Describe the most traumatic event in your life. When did it happen? What caused it? What was the outcome? How did you cope with it?
- How well have you adapted to each major change in your life? Tell me more about that. What else could you have done to better handle each change?
- In what social situations are you uncomfortable? Why is that?
- How open are you? In what areas? Are you open both at work and at home? What don't you care to discuss? How easy is it for you to express your feelings? To whom? Under what situations? How often?
- Describe how you handle stressful situations. Give two examples.
- What's the most important decision you ever made under a great deal of pressure? How did it turn out? Do you have any regrets? Why? What should you have done differently?
- What is your favorite TV program? Movie? Comedian? Magazine? Subject? Why these?
- Describe your sense of humor. How do you apply it in your work? Give an example. Why do you think that's funny? When is taking humor too far? Do you ever use sarcasm? Why?
- Is your profession a way of life to you, or just a way to make a reasonable living? Why do you feel this way?
- Describe your leadership style. How did you develop it? How has it changed over the years?

- How do you maintain your psychological well-being (emotional health) on a day-to-day basis? What obstacles have you had to overcome to do so? What did you do? Why? How would you handle a co-worker who acts depressed?
- How will you be able to adapt to a new position, company, city, area of the country, and climate?
- What didn't you like about the military/some of your prior employers? Positions? Supervisors? People you worked with?
- Do you tolerate others who don't agree with you? How? When conflicts develop, how do you resolve them?
- Describe your working relationship with people of the opposite sex, minorities, people much older and younger than you. Have you ever had a personality conflict with a superior, peer, co-worker, subordinate, or customer/client? Over what? How did you resolve it? Give me some examples.
- If you were having lunch with your boss, what would you talk about? Why?
- Have you ever been emotionally unprepared for an important job challenge? Why? What were the circumstances? When do you feel the least like working?
- How many times have you started doing something and then just quit doing it? Why did you? Do you do it more at work or in your home life?
- Describe a time that you let someone down. How did he or she react? How did you feel about it?
- How do you keep your home life and emotions from entering into your work life? What do you enjoy doing the most when you're not working? Do you gamble? How much? How often? How often do you drink alcoholic beverages? Which ones? When do you know when you've had enough to drink?
- What was your favorite job? Why?
- What are your future goals both in your career field and personal life? Why these? When and how do you expect to attain them?
- If you were to author a confrontational article, what subject would you choose to write about? Why?
- Do you have any question(s) for me? Why do you ask that? No questions at all? Is there anything you feel you should talk to me about? Are you certain?

Assessing 'What Makes You Tick'

All these questions and probing boil down to this: Are you 'put together right'? Will you fit in well with the hiring company and their philosophies, politics, practices, standards and culture—the department, supervisors, peers, co-workers, customers and clients? Do you have the potential to advance and be put into leadership roles? Will you solve problems impressively, and not create them?

In general, as you might expect, job candidates with a strong positive attitude score well. Those who try hard to second-guess the psychologist/psychiatrist in their responses or clam up during the interview usually do not score well. Your goal should be to present yourself as a person who is competent, confident, congenial, forthcoming, tactful, and in control in any situation—the least likely person to panic if things go wrong.

One psychiatrist who screened job candidates for a major airline interviewed candidates while they sat in a rocking chair (a gift from his wife). He would observe when they stayed perfectly still, rocked slightly, moderately, and really fast. At the same time, he would note what question he had asked and correlate it with the amount of rocking going on. The harder and faster the rocking, the more likely the job candidate felt stressed by the question. This was an indicator to the psychiatrist to dig deeper and further into the candidate's response to that particular question. It would be best to maintain a moderate rocking speed throughout their interview. It's much more difficult to notice change in movement from a moderate to slow or fast speed, than from a standstill to any speed. Any change in behavior is a red flag to a psychiatrist to dig deeper for possible hidden problem areas.

Psychologists will place job candidates in one of three categories: positive, neutral, or negative. Just doing as well as other candidates will put you in the neutral group. If you are placed in the neutral or negative category, you will probably be eliminated. Your goal should be to be rated in the positive category.

The psychologist has a lot of clout. Most employers who utilize a psychologist will not hire someone unless HR, the hiring department, and the psychologist all agree that the candidate should be hired. The better you understand what the psychologist is looking for and assessing, the better you can prepare in advance. The better prepared you are, the calmer and more effective you will be, and the more likely it is that you will be placed in the positive category. Again, be yourself—at your best!

"How is your situational awareness?"

16

UNDERKILL VERSUS OVERKILL

The more educated, trained, and experienced you are the more you'll be expected to provide detailed, complete answers in your interviews. When you give some good answers, but leave out other good answers that the interviewer expected someone with your qualifications to give, that's underkill. When you fail to address a critical aspect of something that the interviewer would consider very significant during a discussion—that too, is underkill. Other candidates may have covered these points. You may appear to be one of those people who 'just gets by,' never offering more than the bare minimum to get the job done. Big mistake!

Most people who don't get hired suffer from underkill; far fewer suffer from overkill—that is, talking too much without adding more value. Those who suffer from underkill do so because they don't want to sound long-winded. They don't realize that as long as you are making important, concise, relevant points, you're on track. Don't stop talking, it's time well spent! Note that by keeping each point brief (one to two sentences), you can make more of them in a shorter period of time, and score more points with the interviewer. If you start taking three or four sentences to make one key point, you're leaning toward overkill. Strive to be brief yet not sound like you're reading from a checklist of items.

Overkill happens primarily when you take too long to make one good point and don't get around to other important points. Overkill also happens when you bring up irrelevant or trivial points, or go off on a tangent away from the question. This wastes time that you could have used to answer other questions.

When you come up with significant points that your competition failed to make, you move up and ahead of them. They may have never thought of those points—when you do, you get credit for thinking of them.

While overkill's much less common, you should watch out for it, especially if you have a tendency to dominate conversations. (If you're not sure about this, ask a good friend or close colleague to be brutally honest with you.)

Interviewers want to see if you can think fast enough on your feet to quickly consider all possible significant points, and then come up with the most meaningful ones in a reasonable period of time. They look for freshness in your answers, individuality in developing those answers, the most impressive order in which you can present them, and how well you communicate each point you're giving. They don't want to hear a lot of mundane points that aren't meaningful. Likewise, they don't want to hear answers that sound as though they were memorized from a book you read, list you were given, or a briefing by someone.

Remember, the interviewers will not be choosing between those who answered poorly and those whose answers were satisfactory. They'll be choosing between those who were satisfactory and those who were excellent to outstanding. An average, adequate interview won't win you the job. You have got to stand out from the other job candidates in many positive ways.

The bottom line is: It's better to risk a little overkill than underkill, as long as you are organized, concise, and relevant when answering the questions you were asked.

■ ■ ■

Knowledge without wisdom can be very dangerous.

■ ■ ■

17

INSIGHTS INTO BUILDING TERRIFIC ANSWERS

L et's say a friend who just went through their interview for the same position for which you are applying slips you a list of questions asked by HR and the hiring department. You skim through and say to yourself, "I can answer those! No sweat!"

Most likely you can. Most solid job applicants could. The real question is how much better can you answer them than all those other candidates with whom you're competing? If it's so easy, why do employers turn down so many job applicants? Why don't they hire the majority of those that are interviewed, instead of the minority? Aren't they wasting a lot of their time and money?

Some job candidates look for good answers to a question in the same way some travelers look for a motel while on vacation. Reaching a small town late in the afternoon, the traveler comes across two decent-looking motels within the first three blocks, and checks into one of them. The next morning at breakfast, another restaurant customer strikes up a conversation with the traveler and asks, "Why'd you pick that hotel? There's one four blocks farther down the street that's cleaner, roomier, and much cheaper. Too bad you stopped so soon."

Those same people also 'stop too soon' in finding the best interview answers. They settle for the first 'pretty good ones' they come up with, not realizing that if they'd kept digging they could have thought of more and better answers.

In another analogy, building impressive answers is like pulling tools out of a toolbox. How many things can you build or put together with just a hammer and screwdriver? The more tools you pull out, the more things you can build. It's the same with creating great answers. Don't limit yourself. If you can't come up with a solid reply to a question, you haven't looked and tried hard enough. Your commitment should be clear: "The opportunity to land this job with this company deserves the very best I can give."

When you're thoroughly prepared, interviewers are smart enough to recognize the time and effort you must have put in to build great, full-coverage answers. They know that such an *extra effort* approach makes employees perform very well in the workplace too. That's the kind of person employers want to hire.

Let's talk about what you can do that will put you up there in the top 10 percent of your competition. You'll learn how to build your own, hand-tailored answers to each anticipated interview question—and not give standard, canned answers. Here are the essential elements of successfully presenting yourself as an impressive job candidate:

- Tap into Your Source Material
- Be Comprehensive
- Give Key Points and Supporting Points
- Show Them How You Think
- Bone Up
- Know Their Company
- Put 'People' First
- Show Follow-Through
- Be Loyal
- Add Value to Their Company
- Impress Them with Your Preparation
- Pick Your Most and Least Favorite Jobs
- Say It: "I'm One of the Best!"
- Make It Fresh
- Establish a Positive Image of Yourself
- Handle the 'Bad Stuff' Well
- Fill Your Reserve Tank
- Aim for Perfection

Tap into Your Source Material

You may be wondering where all these terrific answers come from? Use the method described in "Tapping into Your Subconscious" in chapter 10.

As you relax quietly at home, focusing on a particular interview question, your mind will wander and scan through everything you have experienced that could possibly relate to the question.

It's similar to fishing. Close your eyes and imagine yourself fishing at the bank of a fast-running, clear stream. You're noticing the number, type, and size of fish swimming there; catching some, picking out those worth keeping and returning the others to the stream. In this same very comfortable, relaxed, 'open' state of mind, you're catching the good points to use in building your answer, releasing the others. Once you've gathered what you need, you open your eyes and write down the best material. You've had a very productive experience creating a great answer to an important anticipated interview question.

You've got many answers to prepare, so it's good to prioritize your 'answer development' sessions. While you're becoming comfortable with the method, use a few of the easier questions (perhaps those concerning recent achievements, or why you like your job). Once you feel proficient, use your sessions to explore the most important and difficult questions; then the less critical questions, as time allows.

Be Comprehensive

As you build your answers, keep in mind that it's better to give comprehensive coverage of all the *key points* and *supporting points* pertaining to the question you are asked, than to have long, detailed coverage of only half of them. The interviewer can always press you for more details on a certain point if he or she wishes to, but if you fail to even mention major areas, the interviewer may reach one or more of the following conclusions:

- You aren't aware of the importance of these unmentioned areas
- You can't differentiate between more and less important points
- You don't see the big picture
- You are in a hurry to get through your answer
- You didn't anticipate this question
- You have trouble concentrating under pressure
- You are so nervous you can't think clearly
- You aren't a creative thinker

As you build your answers, ask yourself, "Is there anything else I could say briefly that would add another point to my score—something I might have failed to think of that would be worthwhile to bring up?" Don't stop with "I think that's good enough." Instead, think, "I challenge anyone to come up with good points I haven't already thought of—any takers?"

Let's examine some approaches job candidates may take to answering the following question: "How were your grades in college?" Which of these approaches do you think is best?

General	More Specific	Complete and Concise
"Good"	"Had a B average"	"Had an overall 3.1 GPA
"Pretty good"	"Almost a B average"	on my bachelor's
"Not too bad"	"Mostly Bs and Cs"	degree and a 3.3 GPA on
"Not so good"	"Had about a C average"	my masters"
"Pretty bad"	"Mostly Cs"	"Had a 2.9 GPA overall,
		and a 3.1 GPA in my
		major"

When you give more good points than your competition, one of those additional good points may touch a warm spot in the heart of your interviewer. He or she may be impressed that you thought to bring out something none of the other candidates did. This positive feeling about you could permeate the remainder of the interview.

Give Key Points and Supporting Points

When you're preparing an answer to impress the interviewer, think in terms of *key points* and *supporting points*. To illustrate, let's take a common question asked civilian and military pilots being interviewed for a flight position with a major airline:

"What are all the important attributes of a good airline pilot?"

Key point: Safety-oriented.
Supporting point: Safety is the pilot's top priority in flying.

Key point: Competent.
Supporting point: A competent pilot knows the aircraft's systems well, has strong operational skills, and makes sound judgment calls.

Key point: Displays strong leadership skills.
Supporting point: A strong leader brings out the best in each crew member, motivates them as a team, and leads by example.

Key point: Handles stress well.
Supporting point: The pilot doesn't lose his or her cool in an emergency.

Key point: Customer-oriented.
Supporting point: The pilot recognizes and satisfies the most important needs of the customer.

Key point: Profit and cost-containment oriented.
Supporting point: The pilot saves fuel whenever safely possible, and comes up with good cost-reduction and time-saving ideas.

The order in which you present both your key and supporting points is very important. In the illustration used, the most important points—safety, flight skills, handling stress, teamwork, people, leadership, customer satisfaction, cost containment, and profitability—should come first. Time permitting, follow up with less important points.

When you come up with two or three good points in answering a question, and are pleased with the way you presented them, remember that most of the other job candidates who are applying for the same position come up with just as many. You have to consistently come up with more and better answers than they do to be chosen over them.

Don't announce or count off your points by number—for example, don't say, "There are three important points every professional in my position should consider. First of all...second...and third..." You may think there are only three important points—the interviewer may think there are five. He or she may feel that you actually made only two main points—your third wasn't really a key one. Just present your points in the order of their importance to you, in a conversational manner. When you number them it appears that you consider yourself an authority on how many there are and which ones are definitely the most important. There may be five to seven major reasons why someone in your profession would want to work for their company, although you offer just three. You may think the product the company produces is most important; the interviewer may feel their 'team of people' is paramount.

After you make your last point in answering a question, stop talking! Don't go on and repeat what you've already said or try to think of something else to say—you gave it your best shot. Leave it at that. Be aware that whatever you say to the interviewer (in chit-chatting) prior to or following the interview itself, will be noted and become part of their total evaluation of you.

Don't give a summary of the points you made after answering each question; it's best to just present them and let the interviewer draw her or his own conclusions. Interviewers have a good attention span. Your time will be better spent moving on to answer the next question.

Show Them How You Think

Aside from such questions as "Have you ever taken illegal drugs?" interviewers don't want just 'yes or no' answers to their questions. They want you to reveal the logic and analysis that led to your conclusion.

When it comes to decision-making, refrain from regretting a number of important decisions you have made. These may include deciding upon which college to attend, picking a major and certain courses, your study habits, declining a job offer, choosing a company to work for, and so on. When you regret making them or if you want to change them, it's sort of like admitting you made a big mistake or are wishy-washy—not certain of what you should have done. We all regret one or two bigger decisions we've made and it's okay to admit it; but it's not tactful to bring this up voluntarily during a job interview. Bring up a couple of lesser importance—not the real 'biggies.'

Discussing the process, method, and analysis by which you came up with your answers to difficult questions can impress the interviewer as much as the answers themselves. This shows that you approach any situation in an objective, logical, thorough manner, rather than 'shooting from the hip' and hoping you hit your target. Interviewers don't want people working for their company who *guess* how to carry out a job assignment or handle other employees and customers; nor guess in giving an answer to their question during a job interview. It's better to say "I don't know" than to guess wrong.

Should you be asked why you have stayed in your current position for so long, show that you gave that a lot of thought. You liked the company, your department, your boss, co-workers, the type of work you were doing, and your job assignments. However, you were getting up toward the top of your salary range; there were no promotional opportunities coming up; the company's volume of business had leveled off; and there could be some downsizing of personnel. There was also talk of outsourcing the type of work you were doing.

You want to point out that no company will ever owe you something—you will earn whatever you get through hard work; not handed something without putting in the effort to achieve it. You're the type of person who approaches every new job challenge with strong interest and excitement.

Should you be asked about how you could have improved your educational and training background, you could respond by saying that you would have liked to have taken one or two courses that were offered (knowing today what you know) that would help you in job assignments you've been given. Point out the on-the-job value of part-time and summer jobs you held, co-op programs you participated in, volunteer work you did, clubs and organizations you joined, and internships you received.

You may be asked to sell the interviewer (playing the role of a customer) on buying their company's product or some item in their interviewing office. The interviewer hopes to catch you off guard and find out how quickly and impressively you can 'think on your feet.' The interviewer wants to learn how you handle stress, organize your thoughts, prioritize, communicate in words and body language, understand what appeals to a potential customer, the key purposes, functions, and strengths of the product/item, any limitations, cost, guarantee, and so on. He or she will often play an adversary role, questioning just about everything—to observe how you handle criticism and rejection. You are observed on how well you remain calm, pleasant, non-defensive, optimistic, and 'on course' with your sales pitch. Knowing all this in advance of the interview, you can prepare to address every area of the interviewer's questioning and concerns.

Bone Up

Now's the time to strengthen your technical knowledge and expertise in your profession and career field before your interview. Bone up on new approaches; do some research on processes, methods, procedures, practices, programs, plans, innovations, and new ideas that are being discussed and tried out in your field. Go over your job-related education, training, and experience. Review current and prior important job assignments, projects, and programs in which you were actively engaged. Be able to provide technical information and insight into how you think and operate. Recall how you contributed significantly to team success and situations in which you handled the people involved in a very impressive manner. Bring all the 'good stuff' you have to offer to the surface of your thinking. Don't hope it will arise spontaneously when you're called upon to reveal it during a job interview.

Know Their Company

Revisit all the research you did that led you to choose this company. Prepare yourself to talk knowledgeably about every aspect of its history, main operations, products and services. Anticipate discussing their company's current status, relative to its competitors. This could include their team of people; their energetic, positive atmosphere; their top leadership; their impressive track record/history of growth, innovations and other achievements in the industry. Point out their strong marketing approach, pride in what they stand for among their peers and in the communities they service, across the country, and throughout the world. Stress the excellent job and advancement opportunities they offer.

Put 'People' First

Employers like to hire those who express a strong awareness of and commitment to the people they will work with and the customers they will serve. They know that it is their employees who are responsible for their organization's success. Some job applicants do not stress the importance of people, teamwork, and customer satisfaction during their interviews. Instead, they focus completely upon themselves. Prepare some examples that illustrate your successes in understanding and dealing with people in every area of your job involvements. Point out how important teamwork is and how teams of impressive individuals can make any company successful no matter what products and services they provide.

Show Follow-Through

Companies don't like quitters—people who start something but give up and walk away as soon as the going gets a little tough. If you've had any such false starts in building your career, develop good reasons for failing to finish them. The interviewer can conclude that even though they wished you had seen it through, they can understand why you weren't able to.

Be Loyal

Loyalty is a 'make or break' quality with every employer. If they don't have your loyalty, they don't want you working for them. When you hear employees consistently knock their employers, what they say is more damaging to the company's image than if it were said by someone outside that company. An outsider doesn't have firsthand information and insight into what's going on—an insider does.

As you enter a discussion of your present and prior employers, departments, and supervisors, show your strong loyalty to and support of whatever they were trying to accomplish—even if you didn't always agree with them. Point out how much you learned and were able to grow, and how well you worked with those around you at all levels. Play up any positives; play down any negatives.

Add Value to Their Company

Your answers should demonstrate that you are more interested in how you can add value to the company than you are in personal gain (more money, benefits, better location, and so on). Your focus is on achieving success through tackling added job challenges, advancing into greater job responsibilities, contributing significantly to team effort and results, generating ideas for time and dollar savings, and helping others around you. Interviewers notice whether you're a self-centered 'gimme' person or a "what can I do for you?" person.

Impress Them with Your Preparation

The efforts you made to prepare for the interview can impress the interviewer, in and of themselves. You can expect to be asked what you did to prepare, so be ready. Take note of each step, compiling a list to refresh your memory. This may include your having completed the following steps:

- Going over your completed employment application and resume thoroughly. Being certain you had all the dates, places, and experiences you have been through at your fingertips, so that you could readily answer any questions about them and save time for more of the interviewer's questions.
- Thoroughly researching the company—asking friends who work there, and others who know a great deal about its history, present operations, and projected plans.

- Reading many technical and business magazines and newspaper articles covering the company's products and services, its key personnel, business/marketing factors and statistics, and so on.
- Reading everything you could find relating to state-of-the-art developments in the company's field.
- Keeping up with news stories relating to the company and its industry.
- Making a list of questions you could be asked, considering your particular qualifications and job experiences.
- Thinking back over your education, training and positions held, and considering anything meaningful that you accomplished that might relate to those questions. Selecting directly-related examples to discuss.
- Practicing going over your answers with your spouse and closest friend. Working on them to be certain they came out sounding both honest and tactful. Thinking of every way you can improve your presentation—because getting this job at this company means the world to you.

One word of caution: Avoid giving the interviewer the impression that someone working for their company had access to the current list of interview questions and/or preferred answers, and that these were passed to you.

During your interview, *you're better off spending more time on presenting your strengths than on improving your weaknesses.* The effort you exert on impressing the interviewers with your capabilities will pay off more than putting it into softening the impact of your drawbacks.

Pick Your Most and Least Favorite Jobs

Think about how you'd answer the question, "Which job did you least enjoy? Most enjoy?" Sometimes the interviewer specifies "over your professional career," but you should also be prepared to discuss your earliest jobs—those that were part-time and during the summers while you were in high school or attending college. Don't be caught off guard. When asked about the job you least liked, pick out the one that was the simplest to learn, repetitive, and boring. Your most liked job should be the highest in position, leadership, complexity, responsibility and challenge, and most directly related to your profession and career field.

Even when addressing the question, "What courses did you most and least enjoy?" you can tactfully point out that the ones you most enjoyed were the ones in which you made your highest grades. They also proved to be the most helpful to you in handling on-the-job work assignments. You can mention that those least enjoyable were not as directly job-related and you didn't make high grades in those. Also add that you seemed to get much more out of courses when you had a highly motivating instructor.

Say It: "I'm One of the Best!"

When asked about your greatest accomplishment, pick the *most impressive* of all the things you have achieved that is the *most recent.* The fact that you upgraded into a higher position with much greater job responsibilities, in a short period of time, will impress interviewers. You can also describe overcoming a major obstacle that stood in the way to achieving a very important and difficult job assignment. Achievements that had a big payoff value—saving the company money, time, and increasing quality— deserve top billing. 'I did' is always better than 'I could do.' If you have to choose between two alternatives, demonstrated ability and experience are more valuable than potential.

Prepared to be asked "Why do you think we should hire you over all the other well-qualified candidates that we have interviewed for this job opening?" Most interviewers ask this at the very end of the interview. Consider this the equivalent of a courtroom summation—your opportunity to represent (with a fresh twist) all the things you have going for you that set you apart from all other candidates.

Give the interviewer more than just one or two good reasons; bring out all the important things you have going for you, professionally and personally. Highlight whatever you believe specifically differentiates you from the others. Stress your continuous proven record of successful job performance and progression. Point out that maintaining and advancing the *quality* of your track record of performance in your profession has been, and always will be, one of your top priorities.

It's possible to do this without sounding boastful or cocky. You are only relating what you have worked so hard to achieve within a balanced professional and personal life. State your accomplishments as though you were a TV news broadcaster reporting today's news—in a straightforward manner, without commentary. You deserve credit for them. You earned them. Now it's payoff time.

What sets you apart and makes you the best candidate? Keep this ultimate question in the back of your mind as you prepare all your other answers. Compile a list. Whenever something stands out as a key point in response to this question, add it to the list. When you're done, you can rearrange the order as you choose, to end up with a compelling summation.

Make It Fresh

Think about how many candidates your interviewers have faced. When job interviewers and/or selection boards are in the process of deciding who to select to fill each job opening, they must reduce the field of candidates down to two impressive, seemingly equally qualified and well-prepared candidates. They will usually give the edge to the candidate who made positive points in their presentations in a more fresh, original manner. If you take the time to produce your own unique version of a classic answer, you won't fall into the trap of making the exact, same worded points as all the other candidates. You don't have to skip an important point in order to be different. Make the same point; but in your own words, and style of delivery. Give it a fresh look!

For example, how many times do you suppose the interviewer has heard "I'm a real perfectionist." (This is a tried-and-true 'too much of a good thing' response to the "What are your weaknesses" question.) Instead of this tired self-description, you could say, for example (in your own words), that you tend to set extremely high standards for yourself in performing your job responsibilities and wind up not fully satisfied with the result of your efforts—even if others tell you that you did a great job, you don't quite believe them. Describe specifically how your perfectionism manifests itself in your work.

Establish a Positive Image of Yourself

There's a lot of applied psychology involved in successfully presenting yourself in an important job interview. Do your homework on this subject. As a starting point, consider that the interviewer's *perception* of you will determine whether or not he or she will recommend that you be hired. The *image* of yourself that you project to the interviewer is even more important than your actual qualifications. It is the perception that people have of 'things' and those people around them that counts most. What people *think* you are is the basis of their decisions and actions concerning you; it may, or may not, align with the 'actual facts'.

The interviewer perceives many things about you; your looks, appearance, grooming, body language, actions, eye contact, voice, character, values, temperament, disposition, attitude, and overall personality. He or she also notes your reactions to the interview atmosphere and the situations you are placed in, your understanding of the questions asked, your style in answering questions, the breadth and depth of your answers, your level of stress, your job knowledge, skills, and judgment exercised. There is a focus on the examples you give, your leadership capabilities, people skills, team orientation, and potential for development into senior level professional and managerial positions with their company. All these contribute to the hiring decision.

It would be a good idea to point out how you can disagree with someone's ideas and opinions without having a personality conflict. You respect a person's right to disagree with you and not let it hamper your working relationship.

Think about what you do to positively influence everyone with whom you come in contact throughout the interviewing process, from the time you open the door of their HR employment office to the time you leave their premises.

Handle the 'Bad Stuff' Well

Interviewers are especially interested to know about your skill in handling a stressful, touchy, delicate situation—whether an actual past incident, or a hypothetical future one. Let's say your boss does something wrong, or acts in an unprofessional manner, or becomes incapacitated, and the like. What's your approach to handling these? What do you say and do? How tactful are you? Can you effectively correct your boss and defuse a tense situation? What techniques do you use? Do you involve management and/or others? What you choose to say and do will reveal a great deal about you.

Think about the serious problems or emergencies you've faced in your career, and choose the ones that best reflect how successfully and impressively you handled the situation. There may be others that were more serious, but if you played minor or limited roles in resolving them, it won't gain you many points.

Practice going over touchy, negative situations which have occurred in your present or past positions and employment that you may be asked to explain. Work on your description and explanations until you find the most comfortable way to discuss the circumstances. Go over these out loud several times until you feel more self-confident, relaxed, and less emotional when talking about the details. You want to sound like you are not making excuses for what happened but instead are trying to understand exactly what occurred, both for your own peace of mind and to be better prepared to handle such incidents successfully in the future.

As you probe for examples of such situations, you must consider full-blown arguments and personality conflicts to be very serious 'negatives' and avoid relating these if at all possible. Try, instead, to come up with honest differences of opinion, disagreements, and minor conflicts that you can cite and describe; these are more understandable and acceptable to interviewers.

Fill Your Reserve Tank

Don't settle for one good answer to each anticipated question. You should plan to have several to choose from. The more options you've prepared, the more you'll arm yourself to have just the right answer to a specific question. It's common for an interviewer to ask, "What other examples can you give me?" Always have more good examples and points to fall back on than you planned to give.

When you get into the actual interview, you may be more nervous and forgetful than you thought you would be. Extra points are like reserve fuel—don't let yourself run out of gas. If you come up with just one more good point that other candidates didn't think of when answering each of the questions you were asked, think how far ahead of them you will be at the end of the interview.

You should also be prepared for the interviewer to follow up on points you've made, probing for more details and examples to support what you have said. Choose those examples/stories that tie in with their company's culture, philosophies, values, approaches in promoting their products and services, and their people. Develop answers to questions such as:

- What else can you tell us about that?
- How did you come up with that? Why didn't you act sooner?
- What was your gut reaction? Why didn't you follow it?
- What were you thinking about in deciding to do that?
- What were the most important factors you considered? No others?
- What other actions could you have taken? Why those?

- What other timing could you have had?
- What other people could you have called upon to help out?
- Exactly why did you change your mind?

Aim for Perfection

The perfect answer is like the perfect job—it doesn't exist. It is, however, a good target to aim for, knowing that you'll never hit the bull's eye, but will keep trying to get as close to it as possible. More people are hired with some overkill than those who have some underkill. Perhaps there were a lot of things that you were prepared to talk about that didn't come up for discussion during your job interview. Being well prepared allowed you to do a good job of handling everything that did come up. Look what you gained.

The chapters that follow will help you shape your raw material into polished, effective responses for your interviews.

■ ■ ■

You are important! You are the past,
present, and future 'combined' of time itself.

■ ■ ■

18

HOW LONG SHOULD YOUR ANSWERS BE?

Your answers can vary in length from one second for a simple "Yes" or "No," to as much as a minute and a half to describe a very important, highly involved project that you headed—from start to completion. Most open-ended questions can be answered effectively within a range of fifteen to forty-five seconds, providing you anticipated the question being asked and were well-prepared to answer it. Interviewers expect that it will take more time for applicants to answer the 'heavy questions' they ask.

Prepare your answers so that you can speak as concisely as possible, without seeming rushed; don't take three sentences to say what you can in one. You can make one good point every five to six seconds, if you are concise and condensed, choosing meaty words and skipping the fat. In this way, if asked to describe all the attributes of an impressive leader, you can list as many as ten good attributes within one minute. Using this approach throughout your interview, you will significantly increase your chances of getting hired.

After an interviewer asks a heavy or difficult question, you will usually be allowed three to four seconds of silence to gather your thoughts. Wait six or seven seconds, though, and the interviewer will move on to another question—and score you 'zero' on that one. Be prepared to answer immediately to any 'yes' or 'no' question such as, "Ever been fired from a job?" If you don't, the interviewer will be concerned as to why you need to think for such a long time in order to answer such a simple, clear question—and wonder if you are thinking of some way to fabricate an answer. Your chances of scoring high will drop sharply when you hesitate to answer such a straight forward question. Here's where your *advance preparation* will really pay off—you'll have the answers to every antici-pated question 'at your fingertips.'

An answer should be no longer than it takes to concisely cover each key point and its supporting points—no more, no less, be it ten seconds or a minute, or perhaps a minute and a half—some questions call for 'the full story.' Astute candidates can cover twice as much territory as others in a shorter period of time. Interviewers look for lean and meaty answers. Too many superfluous words and long periods of silence are the fat on the body of good answers. (But a little fat is acceptable when you're known to be new to the interviewing game.) Your answer is 'too long' when you add extra words and thoughts that don't add any significant value to what you have already said.

After making your last good point, stop talking. Don't linger on with, "Let's see…hmm…" If you have anticipated the question and are well pre-pared to answer it, you should not have any problem staying within the suggested time frame.

■ ■ ■

There are no bad questions, just bad answers.

■ ■ ■

19

CHOOSING YOUR BEST EXAMPLES OF
'SITUATIONAL-BASED BEHAVIOR' EXPERIENCES

Interviewers often ask a job candidate to give an example from their work experiences to support a statement or position taken. The interviewer is actually thinking "How do I know you didn't just make that up to impress me? I want an actual example of a situation you were in to back it up."

Let's say you've emphatically declared your strong commitment to 'quality' in performing every job assignment. The interviewer asks for specifics to back up your claim. You are well prepared: "My supervisors would all tell you that I'm very quality-conscious. Let me tell you about an extremely important job assignment I was on earlier this year and how I handled it when it came to doing a top quality job. I was deciding how to best cope with a problem our department was facing and I..." Point out that you have always believed that 'quantity' is important, but 'quality' is crucial.

As you work on examples to illustrate a key point for each answer you plan to give, collect several examples and then identify the very best—the one that most favorably conveys how crucial your actions were in resolving a situation, displays one of your greatest strengths, reveals a good idea you came up with, and so on. These can be presented as 'stories' (up to two minutes in length) you want to tell to support the point you made. Build each story into a clear, vivid picture so realistic that it seems as though you are going through the experience as it is occurring. Everyone enjoys hearing a good story. You may recall a story/example that was more serious or had greater impact on others, but if you didn't play a big role in the outcome, find a better story/example to use. Interviewers are interested in the results, not just a lot of activity. Your story must be delivered impressively and have a strong punch line. Practice organizing and delivering each story you tell until it sounds credible, concise, well worded, and clearly sends the key message you want to get across to the interviewer. Should you sense that the interviewer isn't that impressed with that particular example, stop where you are and say, "I just thought of a better story of what happened to me that will more strongly back up the point I made earlier. I'd like to tell it to you. It's not too long."

The more recent the accomplishment and the greater the positive impact, the better the example. Your top example should show that you not only met, but far exceeded performance expectations—especially when achieving time and cost savings or efficiency improvements. Be prepared to explain the reasoning behind the approach you took in handling any situation.

As you think back over situations, people interactions, incidents, emergencies, and other circumstances upon which to draw your stories, try to select those that would be most meaningful to the job responsibilities and typical job assignments of the position for which you're applying. There is a big difference between "I need to do something" and "I've already done it;" between the desire to do something and actually accomplishing it. Remember, the interviewer well understands these differences—it's his or her job to spot them. You will be scored critically if he or she thinks you are trying to receive credit for something you really didn't accomplish even though you had good intentions.

It's also a good idea to convey the impression that you take your job seriously, but don't take yourself too seriously. It's important to show you can 'lighten up' when it comes to self criticism. No one likes to work with someone who can't take any type of constructive critique directed their way and is always serious. There's a time to be serious and a time when it's okay to 'kid around' a little.

Even with your best examples, plan to avoid overkill. Interviewers don't want to hear long, drawn-out minor details, just the important facts. State the problem, how it came about, who was involved, what actions you took to come up with the best solution, the resolution, and how the problem could be prevented from occurring again.

Try to use job titles rather than actual names, especially if the situation involved friction with someone you consider to be difficult to work with. Personal revelations could come back to haunt you; the person in question could possibly be working for their company.

Interviewers also want examples of times you didn't perform well.

Think of those furthest back in your career when you had limited experience in your profession. Pick one that would be the least damaging to your professional and personal reputation. Play it down. The more recent and serious your mistake, the more critically you will be judged.

In preparing to present your examples, choose the best wording and sequence in telling your story. Practice giving it aloud to yourself, spouse, or best friend until satisfied you're telling it to the best of your ability. Try videotaping yourself telling the story. Bounce it off your family and close friends as well. Weigh their assessments and suggestions. You want all your stories to sound interesting and hit their target of supporting statements you have made about your attributes, capabilities, and accomplishments.

You don't have to volunteer an example for every answer you give—just be ready to do so when asked. However, if you've got a terrific example ready and are not asked for one, take the initiative to tactfully work it in at an appropriate time relative to the subject being discussed. Be brief and let the interviewer ask for further details.

Let me emphasize several important observations. Interviewers believe that the more they understand how you behaved in the past in handling job-related matters, the more likely they will be able to accurately predict how you will behave in the future while carrying out job responsibilities for their company. What 'samples' are you prepared to give? Will they reveal your past and present behavior in the best light possible? Have you decided what example to use if they asked about a situation you were in that didn't turn out well? The examples they ask for can relate to almost any questions they could ask you. Choose examples/situations that will be positive reflections of who you really are and how you typically operate. If you present examples of how well you made important decisions and solved problems that arose while performing your job assignments in the past, there is every reason to believe you would do the same in the future—for them.

Interviewers want you (through your examples) to demonstrate to them that you possess certain attributes, traits, skills, and abilities. They don't want you to bluff or give vague or evasive responses to their requests. They hope to 'pin you down' to specifics. They are more interested in learning all about your most significant accomplishments than they are your years of experience. It may take one job candidate several years to accomplish what another did in one year.

Using the 'SPSRP' Approach

You may be asked to demonstrate to the interviewer, in the form of a story/explanation, how you resolved a big problem that had developed while you were working on an important project. You should choose the best example you can think of that worked out very well for you, your boss, the department, and the company—using the SPSRP approach:

S (Situation occurring)
P (Plan of action to resolve)
S (Steps with actions taken)
R (Results achieved)
P (Prevention of problem reoccurring)

SITUATION. Explain what happened—why, when, where, and with whom it happened; the circumstances under which the situation/experience/event happened; the problems it caused; the impact it had on you, your boss, co-workers, the department, and company. Tell why it was so important to address and resolve the problem.

PLAN. Tell about the challenges you faced and how you were able to develop a plan of action to solve the problem. Explain how and why you established goals and objectives Describe how you observed and analyzed many factors and reached several conclusions that proved to be correct.

STEPS. Point out the steps/actions you took; the reasoning behind your action; obstacles you overcame; who was involved; the process you used and the skills you displayed; when these steps/actions were implemented; the timing required; why these particular steps/actions had to be taken—how they would resolve the problem.

RESULTS. State the results you achieved and how you measured them. Relate these accomplishments to the core of the problem and what you did to turn a negative situation into a positive one. Reveal how you behaved and effectively handled every phase which you went through—all the 'good stuff.'

PREVENTION. Point out that the plan, goals, objectives, steps, and actions taken included ways to prevent the problem from reoccurring — and it never occurred again.

Being Placed in a Role-Playing Situation

Some companies have their job interviewers put you in a realistic, comfortable, on-the-job role-playing situation (professional, leader, follower, or coordinator) and observe how you behave and conduct yourself in a realistic work situation. You're presented with a typical work problem (found in the actual position for which you are applying).

The situation typically involves a problem requiring team effort to resolve, with you as the central figure. The problem could relate to a myriad of areas: chain of command; coordination breakdown with another department; satisfying staffing needs; production difficulties; quality control concerns; failure to meet crucial deadlines; misunderstandings over job and project assignments; cost reduction needs; declining sales; loss of customers; training needs; establishing new job goals and responsibilities; and resolving conflicts between co-workers, subordinates and bosses.

There are no right or wrong solutions as such. The focus is on your thought process and your ability to reach logical conclusions and make sound decisions. The concern is whether or not you display leadership skills and can handle multi-tasking successfully.

One, two, or three of the interviewers interact with you. They play the roles of subordinates, superiors, or co-workers. You are asked to utilize them productively in every way you can, as all of you work as a team to resolve the problem. They will provide information to you when requested but will not volunteer information or offer assistance unless you ask for it.

Another interviewer may serve as 'the observer'—taking notes and assessing everything that is happening throughout the session (which may last 15 to 30 minutes). There may be a time limit established for solving the problem. You are expected to formulate a plan of action within a short period of time, establish goals with time plans for completion, and listen closely to your team's inputs. You must quickly grasp the role each member plays and point out the need for each to inform the others of changing circumstances as they evolve. It's up to you to solicit their recommendations and let your intentions be known. You should continuously monitor what's happening, stay alert to unexpected developments, and not overreact. Your display of situational awareness at all times is crucial.

Those interviewers involved in the exercise may also be taking notes. Their goal is to observe and assess your leadership, technical, and coordination skills, analytical ability, reasoning, how well you handle people and stress. They keep a watchful eye on when and how you display initiative, your thought processes in many areas, the way you function in a subordinate or peer role, how you respond to unexpected challenges of authority, role reversal, and your overall ability to remain calm and think clearly at all times. Do you handle pressure and stress well? Are you easily distracted? Are you irritated and lose concentration when interrupted? How do you handle criticism? Do you bully or succumb to one of the players? Are you concise or vague? Do you waste time? Are you easily intimidated? Do you remain relaxed through most of the session? Do you play favorites? Do you give crisp and readily understood directions to others? Do you seek the judgement of those involved? Are you well organized? How cooperative are you? Do you display a lot of 'give and take?' Do you seem reluctant to participate in the exercise? Do you remain personable regardless of what happens? Are you results oriented? Do you focus too much on the others involved instead of the problem to be solved? What problem-solving processes and techniques do you use? Do you take on 'too little' or 'not enough?' How do you behave at the close of the session? Do you act appreciative of the help you received from the other players/participants?

There may be a debriefing situation where you're given the opportunity to explain how and why you responded to particular situations as you did. You are asked how you would have handled them differently if you were to do it over again. Be honest and brief. Highlight what you thought to be the key elements of the problem presented, your rationale for accepting or ruling out various courses of action, and taking full responsibility for the outcome. Give credit where due to team participants for providing valuable input to you. Avoid blaming others for mistakes made. Be open to criticism.

Point out how the whole experience provided the opportunity to learn and gain insight from the exercise in how to better solve problems through making sound decisions and utilizing the help and knowledge of those around you.

■ ■ ■

Acting upon your beliefs is so much
more important than just embracing them.

■ ■ ■

20

ASSESSMENTS MADE DURING GROUP PARTICIPATION

Some companies want to find out how you behave when you're part of a group. There are usually two or more interviewers who gather a group of job applicants (three to five) competing for the same job opening. The interviewers address the applicants as a 'team' as well as 'individuals.' Their goal is to observe and assess each applicant as he or she interacts with the other applicants when the group is tossed a question, as well as when questioned individually. Each interviewer will make a written evaluation of his or her observations and assessments on each candidate. Their session can last up to an hour.

Candidates Address Group

The questions addressed to the group may range from "Why do you want this job?" to "Why should we hire you over all the other candidates?" The interviewers may single out a candidate to answer the question and continue doing this until every candidate has a chance to address their response to the interviewers and the group. You should be prepared to answer the question as you would in a one-on-one interview, but modify your answer so that you don't say exactly the same thing another candidate has said. Use your own unique style and wording when giving your responses. You don't want to come up with an answer that is less impressive than the one you planned to give, just to be different from your competitors. Don't get so wrapped up with what the others are saying that you lose your train of thought when you are addressed. While giving your answer, switch back and forth in your direct eye contact with both the interviewers and the other members of the group. You don't want to appear intimidated by the group and therefore avoid eye contact with anyone.

Role-Playing Problem Situations

One interviewer may create a realistic work situation that needs to be resolved and throw it out to the group to handle. The group is given little guidance as to who plays what role, what should be addressed, the facts that are known, and so forth. The interviewers are interested in finding out how the participants will choose a leader, who he or she will be, what role they will play, what group organizational structure will develop, what goals and sub goals will be established, who is responsible for what, who reports to whom, what assignments are given out and to whom. They observe what decision-making process will be used, whether decisions are made by consensus or certain individuals, what actions are taken, who evaluates what is being accomplished, what follow up there is, what results are expected and how will they be presented as the solution to the problem posed to them. You don't want to be dominating and overly aggressive and just take over as the group leader without any group discussion, nor do you want to sit back and say nothing or do nothing. You want to participate, be assertive, show you can handle any role (leader, follower, coordinator, participant), are action and results oriented, and can help create and follow an agenda. You want to be viewed as a patient, keen observer and communicator, having good timing as when to speak up, a consensus builder, asking good questions and displaying initiative, coming up with impressive ideas and plans, appreciative of the contributions others make, someone who doesn't get frustrated easily and isn't afraid to give others credit for their ideas. Your behavior should reflect your having a good attitude— aren't argumentative or antagonistic, your ability to motivate others to participate in building a realistic solution to the problem posed, understanding of time limitations and deadlines, tolerance of others who might not agree with you, and your exercise of sound judgment. Make it evident that you are assertive and personable, a 'peace maker,' stimulate and help others in the group that are more reserved and hesitant to 'join in', a good facilitator, organizer, and problem solver, goal oriented, and considered one of the people who significantly contributes to the success of a team. Focus on the goal of showing everyone involved in this exercise that you are indeed a 'team player'—the team comes first and individual recognition next.

The interviewers will sometimes confront each individual in the group, aside from the others or in front of the others, with a typical workday problem and ask how he or she would resolve it. You are given a role to play. You are told or given facts as to how the problem arose, provided documents, reports, input, and other forms of tools to work with, and informed that the problem must be resolved by a certain time. Other individuals in your group may be asked to explain what methods, processes, practices, and tools they would use to assist them in coming up with a solution—such as certain reports, memorandums, bulletins, e-mails, direct phone calls, faxes, voice mail messages, one-on-one inquiries, and so on. The interviewers are interested in what you will do, with whom, what sources and contacts you use, what tools you utilize, how well organized you are and how well you manage your time and priorities. They want to know if you can resolve the problem in an impressive manner and meet or beat the time deadline. An interviewer may tell you that he or she will interact with you during this period of time, asking probing questions about what you are doing, throwing unexpected contingencies at you, and interrupting the progress you are making in numerous ways—as often occurs in the real world 'on the job.' They are interested in how well you can handle pressure and how well you can operate and resolve daily expected and unexpected work confrontations, while working with both cooperative and uncooperative people.

Use all the insights offered in this book to help you anticipate such techniques used by interviewers and in preparing, long before your interviews, what you will do and say when the time comes.

■ ■ ■

If you don't manage your mind, it will manage you.

■ ■ ■

21

YOUR STRENGTHS

Interviewers often ask, "What are your strengths and attributes?" or "What favorable things would your past employers say about you?" Give this a lot of thought. Think back over the years. Be selective. Consider all your options, then choose those that, in your opinion, best describe you. Keep in mind the employer's desire to choose impressive individuals who will make great future employees and leaders. That's the image you want to present and support.

Interviewers understand that both experienced and inexperienced job applicants have certain strengths of their own, common to their group.

When interviewing relatively *inexperienced* job candidates, the inter-viewer knows that they are easily trained—no bad work habits to over-come, want to soak up new ideas and learn as quickly as they can, and are eager to 'prove themselves.' Their salary demands are lower than experienced job applicants and they're more likely skilled in today's technology (computers, software, internet, etc.). They approach a job with fresh insights and will likely be more flexible in adapting to new tasks, job assignments, hours of work, and schedules. They don't mind taking less challenging duties. They want to start their career on a successful note, then move ahead.

Experienced job candidates have generally developed good working habits and know what is acceptable and not acceptable behavior in performing on the job. They have a good job reputation to uphold and they're more realistic in their career potential for movement 'up the line.' They also can take constructive criticism better than novices, have a track record of successful job performance, and display a broad and more realistic perspective of their capabilities and limitations. They look at job assignments in a wider scope, have a track record of reliability, dependability, commitment, and appreciation for the job opportunities they are given.

The following list of self-perceived personal strengths, organized in general categories, should stimulate your thinking. Use these suggestions to help develop your own list of the personal strengths that others—superiors, instructors, peers, subordinates/students—perceive in you. If any of the listed strengths coincide directly with your perception of yourself, use them, but don't present them verbatim to an interviewer. Use your own words, in your own style of expressing yourself, and don't refer to one or two of your strengths over and over—it's overkill.

Professional Strengths
- Am good at 'what I do' and enjoy doing it
- Possess an in-depth knowledge of my profession and career field—keep abreast of new ideas, innovations, and state-of-the-art advancements
- Am dedicated to my profession and strive to think and act professional at all times—thought of as a solid professional by my supervisor, peers, and co-workers
- Consider myself a strong leader and follower, good teacher and instructor
- Have strong communication and presentation skills (written and verbal)
- Foresee obstacles and avoid or overcome them in a timely manner—want to prevent negative surprises
- Practice situational awareness at all times
- Have the ability to quickly scan and simplify complex problems and situations into manageable areas
- Have a track record of excellent performance ratings and above average salary increases
- Continuously strive for objectivity in viewing situations and information received
- Am cost, profit, time, and customer oriented—consider everyone I serve (within and outside my department) 'my customer'
- Am proficient at decision-making and problem-solving—believe it's best to do everything possible to prevent the problem from occurring
- Know my capabilities and limitations when approaching any new job assignment and project

- Have a thorough understanding of our company's products, services, culture, philosophies, and mission—supportive of each
- Am very flexible—not set in my thinking and ways of doing things
- Continuously strive to come up with fresh, innovative, practical, and inexpensive approaches to product and service improvements
- Consider myself quite persuasive—possess good selling skills. Serve as a sales person for the company in everything I'm involved in
- Am team oriented—place the importance of the team over that of any one individual member. Believe in team resource management (TRM)
- Am a good negotiator—know when it's time to compromise
- Consider myself very goal and results oriented—seek objectives and targets which strengthen and challenge my capabilities
- Think short range, intermediate, and long range in pursuing job assignments and projects
- Break major goals into sub-goals when planning how best to achieve key objectives
- Am proficient in time management and management by objective techniques
- Am very reliable—can be counted on to consistently set high work ethics and standards for myself and perform up to and beyond those job standards
- Consider myself very self-motivated and committed to doing a good job regardless of what job assignment I'm given
- Am well-organized in selecting and applying those principles and practices which would be most suitable to each job challenge faced
- Have a strong determination to succeed in everything taken on. Don't back off or quit. Am achievement oriented
- Make sound judgement calls based on fact, logic, insight, and and analysis—don't impulsively jump to conclusions and pre-judge situations or people
- Have lots of stamina and perseverance
- Quickly adjust and adapt to new and changing job/work environments
- Take a pro-active, hands-on approach to new projects and programs
- Adhere closely to company standards, policies, practices, and procedures and offer suggestions for improvements when needed
- Continuously strive to become a better supervisor/manager in my profession

- Am systematic in my approach to problem resolution
- Handle stress and pressure well, both on and off the job
- Anticipate the needs of others I work with and am patient in hearing them out
- Have a strong sense of loyalty to my company, department, boss, peers, and co-workers
- Have strong computer skills and utilization of internet sources of information
- Closely monitor the quantity and quality of my job performance—focus on 'end results'
- Accept full accountability and responsibility for all my decisions and actions
- Am concise and 'to the point' when expressing myself, while using a very tactful approach
- Am very trainable and easy to manage
- Take advantage of the experience and training of my peers. Will seek their advice on handling very difficult problem situations
- Am thorough in completing job assignments—never sloppy
- Avoid job complacency and fatigue. Take fresh perspectives on frequently repeated job tasks
- Am told by my supervisor that I set the standards of good performance for others in my profession
- Consider myself proficient at delegating work to the most appropriate people, in a timely and tactful manner
- Can readily perform several job tasks simultaneously on complex job assignments
- Consistently meet or beat deadlines on project completions
- Don't take chances, risks, or short cuts unnecessarily
- Strive to do more than is expected of me, at all times
- Am resilient—can quickly bounce back successfully from situations that don't go well…am not easily discouraged
- Am willing to admit my mistakes and view them as opportunities for improvement
- Apologize when I am wrong
- Am typically the first person to congratulate someone on a job well done
- Don't expect to be rewarded without proving myself and earning that recognition

- Am eager to do job-related research and try out new ideas, methods, and ways of doing something
- Handle constructive criticism well—invite questions and feedback on my performance
- Don't dwell on disappointments—focus on what I can do to positively impact future results
- Avoid overloading myself while successfully maintaining a heavy schedule of job involvements
- Follow a 'lead by example' approach to developing subordinates
- Display an open-minded attitude when asked my opinion on a proposed idea by first recognizing the positive aspects of the idea before providing any constructive critique/drawbacks or other suggestions
- Am very security and safety conscious
- Fall back on 'the way I was trained' when in doubt as to how to best handle a unique problem situation
- Take the initiative in notifying those who have a need to know when making significant changes impacting others in my department
- Never talk down to people nor approach them with a feeling of superiority
- Never 'order' people to do things—ask them for their help and express appreciation for the help they provide
- Not afraid to speak up during our department meetings, but do so at an appropriate time and in a tactful manner
- Concentrate and focus on what the person I'm conversing with has to say, showing my understanding and concern with the issues and circumstances they are facing
- Have a stable employment history—am not a job hopper
- Attend after hours job-related courses on a regular basis
- Don't spread rumors or gossip
- Enjoy a little 'quiet time' each day to think things out—go over what happened that day and what I'll need to do the following day

Practical Job Strengths
- Have a positive attitude, on and off the job
- Know where I want to go in my career
- Like my job, my boss, and the people I work with
- Look for ways to reduce time spent on a job assignment, save money, and improve overall efficiency—think and plan ahead

- View 'the big picture' when taking on new job tasks, assignments, or another position
- Consistently sell/talk up my company, our products and services to my friends, neighbors, and others in our community
- Have 'good chemistry' with my boss, their boss, and the people I work with
- Have a reputation of being highly proficient in my job skills and abilities
- Am proficient at training others how to perform in my job classification
- Am flexible and adaptable to sudden changes in job responsibilities and working for a new boss and/or with new co-workers
- Am dependable, task oriented, insightful, self-critical, focused on end results, and good at follow up
- Manage my time well—make a prioritized list daily of what needs to be done
- Am considered by my manager and previous supervisors as a very promotable employee
- Approach every job I've held with the attitude, "What do I need to do to prepare myself for the next higher position?"
- Provide immediate feedback to my boss when unexpected, significant work problems arise
- Seek the advice and assistance of others who are heavily experienced in my job category, when faced with a new and very difficult problem situation
- Have had a stable, progressive work history—never fired or asked to leave a job, and consistently received excellent performance reviews and above average salary increases
- Am a courteous, respectful, and cooperative employee
- Am imaginative, inventive, and creative in finding better ways to do things
- Consider the customer's perspective when performing services for others
- Have excellent operational skills and abilities
- Am eager to learn new job skills—absorb instructions quickly
- Prepare well for every work assignment I'm given
- Have good insight into what is required to be successful when taking on a new job assignment—stay on top of things

- Learn as much as possible from my supervisors, trainers, peers, and co-workers
- Have been told that I'm very thorough, practical, tactful, and optimistic
- Thrive on new job challenges—not afraid to tackle problems and—make important decisions
- Take the initiative to look for better ways to do my job
- Don't require close supervision—self motivated to do my best at all times—a go-getter who knows what is expected of them and do it without being prodded
- Can identify and prevent problems from occurring in a timely manner—a good trouble shooter
- Overcome adversity and job obstacles whenever and wherever faced
- Am considered company-oriented and loyal to those I work for and with
- Am a quick learner—don't need to be told what to do several times
- Am willing to work extra hours/days in order to complete an important project—whatever it takes to get the job done
- Ask questions to learn and when in doubt—not to impress others
- Am a clear thinker with a good memory—remember people's names
- Won't settle for mediocrity—thrive on quality performance and inspire those I work with to do the same
- Don't get discourage easily—am patient and avoid rushing when making decisions—am not a quitter
- Have strong determination to succeed—keep practicing until I 'get it right'
- Am well organized and fully concentrated on what I'm doing at the time
- Volunteer to help my boss, peers, and co-workers whenever possible, and to mentor those seeking guidance in areas of my expertise
- Still get excited when given a new job assignment, project, responsibility, or challenge
- Peers seek my advice and counsel on difficult job assignments—can count on me when needed
- Provide timely feedback to my boss on how my projects and assignments are progressing
- Pride myself in being reliable and consistent

- Am self-disciplined—avoid distractions and don't take unnecessary risks
- Maintain close and full control of the situation I'm in
- Don't expect a 'pat on the back' every time I do something well
- Handle emergencies calmly
- Am periodically called upon to orient and help train department new hires
- Don't 'pass the buck' to others when I make a mistake
- Work at a fast, steady pace with high accuracy—as though it were my own business
- Know when it's time to slow down or speed up as conditions change
- Interact well with people from other departments—at all job levels
- Work hard but also know how and when to relax
- Am not a 'clock watcher'
- Don't use abusive or foul language to 'put down' people
- Don't approach my boss with minor problems—expected to resolve them on my own
- Don't discuss personal problems, politics, or religious beliefs at work
- Have an excellent attendance and on-time record—seldom late for appointments
- Can speak a foreign language spoken by many of our customers
- Am self-confident but not cocky—open to constructive criticism
- Pay attention to details—don't overlook important items
- Am told I'm fun to work with and am highly respected at the same time

Intellectual

- Am a sound decision-maker and problem-solver
- Have strong learning, reasoning, and analytical abilities
- Am thought of as a logical person with good common sense
- Have good focus and concentration
- Don't underestimate or overestimate my own or other people's intellect
- Am able to comprehend complex ideas, break them down into simpler concepts, and explain them clearly to others
- Display strong situational awareness and perception
- Have strong curiosity and a thirst to lean new things

- Am well-organized, creative, and inventive
- Have submitted several ideas and suggestions which were adopted and implemented throughout our department, resulting in significant time and cost savings
- Have a photographic memory—easy to train and readily retain what I learn
- Can separate 'the person' from their actions
- Have good visualization and intuitiveness—able to comprehend what must be accomplished to resolve major problems and obstacles
- Have an insatiable interest in people and the insight to understand what motivates them
- Am considered a very resourceful person
- Readily gain the support of others when I need them—able to tie in their needs and concerns with the situation I'm faced with
- Am well-versed in many subjects

Character and Values

- Have high integrity, morals, and values—set high standards and expectations for myself
- Never compromise on work ethics, principles, standards, or personal values
- Take pride in my job and family values—believe in myself and have strong work ethics
- Am dedicated to my career, family, friends, community, and country
- Am considered honest, open, trustworthy, loyal, unbiased, and a good judge of character by the people I work with
- Have gained a reputation of being credible, lever-headed, sincere, and understanding—am highly respected throughout our company
- Have never falsified anything or deliberately violated rules
- Am someone who lives up to their promises, commitments, and responsibilities
- Take pride in my integrity and the quality of my work—receive great satisfaction from 'a job well done'
- Don't lie or attempt to deceive others by stretching the truth
- Respect the values and opinions of others—consider myself a very tolerant, impartial, fair, and caring person
- Am not quick to judge others, prejudiced, or easily intimidated by someone

- Am self-controlled, non-judgmental, self-disciplined, and self-assured
- Deal with people, problem situations, and challenges realistically—in an emotionally mature manner
- Strive to prevent 'abuse'—whether that of people, equipment, or property
- Maintain confidentiality with those who entrust me with sensitive information
- Never exaggerate my capabilities—avoid being self-centered
- Am consistent—don't vacillate back and forth on issues
- Give the other person the benefit of a doubt—respect their viewpoint, even if I'm in disagreement
- Don't bad-mouth people, or talk behind someone's back
- Am appreciative of all that I have and what people have done for me
- Enjoy helping people in every way that I can

Personality and People Skills

- Maintain a positive attitude, day-in and day-out—it becomes contagious
- Am a self-confident and optimistic person who believes that tomorrow could be the greatest day in my life
- Possess strong leadership and communication skills—one-on-one and withing a group
- Have excellent supervisory skills and abilities—am sensitive to each subordinate's feelings, needs, problems, and concerns
- Am proficient at delegating work assignments to subordinates at an appropriate time, taking their current work load into consideration
- Avoid getting bogged down or dwelling on matters of lesser importance—focus on major goals
- Am told that I'm a boss who is easy to work for and very approachable
- Am able to quickly get to the core of a very difficult people problem
- Avoid preconceived notions about people, ideas, situations, and events—seek the facts
- Consider myself an effective team builder
- Have the ability to 'size up people' quickly and accurately—read their facial expressions, body language, and 'what is on their mind'

- Treat everyone on our team equally—believe that ideas should be considered based upon their merit, not their source
- Have good PR (public relations) skills and exercise good diplomacy when dealing with people and issues—am very people and service oriented
- Believe every individual is important and deserves respect and recognition for the value of their ideas, beliefs, and opinions
- Never attempt to 'put down' someone's suggestions out of jealousy for not having one of my own to submit
- Am told that I'm personable, tactful, open-minded, decisive, and have a relaxed style and easy-going temperament
- Am a go-getter, assertive, but not overly aggressive in approaching people and situations
- Have lots of drive and enthusiasm
- Am told that I have a pleasant disposition, am witty, smile and laugh a lot—but not at the wrong time
- Display a good sense of humor and have learned to laugh at myself and take a joke at my expense without feeling offended—'back off' when I start taking things too seriously
- Am the type of person who can be counted on to stand by and support a friend in need of help in getting through a rough time in their life
- Fit in well with those around me—adapt quickly to new people and situations—seem to establish an immediate rapport
- Take the initiative to introduce myself to those around me when joining a new group of people
- Am compassionate, understanding, humble, and fair-minded—someone who people believe they can confide in
- Handle constructive criticism well—view it as an opportunity to improve
- Am a good teacher, facilitator, counselor, and motivator
- Am a curious person—seek new perspectives, methods, processes, and approaches that will improve the ways we accomplish things
- Have been told that I'm an interesting, likeable person with many interesting stories to tell
- Have learned many ways to effectively cope with stress, and avoid arguments and confrontations while debating a problem resolution

- Am effective introducing humor into a group discussion which has become heated—lowers the tension level
- Avoid asking people personal questions at inappropriate times—don't want to cause them any embarrassment
- Never exploit a person's weaknesses
- Know when to 'back off' when someone is feeling threatened or doesn't what to talk about something—recognize the indications of anxiety and stress developing
- Don't overreact or under react to a situation
- Am encouraging to people who underestimate their skills and abilities to take on new and more challenging job responsibilities and assignments
- Listen closely, with empathy and sincerity, to those facing difficult circumstances—just having someone who cares helps them to cope with their concerns and instills self-confidence
- Have learned to pause a few seconds to gather my thoughts, before reacting to a serious situation or responding to an important question
- Take pride in remaining calm and in control of myself when situations become hectic—calm down others who become agitated
- Am considered upbeat, friendly, good-natured, unbiased, reliable, and generous
- Can 'switch gears' quickly when dealing with people from different backgrounds and under unusual conditions and situations
- Have been described by my peers as resourceful, tactful, considerate of others, cooperative, and 'down to earth'
- Am not easily upset nor frustrated, or am I guarded, defensive, confrontational, or arrogant
- Consider myself 'thick-skinned'—not easily intimidated
- Am willing to introduce an unpopular idea which I consider valid and significant to resolving a major problem
- Am thought of by many of the people who I have worked with as very approachable, level-headed, thoughtful, diplomatic—someone respected that makes you feel relaxed and comfortable whenever you're around them
- Go out of my way to congratulate those who have achieved a major success in their job accomplishments
- Am not self-centered, egotistic, sarcastic, hard-headed, tempera-

mental, or selfish—feel grateful and appreciative for what people do for me
- Am understanding of people who aren't able to grasp new ideas and information quickly, and take that into consideration when instructing and training such individuals
- Go out of my way to ask the opinions of those who haven't spoken up during a department meeting
- Am not afraid to express my opinion on controversial issues, but do so in a tactful and timely manner
- Give the person that I'm interacting with at the time, my full attention—make that person feel that during the time we're spending together, they are the most important person to me
- Never belittle, demean, embarrass or humiliate people—there is no justification for treating people in such a manner
- Have learned how to get people who strongly disagree with one another to compromise their differences and come up with a unified approach to resolving a problem situation
- Believe that you should never try to prove you are right on an issue at the expense of destroying a close working relationship with the person you're conversing with—give that person the benefit of a doubt when it's a 'toss-up'
- Believe that the person I'm dealing with wants and tries to do the right thing from their perspective
- Take people at their word, unless their reputation for telling the truth is questionable
- Have the ability to remain calm when others are beginning to panic
- Have a strong enough track record of successes to be able to admit my shortcomings
- Am not easily offended—understand that people will often say things they don't really mean during a moment of anger or hurt
- Am considered mature for my age—make the most of my limited job experience and formal education
- Never make light of a serious situation or inflate the importance of a less serious one
- Never attempt to 'back people into a corner'—allow them to gracefully get out of an awkward situation
- Realize when I'm beginning to become mentally stale and move on to other important matters

- Never attempt to mislead or cover up by telling half truths or putting words into someone's mouth
- Am not a complainer—pose suggestions for solutions to problem situations instead
- Never disguise problems by referring to them as challenges
- Avoid dominating a discussion—recognize when it's time for others to add their inputs
- Do favors without expecting some in return
- Believe in having a strong opening and closing every time I interact with someone
- Am comfortable with who I am—know and act myself
- Have learned, over the years, that everyone needs a big hug from time to time—especially when things aren't going well for them

Physical Attributes

- Maintain good health habits—eat smaller, balanced meals, exercise daily, and stay within a reasonable weight level
- Undergo periodic, thorough medical examinations to monitor my overall health—received a 'clean bill of health' on my last one
- Manage stress well—believe in stress prevention by avoiding conditions and situations that can cause stress
- Know when and how to relax, using numerous techniques [list]
- Make a concerted effort to stay in good mental and emotional health
- Don't smoke, drink alcoholic beverages in moderation, and have never taken illegal drugs
- Take pride in my appearance and cleanliness
- Am energetic—have lots of stamina and don't tire easily
- Get sufficient sleep (seven to eight hours nightly)—am well rested and have a clear mind facing each new day of work
- Have good vision and hearing, excellent eye-hand coordination, manual skills and dexterity
- Don't have any health restrictions which would hinder or prevent me from performing the job for which I'm applying

Personal Life

- Consider family impact before making any major decisions
- Consider myself a good spouse, partner, parent, friend, and neighbor

- Do volunteer work with children with special needs, disabled military veterans, and elderly people living in care centers
- Am a mentor to youth groups
- Support several charitable organizations, through donations and participation—hold memberships in several organizations
- Am an avid reader—mainly non-fiction, covering many diverse topics
- Enjoy surfing the internet—have my own blog
- Am active in sports and engaged in several hobbies and interests [list]
- Have several avocations [list]
- Am a defensive automobile driver
- Enjoy music—all types, play several musical instruments [list] and compose music

"Alright already! What are some of your other strengths?"

22

YOUR WEAKNESSES

The interviewer may ask you, "What would you say are some of your weak points?" That is a question that may strike fear into even the most confident, experienced job candidate. Like most people, you may find it difficult to address your weaknesses. You can't imagine talking about them without making the interviewer think, "I would never hire anyone like that!"

Put yourself in the interviewer's place. A candidate claims to be a perfect person, without fault of any kind. Do you believe this? Of course not. Every one of us has room for improvement. You're no different. You've made some mistakes, received some constructive criticism, not completely lived up to what was expected of you, lost your temper, and so on. These aren't major faults. Naturally you don't want to volunteer giving them an extensive listing of all your weaknesses. But if you try to evade answering the question, the interviewer may well suspect the worst.

Consider a weakness something you do but don't do well, or something you haven't done or do very little of but would like to do well. Let's say there is an area of your behavior or performance which you're trying hard to improve, but you're not quite there yet. Perhaps you don't have the ability to speak a foreign language well—you're weak in that area. It's not your fault. You just haven't thoroughly studied the language; you've picked up what you could on your own. If you haven't become heavily involved in community activities, you're weak in that area, but it's understandable; you've been so busy pursuing your career, researching the companies you would like to work for on the internet, faxing and e-mailing, networking with friends, spending time with your spouse/live-in, family and friends, and engaging in hobbies, sports, music and other special interests. You plan to take a fresh 'time management' approach and vigorously pursue and attain your goals in these areas.

Be careful not to present a weakness that sounds like a significant, intractable problem, especially when it comes to working with people. Some examples of this might be: "I'm somewhat impatient," or "I'm sort of high-strung," or "I don't hit it off too well with some of our customers," or "People say I'm too laid back, as though I don't care." These can raise a red flag. Employers won't accept these or other fundamental personality weaknesses.

The key to preparing for this question is to choose your weaknesses from one of the following categories:

- **Too Good.** Work too hard, take the job too seriously, need to achieve a better balance between your job and your personal life.
- **Goals You Haven't Yet Reached.** Need to speed up your effort to attain them.
- **A Soft Touch.** Tend to bend over backwards to help or accommodate others; need to be more self-protective.
- **Too Humble.** Am too self-effacing. Need to take credit where and when credit is due.
- **Inconsequential Faults.** Like anybody, have some small, correctable on-the-job weaknesses that wouldn't really affect your performance as a professional: in a hurry to eat a meal in order to return to a pressing job assignment, get behind in filing paperwork from a completed assignment.
- **Common Personal Weaknesses.** Have a sweet tooth, a cluttered garage, basement, or attic. Any interviewer who's half human can sympathize or even commiserate with these.

Let's look more closely at each category of weaknesses. Here are some suggestions for acceptable answers that could be applicable to you. Try, whenever possible, to present them with some kind of positive spin. Offer the 'least serious' and 'less recent' ones first. If prodded, give the others. Avoid those that you feel will 'blow you out of the water.' It's important that you convey the idea that you have consistently overcome weaknesses in the past and expect to continue to do so in the future. Some of the following may strike a chord, or at least remind you of others that you could safely use.

Too Good

- Talk about my job and career too much with my family, friends, and others who aren't in my profession—once I get going, it's hard to stop
- Take my job too seriously at times—need to laugh and lighten up more often
- Keep abreast of new developments in my career field but am not as on top of today's news stories to the extent that I should be
- Am overly conscientious when it comes to being on time with projects and job assignments—hate missing deadlines
- Sometimes set standards for myself that are too high
- At times, try to cover too much in a short period of time, perhaps an overachiever—but making a lot of progress in this area
- Overplan and over prepare once in a while
- Working 35 hours a week to pay for my education, my grades could have been higher. Had a 2.7 GPA
- Occasionally spend too much time in preparation for something that's coming up. Need to avoid overkill. Could be a little more spontaneous. Making progress
- Well-organized, at times, to an extreme—ask my wife when I try to help her reorganize our kitchen appliances and the food in our pantry
- Tend to be somewhat of a workaholic—am working on it
- Need to better balance time spent working on my career progression with time spent doing things with my family and personal interests—no big problem but could use some improvement
- Am too focused on my own career—need to spend more time focusing on my spouse's goals and interests

Goals You Haven't Yet Reached

- Don't savor my successes long enough before pursuing new goals
- Don't care to receive continuous close supervision—need to completely convince my boss that I am to the point that I need only guidance and can carry the ball on my own
- Don't have much experience supervising a larger group of employees but hope to gain more if I can join your company

- Need to formalize an idea I have to speed up some of our department's procedures—still have a few loose ends to take care of
- Want to learn more about my boss's job and career aspirations—should be able to help her to achieve them in some way
- Should learn more about how the other departments in our company operate—plan to talk to some of the supervisors in each of their operations
- Need to learn more about the families of the people I work with
- Need to improve my public speaking skills—still get nervous when I address a group
- Don't have a photographic memory
- Don't have an advanced degree yet, but it's my goal to receive it within the next three years
- Could learn more about computer programming
- Feel I'm too concerned about my future career and need to enjoy today more
- Can't speak a foreign language well—plan to take an evening course in Spanish
- Need to do more reading outside my career field—have a heavy technical background but weak when it comes to having taken courses in business and psychology
- Need to join more clubs—become more active in my community
- Can't play a musical instrument—would be great to be able to play the piano

A Soft Touch

- Get burned at times trusting people to be honest with me. Too quick to forgive them when they mislead me deliberately
- Am too compassionate at times—have a hard time saying no to someone who needs my help, even if it means having to work overtime to get caught up with my own work
- Put others before myself at times when I shouldn't
- Am late at times getting home to my family because I just couldn't let down someone I closely worked with who was having unexpected problems
- If in doubt about who was at fault, will accept the responsibility even though it could have gone either way—maybe I shouldn't

- If one of my subordinates falls behind in their work, will accept part of the blame even though I spend more time and put in more effort helping that particular person than I do my other employees
- At times, am too sensitive to other people's feelings at the expense of my own

Too Humble

- Feel awkward talking about my strengths and accomplishments—too modest
- Don't take compliments as well as I should—not sure how to respond without sounding egotistic
- Get somewhat uptight when asked to speak (unexpectedly) on a subject I'm knowledgeable in—feel I'm not an expert

Inconsequential Faults

- Sometimes go into too much detail in explaining something
- Occasionally repeat a question I was asked before giving my answer
- Tend to talk with my hands a little more than I should
- Use clichés more often than I should
- Talk a little too fast when excited about something
- Could improve my spelling
- Say 'um' too often when trying to think of something else to say

Common Personal Weaknesses

- Don't kid around as much as I should—take my job and my life a little too seriously
- Have little tolerance for those who try to deceive others
- Am a sucker for buying new gadgets
- Don't care to window shop—know what I need and buy it
- Eat too many Oreo cookies—and anything else that has chocolate in it
- Need to lose at least five pounds
- Need to exercise more on a daily basis

- Been losing touch with some relatives and old friends—am determined to contact them this year
- Not too sophisticated or formal—guess I should be—am just a regular person who wants to be themselves

"Do you have any problems handling stress?"

■ ■ ■

With the passage of time, your 'emotions'
will turn into 'thoughts and memories.'
Re-kindle the pleasant ones, let the unpleasant fade away.

■ ■ ■

23

MILITARY JOB CANDIDATES

An impressive job candidate can have roots in military or civilian training and experience. Military job applicants should never knock civilian training and experience, nor should civilian job applicants knock those of the military. Both should display respect for each other—employers hire both.

Tips for Military Job Candidates

If you're coming from the military, you must put in significant effort to make a successful transition into the civilian job world. You want to gracefully relinquish your military past and start visualizing your future working as a civilian. Start perceiving yourself as a civilian in your profession, talking and acting like one. For example, you'll have to overcome the reflex to pull rank and give orders. When you're a competent professional working for a major company, you'll *ask* people to do things for you—just don't infer that they must do them because of your higher positional level.

You'll need to make another major mind-shift: In the military, profitability and cost containment are generally not a pressing issue. As a candidate for a highly profit-oriented, competitive company, you must show that you understand their critical importance and will do your best to lower costs and increase profits in any way you can.

When a military job applicant has had limited or no exposure to civilian job assignments and few close friends who are civilian professionals, he or she should reach out to those doing the same type of work in the civilian world—those who are impressive. They should consult with them for a better feel and understanding of how civilian professionals think and operate. How and in what ways are they different from military professionals? Develop some contacts with civilians in your field of work (through networking) that could give you a good feel for what performing the skills of your specialized field is all about. These could also lead to close friendships with them and, in turn, result in their recommending you to the company you're pursuing.

Some military job candidates think that because all their job experience is military and they haven't had the opportunity to gain much interviewing experience in the civilian world, interviewers will go easy on them. Not so. They'll expect you to work hard in preparing for your job interview—just like every other job candidate—in order to be successful in getting hired. You need to take every suggestion in this book doubly to heart, because you're newer at this than most civilian job applicants.

You should begin applying to companies at least six months prior to your military separation or availability date. You want to be on file with them well in advance of their having a job opening in the type of work you do.

Try to avoid a prolonged period of unemployment or working outside your career field. Maintaining 'currency' in your profession and career field is a big plus from the interviewer's perspective.

In civilian interviews, many military job applicants make the mistake of giving short, quick answers. After all, that's what you do in the military when someone's quizzing you. But in the civilian world that technique could cost you a career with a highly desirable employer. It makes interviewers feel rushed and uncomfortable. Allow yourself time to make meaningful points. This may result in a longer answer, but it will be more comprehensive and impressive. For example, the interviewer may ask, "Have you ever refused to obey a direct order?" Instead of an automatic "No, sir!" you can offer more detail and show your understanding that this is not a black-and-white issue. You may want to respond: "No, sir, as long as I'm not asked to do something obviously unsafe, illegal, or against military policies, practices, and procedures."

Those who tell you that civilian interviewers want you to make it 'short and sweet' are misinformed. Do you talk to your spouse, family, friends and neighbors that way?

Try not to use military jargon; if some slips in, you can catch yourself, smile, and acknowledge that old habits die hard. You will impress the interviewers by using civilian wording.

Some military professionals have frequently had to raise their voices to get their message across to a subordinate. Watch out for the temptation to do this in a civilian job interview. Again, the key is *persuasion—not demand.*

Pay close attention to the questions you're asked. Do they relate solely to your military or civilian work experiences, or both? If you have both military and civilian experiences to share, lean towards the civilian ones and give the most important first. If you're a member of the National Guard or military reserves, include your professional experience while working for them in your answers. The more extensive your professional work opportunities, the more extensive your professional expertise.

■ ■ ■

Decide what's best for you—
not what you want.

■ ■ ■

24

INTERVIEW COACHES AND PREP SHEETS

Most job applicants (both military and civilian) don't have extensive knowledge, training, and practice in interviewing. This is understandable; all your experience may be with just a few companies or just within the military, which has limited your interviewing experience. You certainly don't intend to present fake or misleading credentials and images —only the real ones that truly reflect the best picture of your job experiences and skills.

You can gain some good pointers on interviewing by selectively reading many of the prep sheets that are passed around from one job professional to another by mail, fax, or internet throughout the country. These often cover hints on what other job candidates have learned through their interviewing experiences (both successful and unsuccessful). Scrutinize the validity of each you read and be cautious; times do change. The source may state that the company you will be interviewing with asks certain basic questions and all you need to do is prepare for them; by the time you read them and begin to prepare, those questions may have changed or been eliminated and new questions added.

Prep sheets provide another perspective on which approaches work and which don't—mainly, however, from the viewpoint of other job applicants, not from seasoned interviewers. Again, be cautious. Consider the source; it has to be proven valid or you could parrot the suggestions you've been given in your interview and be turned down. Verify what you read in these write-ups with other reliable sources. Even if what you say in a job interview is valid, if it doesn't sound to the interviewer like it's coming from you, you won't be hired.

Some companies are not as critical in their assessment of job candidates as others; interview preparation based upon that employer's practices would fall short if applied to a more critical one.

Some companies are anti-prep sheet; they believe that in using these, you are not thinking for yourself but merely copying others' ideas. If you follow those prep sheets and the company you're interviewing with makes it clear that they don't approve of them, don't volunteer the fact that you've built answers around the questions and answers that these sources recommended for study.

Other companies expect you to use every resource possible to gain a full understanding of how you can best develop and present the qualifications you worked so hard to attain, in the most impressive ways possible. There's a significant difference between utilizing sources of information—that is, researching—and simply copying information, which requires no thought on your part.

After you have read the most informative, realistic books on job interviews and done everything you can think of to prepare for your interview (including review and follow-up of any prep sheets you've obtained), you may want to set up an appointment with a competent interview coach a few weeks before your interview. He or she will put you through a mock interview and together you can work on fine-tuning your interview techniques.

A competent interview coach will ask you a cross section of the most challenging questions posed to professionals in your career field. The coach should critique each of your answers immediately after you give it. You should also receive an overall assessment (at the close of your mock interview) of how you performed, and which answers you need to modify, delete, or add to. Your coach should also tell you what and where you did well on an ongoing basis. Your sessions should include one or two role-playing questions, where your coach assumes the role of the company interviewer and you become the one who is confronted with a tough problem or a delicate situation.

Shop around for a coach who has a strong reputation and is recommended by your friends who have gone on to be hired by a major company. Ideally, the coach should have received extensive training in how to interview professionals, with an emphasis on questions about handling personal interactions and situations encountered in your industry. Ask if the coach has had the opportunity to actually sit in the interviewer's chair at a highly reputable company and interview professionals in your career field or similar fields. Find out if the coach has been directly involved in the screening, interviewing, and selection process; such direct experience strengthens the coach's authority on the subject. It's not mandatory that the coach has this exposure—just a bonus for you.

Your interview coach should be able to objectively answer most questions you ask during your session. He or she should also be able to explain the logic behind his or her suggestion. It has to make sense to you.

A proficient interview coach will be very open, direct, and straightforward with you, yet always tactful. The coach will gear advice to your particular education, training, and job experience as it relates to the company's profile of what it seeks in its job candidates.

If you have a sensitive area—a problem, explaining something negative or any other concern you may have about how to address something in your interview—your interview coach should be able to help you to your complete satisfaction. Your goal should be to find out what you're doing well and what you need to do to improve. You need tactful, constructive criticism. You want to work with a coach who will come up with good insights and fresh points to add to your answer—covering each question asked during an interview, as well as covering your problem areas that require specific counseling. Knowing and applying what you have learned to perform better will give you more self-confidence.

Some job applicants have themselves videotaped in a practice mock interview with an interview coach or friend. This technique works for those who are very open to constructive criticism and handle it well.

We would all like to believe that a job candidate with a strong education, excellent training, and an impressive technical work record could not possibly fail in the interview phase. The majority of the job candidates who don't get hired cannot find anything significantly wrong with the way they presented themselves in their interviews. They probably did many things right, but made some mistakes that hurt them; left out a great many good points in the answers they gave. They could have received a job offer if they had prepared more and looked for every way to improve before they showed up for their interviews.

■ ■ ■

Bias: Taking a position on something,
then looking for facts to support it.

■ ■ ■

2 5

SELECTING, PRACTICING, AND PERFECTING YOUR FINAL ANSWERS

Presumably, you've followed the game plan presented earlier. Now you're ready to prepare your final answers—the best ones you can come up with.

First, get a stack of scratch paper ready—or ideally, since you'll be playing around with possibilities—use your computer word-processor.

Work from your original list of questions, developed in chapter 14. Pick the ones that merit the most preparation. For each question, brainstorm and record every possible good point and example/situation you can recall from your past experiences. Take a comprehensive inventory of everything you have accomplished in building your career and enhancing your life. Use any notes you've taken after your memory-tapping sessions. Include every success story. Eliminate borderline cases; don't use any that you're not comfortable with, for whatever reason.

From each list, pick out your very best points and examples. Try out different ways of wording them. Emphasize key thoughts. Keep going until you come up with the most tactful and effective presentation you're capable of delivering to a very observant interviewer. Use wording you'll be able to deliver comfortably, talking in a relaxed, sincere, conversational manner. Think about your final choice of words, diction, clarity, speed of delivery, voice tone and level, and overall body language (for suggestions about improving these, see chapters 32 and 33). Bounce your thoughts and ideas off your spouse, family, closest friends, and mentors—especially highly respected professionals in your career field whose judgment you trust.

Now, go through your points and rank them in the order of greatest importance to you as they relate to demonstrated professional expertise in your occupation, important job accomplishments, key projects, high quality results, teamwork, customer satisfaction, and so on. This can be crucial in conveying to the interviewer what is most important to you.

At the top of a blank page, write each question. Then list the points you've chosen to give directly below each question. Start with the most important point at the top of your list and work your way down.

Now practice saying your answers to these questions out loud to yourself. The object is not to memorize your answers, word for word, but to become familiar with discussing your key points and to craft the best approach. Trust the words that come to you, even if they are different from what you'd been planning in your mind. Work on each answer until it sounds as good coming out of your mouth as it does stirring in your brain.

Keep one suggestion in mind as you practice. Most of us have favorite 'filler' expressions we use in our speech: "You bet!" "You can say that again." "To be honest with you…" "You know?" "Sure enough!" "Is that right?" The habit tends to worsen in a tense situation such as an interview. These recurring fillers can irritate any listener, and you don't want to irritate your interviewer. Try to eliminate most of these crutches. It's okay if a few slip in—you're only human.

When you feel comfortable with an answer, it's time to try it out on a coaching partner – a close friend or family member who you also believe can be as objective as possible, serving as a surrogate interviewer.

You may be thinking, 'I feel perfectly ready to go straight to the real interview.' Many job applicants feel this way and resist this final step of preparation. But do you truly want your actual interview for the job you really want and company you really want to work for to serve as your practice session? Probably not. That's much too costly a mistake to make. Go find a partner to team up with in preparing for that very important interview. You'll be glad you did!

Give your partner your practice list of questions and answers and ask him or her to read each question to you. As you answer each question, your partner should listen without interrupting and check off each of the points you're giving as you make them. Do this with every question, sheet by sheet. In addition, any time that you don't present your most important points *first*—at the start of your answer, the person should circle those points.

Now review the annotated sheets to see how you did. Set aside the ones with points that were either not checked off, or were circled. Study and practice them on your own, then try them out again with your partner until you don't miss any (or very few) and can present them in the order of their importance. You may want to video tape your 'final cut' of presenting your refined answers, in a mock interview with your partner. Note the number of times you repeated yourself, used 'fillers', didn't make your points clearly, times you made negative statements versus positive ones, and other pertinent observations. Implement, through practice, your improvements in these areas.

When you reach a point where you have done the best you can, stop practicing and just relax. That's it! You've done your homework. You should feel that you have come up with answers that will be better than those given by other candidates, covering more impressive points and more key areas, with a fresh personal approach. You should be able to honestly and sincerely tell yourself, your spouse, your family and close friends, "I have done everything I can possibly do to prepare for this interview. I really have."

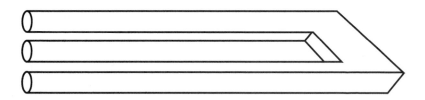

Blundering's 'Blivet'

26

PAPERWORK TO BRING TO YOUR INTERVIEW

In preparation for your interview, make a checklist of all the things you need to do and the things you need to bring to your interview. Take notes as reminders.

Some companies request that you bring certain documents for their review. You will usually be told what documents are needed. Bring others that you may be asked for, just in case. Don't give away any original documents—provide copies.

To be well prepared for the most demanding employers (such as major airlines and companies requiring security/government clearance), bring copies of the following:

- College degree(s) and transcripts, certifications, licenses, and completion of advanced training programs and classes
- Birth certificate, driver's license, and social security card
- Impressive job performance appraisals (both civilian and military)
- Articles you've written
- Summaries of programs and projects you successfully completed
- Your military release (Form DD214)
- Extra copies of your resume (to offer to someone on the interviewing panel who is sharing your resume with another panel member)
- Letters of recommendation from your last two or three supervisors
- A list of the names and current phone numbers of all your supervisors over the past ten years

Some employers welcome personal references; most employers want only job-related reference information. Employment applications and other pertinent forms provide for the listing of schools attended, and so forth. Gear what you bring to each potential employer to how much you expect they will want to cover with you at your visit with them.

Some employers have been known to make job offers 'on the spot.' They want to review your written credentials and other pertinent paperwork before they offer you a position.

You might want to slip in a few photos of your spouse and children— it can create a lot of positive comments and convey the image of 'the family-oriented person.'

Some companies (especially those doing highly-security sensitive work) require verification of your employment with companies no longer in business; Bring copies of your paycheck stubs, W-2 forms, income tax returns, training records, performance reviews, company ID cards, notarized statements from those you reported to, and whatever other documents they need to assess their validity.

Reference letters from your previous supervisors are useful to the interviewers for making phone or written contacts with past employers to verify your employment and performance record. Organize your paperwork so that, should the interviewer want to view specific documents for verification, you can readily pull them out of your briefcase and hand them to the interviewer. Know exactly where they are—no fumbling through everything that's in there.

■ ■ ■

In getting ahead, be sure to stop at the top of the hill or you'll start going back down.

■ ■ ■

27

TRAVELING TO YOUR INTERVIEW

Numerous companies will fly in job candidates for certain profession-al positions. While in transit, carry your documents and other paper-work on board with you in your briefcase. Don't pack these in a suitcase you're checking in—you can't afford to have those become part of lost or delayed luggage.

Schedule your flight, if at all possible, for arrival on the day before your interview. Don't take the last flight out! Have two or three backup flights in case your flight is cancelled. Allow yourself sufficient time to relax and get a good night's sleep after you arrive. Don't cram the night before your interview; your mind might become so active that you have a difficult time falling asleep. In any case, you should have done your home-work by this time, and you'll have time to brush up during the flight. You can quickly review whatever key notes you have between your arrival and the interview.

Wear comfortable, presentable clothes and shoes on your flight—not one of your interview suits. If you wear your interviewing suit, you risk spilling food or beverages that can stain it. Carry two interview suits on board. You don't want to wear the same suit and other clothes twice should you be asked to return for a second day of interviewing and review. The typical dress for airline travel has become much more casual in recent years, but you will be on a career-changing mission. You don't want to look like you're prepared to do some yard work or play a game of volleyball.

Remember to lay out your interview clothes the night before and double check the paperwork you plan to bring with you to the interview. Avoid a last minute rush.

You may be seated next to someone who is a major customer or provider of services and products to the company you'll be visiting. The person could be a prominent person in the world of business, industry, politics, or entertainment. If you can hit it off with him or her, that person could go out of their way to 'put in a good word' for you to your prospective new employer. You'd be surprised at how many times this has happened.

Be on the conservative side when it comes to drinking alcoholic beverages during the flight. Avoid getting into a conversation with anyone around you that could develop into an area of discussion that is controversial. This may seem like a no-brainer, but I know of at least one incident in which a job candidate for a pilot's position with a major airline let his guard down and became rather loud, boisterous, defensive, and argumentative during his flight. A flight attendant observed it all and reported the situation to the captain. The captain, in turn, radioed ahead to the airline headquarters' recruitment staff and gave them a 'heads up' on what had happened. The candidate had introduced himself to the captain when he boarded the aircraft, and mentioned his upcoming job interview and the name of the airline—so the captain knew where he was headed. When the job candidate showed up at the airline, he was given a short 'courtesy interview' and sent on his way. They had already made up their mind about him. He didn't get hired.

You can use the time you spend on your flight to consciously visualize your upcoming interview. Form a mental picture of yourself arriving at the company. You're dressed well. You feel good, excited, but calm, looking forward to the meeting. The moment you meet the interviewers, you hit it off with them. You sit down, relaxed and ready to talk. You hear the questions you anticipated and give the answers you prepared. You remember to give all your prepared answers—they seem to like them. They treat you well. You smile often and laugh at their funny stories. You didn't fail to anticipate any question they asked you—you are never stumped. The interviewers seem very interested in what you're saying and give you their full attention. Their comments and reactions seem very positive. Put yourself in this state of mind and you are very likely to be at your best during the 'real thing.'

If you are driving to your interview, you can also do some visualization of positive images of your job interview performances. Should you be unfamiliar with the city/area/location, take a trial run the day before your interview (time permitting). You'll have a more accurate estimate of the driving time required. Be sure to include heavy traffic and unexpected accidents, finding a parking place, and your walk to their facility entrance. While driving, sing aloud to 'warm up' your voice.

"I noticed that I forgot to sign my employment application."

■ ■ ■

*Your technical expertise 'loads the gun,'
your interview preparation 'cocks the gun,'
and your presentation 'pulls the trigger'
to hit the bull's-eye: getting hired!*

■ ■ ■

PART TWO

Presenting Yourself Impressively **During** Your Interview

"It's showtime!!"

28

IT'S SHOWTIME!
REPORTING FOR YOUR INTERVIEW

It's a good idea to practice a few relaxation techniques the night before and the morning of your interview. Sit in a comfortable chair and concentrate on completely relaxing your body in gradual steps, saying to yourself, "My toes are relaxing...now my feet...now my legs," continuing upward until your entire body is at ease. While in this state of complete concentration and relaxation, you can again visualize being interviewed: picture the interviewer asking you questions and hear yourself give impressive answers. This repeated exercise creates and reinforces positive images, reduces stress, and builds your self-confidence.

Plan to arrive early—at least fifteen minutes to half an hour. It's important to build in this cushion of time for several reasons. First, emergencies do happen. Perhaps one of the interviewers has to attend an unexpected, important meeting that afternoon, and would appreciate the chance to start and finish his or her interview with you early. Perhaps he or she wrapped up his or her interview with the last job applicant sooner than expected and was ready to begin yours.

While seated in your car in the employer's parking lot with the car windows rolled down, take several deep, long breaths. Slowly inhale and exhale. Doing this repeatedly provides more oxygen to your brain and relaxes your muscles. It will enable you to think more clearly and remain relatively calm during the interview. You can repeat this approach seated in the interview waiting room, in an abbreviated and more subtle manner. This approach has been successfully taught at seminars to people who perform assignments under stressful conditions and must learn to relax and handle stress more effectively.

The first person you are likely to meet is the receptionist. Approach him or her with a pleasant greeting and tactfully ask if they have time to provide the names, spelling, pronunciation, and titles of the interviewers. Jot them down on a very small note pad you should carry with you in your suit breast pocket or briefcase. This information will also help you to accurately address the thank you notes or letters that you should send to each of the interviewers after you return home.

While you are waiting in the lobby, try to further relax. Unbutton your suit jacket (button it again when you spot the interviewer headed your way). Take a break from your mental interview preparation—it's more important now to just relax and ease your nervousness. Think about pleasant settings and experiences, or read something light. If you need to use the restroom, do it now. Avoid drinking coffee; it acts as a diuretic.

If there are other job applicants in the waiting area, feel free to mingle and chat, but avoid getting so involved in a conversation with another job candidate that you don't notice the interviewer approaching you. The interviewer should not have to gain your attention. You should be waiting alertly for him or her to arrive. You want to be on your feet just before the interviewer approaches you.

Some companies present a short briefing on their organization to all the candidates as a group, and follow with a brief question-and-answer period. Then come the individual interviews.

■ ■ ■

What appears to be the truth
is often just opinion, in disguise.

■ ■ ■

29

BRINGING IT ALL TOGETHER FOR YOUR INTERVIEW

During the interview, how can you make the best possible presentation of all the answers you've so carefully prepared? Study and practice these winning techniques:

- **Take Center Stage**
- **Sell Yourself**
- **Keep It Positive**
- **Relax...But Not Too Much**
- **Know the Questioning Approaches You'll Face**
- **Develop the Art of Fielding Questions**
- **Give Key Points and Supporting Points**
- **Be Specific**
- **Be Concise**
- **Demonstrate Convictions and Compromise**
- **Expect the Unexpected**
- **Make a Rapid Recovery**
- **Handle the 'Bad Stuff'**
- **A Final Word of Incentive**

Take Center Stage

In a job interview, you want to be *you*—at your best! Not a different you. Be flexible and adaptive but not a constantly changing chameleon. Should you be hired, you don't want your new boss to say, "This isn't the person I hired. I've been had!" Just be yourself (at your best) in the way you dress, your grooming, your smile, your laugh, your gestures, your walk, your voice, the sparkle in your eyes, your level of interest and enthusiasm, the way you communicate, the way you show initiative, your sales savvy, assertiveness, and organization of your thoughts. Reflect it as well in the way you listen closely to others, your display of patience, assertiveness, consideration for others, compassion, and empathy. Show it in your energy level, sincerity, openness, quickness to adjust, freshness in ideas, clarity in expressing your thoughts and ideas concerning your training, education, experience and accomplishments, and on-the-job behavior.

Think back to your best interview—when you received a job offer—a time when you 'clicked well' with the interviewer and felt real good about yourself. The positive thoughts and feelings of that time will start pouring back to you as though you had just gone through it yesterday.

To make the most of your interview, you need to have a little 'actor' in you. Address the interviewer as though he or she is the most important individual in your life for the brief time you spend together. You may not be in the best state of mind (for whatever reason) when you enter the interview, but you must act and appear 'up'—in a good mood, at ease, and quite likeable. You do this every day in both your career and personal life. How many times have you laughed at a joke that you really didn't think was funny? How many times have you said, "How are you doing?" when you really weren't overly concerned, or replied, "I feel great," when you didn't? Can you imagine what would happen to marriages, friendships, and employment relationships if we said exactly what we thought at the time, and expressed our feelings at that moment completely uncensored? Let's not even think about the results! So even if you don't feel like it, you have to project yourself to the interviewer as a warm, friendly, likeable person. The amazing thing is, when you do this for a while, you actually do start feeling that way. *Positive thoughts create positive feelings.*

Sell Yourself

You've read all about it in chapter 8, but it bears repeating. Your resume and employment application got you to the interview—from that point on, you have to *sell yourself.* The interview isn't designed just to verify what you have stated on your resume and employment application. It's to find out what's behind them—how and why you achieved all that you've accomplished. The interviewer wants to know what you were like then, how you are now and how you will be in the future if they should hire you. Will you turn out to be one of their best employees with lots of growth potential? Have you convinced them that you will be?

Point out what skills you believe are necessary to do a good job in the position you're seeking. Provide the interviewer with evidence/examples to support the fact that you possess these important job skills.

Don't use your employment package as a crutch and say, "If you look at my resume and application, they'll pretty much answer your question." That's like an airline pilot applicant telling the interviewer that they can skip putting him or her through a flight simulator test ride—all they need to do is take a close look at their flight training record and flying experience to conclude that they're a great pilot.

Stress that you'll be a very impressive sales person and representative of their company's standards in all your contacts with people within and outside the company. You'll reflect a positive image of them through your behavior and actions. And you'll encourage everyone to buy their products and use their services.

You are unique. Your image must reflect your uniqueness. Your background, education, training, and job experience are different from the other job candidates being considered. In selling yourself to the interviewer, point out your uniqueness in these areas of comparison in the most positive ways you can: "I believe that my experience is directly applicable to the product line you provide to your customers. And I have had interaction with 80% of your present customers, selling them on the benefits of using these particular lines of products." Your uniqueness—no matter what area it is in, will make you stand out from the other job applicants in the minds of the interviewers. Make that uniqueness as positive as you can. You want the interviewer to remember you after you've left, when they are deciding who to hire. "He's the well-spoken guy who sold their biggest customer on doubling their order for the new product line." "She's the sharp, well-dressed woman who came up with that great idea for cutting operational costs by 12% this year. Quite a savings to her company"... and "He's one of the 'good ones'—doesn't try to snow you."

Keep It Positive

The #1 problem for many people in performing well in their profession is that they have a poor or questionable attitude. A negative, defensive, self-pitying attitude becomes very noticeable and annoying, whether it's directed toward the company itself, their department, the job assignments they're given, the equipment, tools, and services they have to work with, their delayed promotion, their boss, higher ups, people they work with or that they supervise, and on and on. More people are terminated from a company for their bad attitude than for a lack of professional job skills. Many job applicants are not offered employment for the same reason.

Interviewers perceive that such people feel they are the victims, and that everything and everyone around them are the villains creating problems for them. Don't become one of these people. Even if the nature of a question calls for directly critiquing something or someone, try to begin your answer with something positive, then proceed with a critique that is a fair evaluation.

After answering a question, don't say to yourself, "Wonder what the interviewer thought of my answer?" You shouldn't be concerned with keeping score as you go along. Concentrate on making the best presentation you possibly can.

Don't try to inflate a point in your favor beyond what it's worth by comparing it with something less desirable; for example: "I like exciting job activities and assignments—sure beats routine, repetitive tasks!" or "I would really enjoy living out here, rather than on the East Coast." This could backfire on you. The interviewer could respond, "We are thinking of moving our operations to New York and Baltimore—you wouldn't want to work for us then, knowing how you would dislike those changes. Maybe you should look elsewhere."

Any time you put down any company, position level, type of job assignment, working conditions, schedules, or locations, you're setting yourself up for all kinds of touchy interview situations. You're viewed as hard to please, a complainer, overly critical, subjective, tactless and inconsiderate. Try to avoid doing this.

Try to be as spontaneous as you can throughout your interviews. It makes all the carefully planned and prepared answers you're giving appear to be 'off the top of your head.' Most people who do complex and challenging things very well, make it sound easy and natural to do. Be one of them.

Relax...But Not Too Much

No two interviewers use the same style while interviewing job applicants. Their personalities, sense of humor, standards, and perspectives differ. One may be more tactful, soft spoken, and appear more comfortable with you than another. Yet another might be louder, more blunt, speak more rapidly, be impatient with long periods of silence, interrupt you frequently, and be very anxious to conclude the interview. Yet, another may appear highly interested in what you have to say and how you say it, give you the benefit of the doubt on borderline assessments, and try their best to put you at ease throughout the interview. It is very important that you quickly determine what type of interviewer you're facing. Read the interviewer in order to determine what would be your best approach to that particular person and his or her unique style. Think about how to best present and handle yourself and what to do and what not to do.

Try, despite any nervousness, to be warm, friendly, relaxed and down-to-earth. If you seem ill at ease, the interviewer will tend to feel the same. Express your sincere enthusiasm about the opportunity you have been given to interview with their company. Look and act interested in what the interviewer is saying and doing at all times. As you relax, let yourself begin to enjoy meeting and talking with the interviewer. Remember, *an interview is a conversation between two people.* It's not a debate. Show that you have a sense of humor and are alert to pick up quickly on the messages the interviewer is sending you. Your goal is to make it a pleasurable experience for both you and the interviewer. Relax. You're acknowledging your understanding of the interviewer's intentions when you say, "You probably want me to elaborate on exactly how I developed that particular skill." Shoot for both being relaxed and at the same time exciting the interviewer to want to find out more about you.

Another word about nervousness. To remove it quickly, focus first on the *message* you're delivering to the interviewer—not the interviewer and not yourself. What you have to say is most important. Concentrate more on the content, than on the delivery of your message. Speak the words aloud to yourself in a practice session and go over them again. Do this as many times as it takes to get the words to sound right and natural to you.

On another note, avoid eating a heavy meal and or drinking diuretic beverages just prior to your interview—you don't want to be constantly excusing yourself.

You and the interviewer should be in sync. When the interviewer acts serious, you should too. When the interviewer smiles and laughs, respond naturally with your own smile and laugh. One interviewer once told me how he deliberately said something witty to put the applicant at ease—and saw a look of bewilderment on the applicant's face! Show the interviewer that you can 'read people' well by responding and adapting appropriately and quickly.

Some interviewers will dress and act casual, in an effort to make you feel so comfortable and relaxed, that you begin to forget you're in an actual interview. They hope to catch you off guard to see what you really are like. You start thinking, "These guys are great. I can say anything I want to and they seem to go along with it." Don't forget that this is a professional interview, for a professional position. You are competing with dozens of others who want the same job as badly as you do. You're not at home, talking to your spouse, family and friends in a social setting, where you can feel free to say whatever pops into your mind. If you get too relaxed, you could inadvertently say things that might not be appropriate or in keeping with a positive image—things that you will later regret saying. Those things might cost you a job offer. Stick to your game plan of giving the answers you've already prepared after having given a lot of thought to them.

Again, throughout your interview, be yourself in the most impressive manner possible—at your very best—no less.

Don't let yourself be diverted by the interviewer's reactions to your answers, or allow these to make you tense up. Certainly it's important to pay attention, in order to determine whether you should change your approach or strategy, but it's more important to focus on what you are going to say, how you are going to say it, and in what order. In sports, the baseball batter doesn't concentrate completely on the pitcher; he's thinking about what type of ball may be thrown (fastball, slowball, curve and so on) and how best to approach the pitch and swing his bat in order to get a hit. Worry doesn't score runs—hits do.

Know the Questioning Approaches You'll Face

It's not just what the interviewer asks you, but how it's asked. You should expect a variety of questioning approaches:

Open-ended questions. Example: "Tell me about yourself?" This is your opportunity to make and score many points. There are no restrictions on the type or extent of your answers. You can really shine in your answers to open-ended questions, if you have prepared for them. Use the latitude provided to bring up many good points you may not otherwise have given. While your competition is thinking about what to say, you're providing the interviewers with meaningful, key information about yourself and raising your score.

Closed-ended questions. Example: "Have you ever taken illegal drugs?" These 'yes or no' questions force you to give a specific, direct answer. Interviewers often use these to pin the applicant down, especially if preceding answers have been too vague or general.

Leading questions. Example: "Bet you weren't too happy when you didn't get the promotion you expected, were you?" In a courtroom, this is called 'leading the witness.' The interviewer is putting words into your mouth; it's up to you to confirm or deny the statement. A leading question is not always a trap; it can be used to simply draw you into a conversation about any area of concern to the interviewer.

Reflective questions. Example: "You say you didn't like what your supervisor said. Hmm." Not really a question, but a reflection of what you've just said, these remarks invite you to expand on a point you've made or implied. The interviewer wants more input from you to reveal your perspective on the matter in greater depth.

Reversible why questions. Example: "Why do you ask that?" The interviewer bounces your question right back at you to understand your motive for asking it. Your response can reveal a hidden agenda.

Intimidating questions. Examples: "Are you bothered by the question I just asked you?" "Is this something you're not comfortable talking about?" These put you on the defensive, deliberately creating a stressful situation to see how well you handle pressure. Keep your cool no matter how intense this type of questioning becomes. Show that you're not easily intimidated by people, that you can remain calm, and can think clearly in giving an appropriate response. You'll score more points.

Listen closely to each question asked. It may sound like one you have read or heard before, but may not be the same. Which version have you just been given? Decide how broad the question is and how much latitude you have in working in some good stuff. You might have plenty of room to cover things others didn't think of because they interpreted the question too narrowly. Does it apply only to your education, training and job experiences, or to your personal life, as well? If the question doesn't specify which, assume it applies to both—all areas that might directly and/or indirectly be job related.

Interviewers can rotate the questions they ask, applicant to applicant, day to day, week to week. The questions can be modified, altered, or reworded significantly month to month. It may sound like the same question a friend was asked a week ago, in his or her job interview for the same position, but if you listen closely, you will notice that it's different. Some questions will be dropped from their current list but asked again weeks later. New questions are added. Some questions are broadened or generalized to pertain to both your career and personal life. Other questions may be narrowed to cover only a very defined and specific area of your knowledge and experience. Some are timeless, covering anything applicable over your entire life; others are restricted to the last one or two years of your career.

When interviewers notice that you have a heavy background in particular areas, they can deviate from their prepared list and ask questions directly applicable to those areas. In some cases, they can create a question (on the spot) that they feel you should be able to answer well, such as: "Why do you think he said that?" or "Why did you decide to handle it that way?"

Try to gain insight into the interviewer's intent as they ask each question. It may be obvious in certain cases; in others it may not be, or perhaps you may not have interpreted them correctly. Ask yourself, "Exactly what is he or she trying to find out about me? Is it professional or personal? Is it my attitude? Does he or she want to understand my decision-making process? Does he or she want to know what's most important to me? Is he or she looking for my strengths and/or weaknesses?" Even the interviewer's small talk can be an indirect approach to finding the answers to these and other important questions. Don't underestimate the competence of the interviewer. You may feel that this person is a push-over and that you can ask him or her enough questions to find out what they're looking for. Then you can tell them what they want to hear. Sure, you might be able to pull it off with a few interviewers but why take a chance? Aren't you self-confident enough in your interviewing skills to be able to do well through extensive preparation? An astute interviewer will soon recognize the game you're playing—role reversal—and 'straighten you out.' His or her "Who's doing the interviewing— you or me?" will most likely kill your chances of getting hired. No interviewer wants to be 'had'. Don't take the risk.

Failure in matters involving your job assignments that are beyond your control or that you have no knowledge of is understandable to an interviewer. You must be credible, however, in convincing the interviewer that the failure was beyond your control.

Developing the Art of Fielding Questions

Think of all the people you have met. Which ones impressed you the most? What was it about them that impressed you? How did they field questions? What techniques did they use? Do you have or could you develop the same attributes and display them in your job interviews?

The first step you must take to effectively field a question, is to listen very closely. If you misinterpret it, you can give the interviewer the wrong impression of the scope of your knowledge or your viewpoint, opinion, or perception. How was the question phrased? Was there emphasis placed on certain words? You can instill a feeling of doubt as to whether or not you represent the type of professional and individual they are looking for someone who could become one of their best employees.

Be prepared to answer questions involving who, what, why, when and where of your career development without glancing at your resume for answers. Know your resume—don't memorize it. Don't expect to be allowed to look at your interview preparation notes for answers. Keep in mind, the interview is a test, and no notes are allowed.

Should you have anything in common with the interviewer, take advantage of the opportunity to talk about these things during the course of the interview at appropriate times. If the interviewer wishes to talk about them—he or she will. You'll soon be able to tell, so don't force a discussion. It's difficult for an interviewer to dislike a person who enjoys the same interests and hobbies as he or she does.

Try to avoid using the reversible why technique some interviewers use. Don't, for example, ask "Why do you ask that?" or "What do you mean?" or "Why wouldn't I?" or "Do you want to know…or…?" Interviewers may comment, "I ask the questions, you answer them. That's the way the game is played." You may (rarely) get a question asked by a new interviewer that simply isn't clear. You can tactfully say, "I'm sorry, I don't quite understand your question. Could I ask you to repeat it?" Usually the interviewer's questions are quite clear. Stay focused and listen closely.

Try not to say "That's a very good question!" Many well-known people being interviewed on radio and television news broadcasts and talkshows frequently use this phrase and it's okay for them to do so in that setting, but not in presenting yourself in a highly competitive job interview. When you've just been asked a tough question in a job interview and your mind goes blank, this phrase may come to you as the perfect stalling tactic. But take the interviewer's viewpoint—he or she has heard this many times before. Consider the implication: "Do you mean to say the other questions I asked weren't very good ones?" Instead, just give the honest response you planned to give.

Another opener to avoid is "I believe…" Interviewers may think you're trying to leave a loophole for yourself should you be wrong. After all, it's just your belief, not a firm statement by which you'll stand. *Interviewers don't want you to guess.* They want to know what position you take on certain matters. They aren't going to let you weasel out of having to answer a question or let you give an evasive response.

After you are asked a moderate to heavy question, take a deep breath (inconspicuously) and allow yourself a pause of three or four seconds to gather your thoughts. Don't immediately start talking, not knowing exactly what you are going to say, in hopes that something worthwhile will come to you. Even when you have prepared to answer the question long before your actual interview, realize that there are so many questions to prepare answers for that you may need a few seconds to gather your thoughts—especially if it's a tough question.

After taking a deep breath, you can begin giving the points that make up your answer. Give them in the order in which you arranged them, and in the manner in which you planned to explain them. You don't know if you will have the opportunity to cover them all, but cover as many as you possibly can.

Don't be afraid that interviewers won't give you time to present all your points. Once they realize that you know what you're talking about, have done a great deal to prepare good answers, and don't waste words, they will want to hear more. It doesn't take a lot of time to say something planned and organized. It takes a lot more time when your responses aren't planned.

When you reach a point when you think, "Perhaps the interviewer has heard all he or she cares to hear," pause for a second or two—no longer. If, indeed, the interviewer thinks it's time to move on to the next question, he or she will do so. But if the interviewer doesn't introduce a new question, you can assume that he or she is thinking, "You seem to know what you're talking about, maybe you have some more 'good stuff' to tell me." Watch for the interviewer to look you in the eye, nod, smile, or prompt you with "So...?" or "And...?" These indicators, and the fact that the interviewer remained silent for two to three seconds, are your green light to continue giving more points. You can pause briefly again after giving one or two more points, then ask the interviewer whether you should continue. If you hear "yes," offer the points you've kept in reserve. If you hear "no," that's okay; you've most likely scored higher than other candidates who just stopped talking after they gave a few points, deciding for themselves how much the interviewer wanted to hear. As they sat there in silence, the interviewer assumed they had nothing more to say and moved on to the next question.

Allow yourself occasional short pauses of one to two seconds between some of the points you're making. Your answers will sound more natural and spontaneous and more like a typical conversation at work or with family and friends. Pauses give a conversation breathing room—much like 'white space' in a publication, which breaks up long sections of text, making it easier to read.

Use Your Key Points and Supporting Points

If you've followed the suggestions given in "Insights into Building Terrific Answers," you'll make good use of key points and supporting points. You'll present the most important ones first and avoid numbering your points aloud. No mundane or trivial points—just meaty, meaningful ones.

Pay attention to the interviewer's response. Is he or she listening with interest? If so, then keep going. Is he or she looking less interested or getting ready to interrupt? Then you've probably delivered your key and supporting points to the interviewer's satisfaction and it's time to wrap up your answer. Don't continue to bring up unimportant points or give minute detail, or try to recap all the points you've made with a summary statement.

Be Specific

Most people want to avoid answering a question for which they don't have a good answer. They want to also avoid questions concerning 'bad stuff' they'd rather not address. They believe they can do this by speaking in generalities, with an assumed 'air of authority.' They think this will get them off the hook, but seasoned interviewers can see right through such responses. Avoid generalities or you will sound like a politician who doesn't want to be pinned down and gives fuzzy, vague and general statements, hoping to bluff their way through the question they were asked. If pinned down by the interviewer as to why you were turned down for promotion or why you didn't receive a job offer for a position similar to theirs at one of their competitors, give your opinion as objectively as you can, with specifics. Describe how stiff the competition was, or mention the particular qualification requirement you hadn't met. For another example, you might say "Another employee in our department was more deserving of the promotion. This person had more related training and job experience than myself. I thought I would give it a try, just in case he or she decided not to put in for the promotion."

Tell it as it is…

> "They told me they have over twenty qualified applicants for every job opening they had. The competition was very stiff. Thought I did well in my interviews with them—would like to think I came very close to being chosen. My GPA in college was 2.4—not the greatest when you have a dozen or more people to compete with."

Rather than…

> "All companies play favorites when hiring. I didn't have an 'in' with anyone."

> "I was one year short of the required job experience in that type of work. I think they were too critical and should have still considered me."

> "You know how it goes—they can always come up with some excuse for not hiring you to cover up their bias."

Be Concise

This point bears repeating: If you want to meet your goal of presenting all the great material you've prepared, you must be concise. You can't be wordy. Don't spend more time building up to the point you want to make than stating the point itself. Whenever an interviewer asks, "What's your point?" you know you'd better cut to the chase.

You should also avoid getting so wound up in making an important point and giving elaborate examples that you use up all your time on just that one area, leaving out several other important areas. That's like spending most of your time focusing on one job you've held and failing to cover another equally important one. You will never have time left to give all your other prepared responses because you've spent too much time on each point you made. Multiply this by all the other questions you are asked; you'll end up with a total score that falls below the cut-off point for getting hired. By starting with the most important points *first*, with minimum build up, you don't risk leaving out the most significant things you want to tell the interviewer.

Whenever an interviewer 'cuts you off' while you are giving an answer, it's a sign that it's taking you too long to make your point, or you already made the point and now you're milking it. You may also be cut off when you've gone off on a tangent, into an area irrelevant to the question.

Demonstrate Convictions and Compromise

Interviewers want to hear candidates take a stand on important work- related matters. When you're asked your opinion, it's fine to express your convictions. If you defer to their viewpoint or claim no opinion, you may come across as 'kissing up to them' or as being wishy-washy. Just state your convictions in a thoughtful, pleasant manner. Don't allow yourself to become harsh or argumentative, to do so, even if you're taking a popular stance on a debatable job performance issue, you may be perceived as rigid and inflexible or not open to the views of others.

There's one strong conviction that you certainly should express: Tell the interviewer how much you want the job (without sounding as though you are begging for it). Emphasize how much working for their company means to you in terms of job satisfaction and attaining your future career goals.

Let your interviewer know, too, that you appreciate the value of compromise, especially in the interests of cooperation and team effort. Make it clear that you won't cling to 'being right' at the expense of what is best for all.

Expect the Unexpected

Be ready for any question, at any time. Often, a question is asked to get you to say something that you didn't plan to talk about. For example, they may ask, "Why didn't you bring that up earlier in the interview?" or "Why didn't you speak up when I questioned the decisions you made?" or "How does your spouse feel about that?" Every time you are taken off guard, it's an indication that you didn't prepare as well as you should have for your interview. Sure, you're expected to be 'thrown off' by a few of them, but only a few.

Don't rush to answer an unexpected question. Allow yourself a pause of three or four seconds in which to think about why are they asking you this and what are they looking for. Deliver a well thought out response. If you wait much longer, the interviewer will begin asking the next question, and you will have lost an opportunity to score some points. No answer, no points. If it's a 'yes' or 'no' question such as, "Have you ever been fired?" your answer should, of course, be immediate with no pause.

If you feel you truly gave the best answer you could come up with and the interviewer appears to have expected a more comprehensive reply, it's okay to ask the interviewer what part of the question you didn't seem to cover. You're just asking for clarification, in a sincere manner, which is a thoughtful, proactive response. But use this method sparingly, only when absolutely necessary. You don't want the interviewer to think that all other job applicants fully understood the question—why doesn't this one?

The repeated question—hearing one that you know you've already answered—may throw you for a loop. It's possible the interviewer's mind wandered and the repeat's unintentional; it's more likely to be a deliberate strategy, for various reasons. It may serve as a test to see if you are answering consistently. The interviewer may think you are twisting the truth, or are disorganized, or are having difficulty understanding the questions. Perhaps your first answer failed to satisfy him or her in some respect but you seemed to be 'getting warm.' Maybe you didn't express yourself clearly. It may have appeared that you were half guessing, or that you actually knew the correct answer but, for one reason or another, couldn't think of it at the time. This interviewer is giving you the benefit of the doubt. You are getting a second chance to score more points, and you should take advantage of the opportunity. Take a deep breath, dip into your reserve tank, and try again.

You can reduce your chances of having the same question come back to bite you, by interpreting each question as broadly as you can. Try to include additional strong points that other candidates might not have thought to include because of their narrow interpretation of the question.

Never say to an interviewer who asks the same question you were asked earlier, "I have already answered that question—I covered it with the other interviewer." If they ask it four times, answer it four times, each time as though it were the first.

Make a Rapid Recovery

If something goes wrong during the presentation of your answers, don't panic and say to yourself, "They'll never hire me now!" Just keep going strong, like any professional athlete or performer does when he makes a mistake, knowing you can overcome it with better answers during the remainder of the interview. Interviewers look for resilience and for that candidate who can bounce back from failure with strong determination to succeed. They don't like someone who gets discouraged easily.

Handle the 'Bad Stuff'

Interviewers tend to more readily recall those things that you spend the most time explaining. Clearly, you should spend much more of your time telling the interviewer good news rather than bad news.

In talking about a mistake you've made, don't try to lay the blame on others who were involved. Your refusal to take full responsibility for errors you have made will not sit well with most interviewers. Take full responsibility. If it's not a very serious mistake, you can say, "I did a dumb thing when I… I should have known better. I sure learned a lot from it; what not to do and what to do, instead."

However, it's sad but true that *just one negative remark seems to carry much more weight than one positive comment.* In fact, your one careless negative comment can offset many positive comments you've made. Badmouthing, for example, is a sign of someone who easily finds fault with people, things, places, and so on. It is not a quality that supports your candidacy for a professional position.

If you don't have something positive to say about something, it's better to not say anything, unless you are forced to. *When in doubt, leave it out.*

A Final Word of Incentive

Your spouse expects you to go to your job interview and deliver all the good things you have planned to bring out regarding your career achievements. Don't disappoint him or her by bringing a lot of those good things back home with you. Don't leave them unsaid when there were many opportunities to work them in. Think of your spouse asking you, "Did you tell them about…and about…?"

■ ■ ■

Don't mistake activity for achievement.

■ ■ ■

30

CRUCIAL FIRST FIVE MINUTES OF YOUR INTERVIEW

Now it's time for the interview itself. It's an important moment, one that may determine the whole course of your future career. You have prepared good answers for questions you anticipate being asked. Naturally, you are both excited and apprehensive. And you want to make a favorable first impression.

When does your image building begin? It starts with your arrival for your interview and is the first of many impressions you will make on those with whom you come in contact. Make each interaction a positive experience, for you and for them. The first five minutes of your interview are crucial to success. It will take at least that long from the time you meet each other to the time you finish answering the interviewer's first meaningful question, in order for them to establish a reasonably valid sample of your behavior and make a judgment call. Many interviewers will form their overall opinion of you during this period of time. They often decide whether or not to put you through the entire interview, or 'cut it short' if it's not likely you'll be hired. During this time, you of course have the opportunity to impress the interviewer in many ways.

The very first impression you'll make on each person you encounter is, of course, your appearance. Follow the detailed suggestions recommended on dress and grooming in chapter 31. Let's continue on and focus on the other aspects of making a strong first impression.

Any support personnel you meet—such as administrative assistants, receptionists, secretaries, people involved in testing, and the like—can and will volunteer favorable or unfavorable comments about you to the interviewers. These comments can add to or subtract from the points earned on your 'image score.' Here are some typical comments: "You're going to hire that engineer, aren't you? He's very nice! Mixes well with the other candidates" or "You're not going to hire him are you? He's not too personable. Seems a little pushy." You should consider providing one or two sincere compliments to these support people—about their voice, smile, personality, professionalism, brisk work pace, or some other real attribute (no B.S.). A little sincere flattery can go a long way.

Time to meet the interviewer. (I'll keep referring to the interviewer as an individual; yours may be a panel.) When the interviewer approaches you and greets you, quickly stand up, make direct eye contact, smile, shake hands firmly, and say enthusiastically, "It's a pleasure to meet you, Mr./Ms./Mrs./Miss…!" (according to how the interviewer prefers to be addressed). When an interviewer first meets a job candidate, looks into his or her eyes, and observes his or her facial expression, the first thing they're thinking is: *How would supervisors, peers, co-workers, customers and clients react to him or her when first they meet and begin carrying on a conversation?* Show from the outset that you are pleasant, polite, relaxed, enthusiastic, energetic, and alert. Establish a 'conversational tone' right from the start. If the interviewer does not introduce himself or herself and remains silent to see what you will do, it's okay to introduce yourself. You'll be demonstrating tactful initiative under stress.

It's okay to ask an interviewer (early in the interview) for his or her business card in order to correctly identify that person and his or her job title. It is important information to have when mailing a brief thank you letter. The receptionist might be able to supply the same information to you, should you prefer.

Snap Decisions

Interviewers 'like' some candidates, and dislike others. Often, this can't be explained based on the person's training, experience, and other 'hard' qualifications. As described earlier, the interviewer's own subconscious associations play a part. The real pros will, of course, recognize and try to control their biases, but you also can do a lot to overcome any negative associations. If you start thinking, "I'll probably blow this interview," you're likely to do just that. People who think positive thoughts perform better and are healthier.

Don't address the interviewer by his or her first name unless invited to. Many people take offense when a total stranger assumes personal familiarity before it's mutually established. Follow the interviewer's lead—don't lead the way. Begin by addressing them by their last name, "Well, Mr./Ms./Mrs./Miss Jones." Be certain you have the correct pronunciation of their name—supplied by the receptionist. You can answer the question directly without formally addressing the interviewer. It would be wise, however, to insert the interviewer's name every five to eight minutes—at least once every four to five questions asked. Most people never tire of hearing their name spoken.

As you accompany the interviewer to the interviewing office, never drop behind more than half a step…to do so would make it difficult for him or her to carry on a brief conversation with you while walking. Keep up the pace—you're not going to a funeral (you hope). The interviewer should not have to slow down for you. Walk briskly, but not so fast that you appear hyper.

After you enter the office, stand and wait at the doorway until you are asked to be seated. Don't immediately sit down in the first chair you see—it might be the interviewer's chair! You should sit down at the same time as the interviewer sits down. If it's a board interview, sit down at the same time the last board member sits down. As you sit down, unbutton your suit jacket. The interviewer may ask if you would like to remove your tie, unbutton your collar and take your suit coat or jacket off. Don't do this unless you are asked. If people in your position typically wear a suit and tie, you could comment, "I'm perfectly comfortable with it on—thanks though for asking."

You should not initiate the interview—that is the interviewer's prerogative. Some candidates mistakenly think they can show initiative and assertiveness by 'getting the ball rolling.' However, this generally comes across as taking over the interview. Don't sabotage yourself at the outset by appearing forward and pushy.

Try to become as relaxed as you possibly can. Interviewers expect you to be a little nervous at the start. If, however, you appear too laid back, it can project an image of someone who is overly self-confident or smug—and maybe lacking enthusiasm.

Most interviewers strive to put you at ease and establish rapport with light conversation, usually unrelated to your qualifications—such as your drive or flight to their location, the weather, a highly publicized current event or news story (especially if job or field-related), or having a mutual acquaintance. Join in this conversation with interest and enthusiasm. If you've noticed something positive in what you've been observing—how friendly their employees are and how well they've treated you, the office décor, or something else that impressed you—then mention it. Just be sincere and don't go overboard.

You must be especially impressive at both the start and finish of your interview—they are equally important.. This will help override any so-so answers you gave in between. You may start out well but end on a negative note—leaving the interviewer thinking, "I was impressed when he or she first started answering my questions but then he/she sort of fizzled out at the end." Put 'feeling' into what you are saying throughout the interview—especially when you're making your most important points. Reveal your positive relationship with supervisors, peers, and co-workers and the work values you've established and maintained in every job you've had.

During those crucial first five to eight minutes of your interview, you need to get a feel for the interviewer and adjust your approach accordingly. Observe closely whether the interviewer establishes a light or serious mood, is relaxed or uptight, is quiet or talkative, seems to be in a hurry or has a lot of time, is very aggressive or laid back, displays continuous or sporadic eye contact, uses lots of body language or a very limited amount. Determine if the interviewer likes to get 'straight to the point' or is round about in making points, very detailed or generalizes, 'idea' or 'feeling' oriented, neat or somewhat disorganized. Notice if he or she speaks rapidly or slowly, dresses professionally or casually, appears formal or informal, is very 'hands-on' in controlling the interview or allows you to take initiative at times, and so on.

During this time, your facial expressions and body language should readily reveal that you're hanging on to every word he or she is saying. This shows you're a good listener and that you closely observe everything that is happening around you, and aren't easily distracted.

By following the interviewer's lead, you can make some adjustments and modifications to accommodate the interviewer's style, and still be cheerful, optimistic, enthusiastic, and self-confident. You may have to speed up or slow down your delivery somewhat to keep in sync with the interviewer while still maintaining your own unique style and personality. Don't we do this daily with the people we deal with in order to get along well with them? You don't want a drastic change or shift that would make it appear that your personality is changing. You just want to interact with this particular interviewer in the most productive and constructive ways possible. A word of caution: don't directly adopt the interviewer's speech pattern, body actions, facial expressions, voice inflections and speed of delivery—he or she will quickly detect your intent to mimic him or her.

Treat all interviewers equally, whether male or female and regardless of level of position, age, race, nationality, or other distinguishing characteristics. Any special treatment on your part will be readily apparent.

The interviewer will ask many questions on many different subjects. Be consistent in what you say—inconsistency is viewed the same as lying. You are expected to give logical, clear, candid replies, with occasional comments on the subject; however, you must not attempt to control or dominate the interviewer at any time. Whenever you have the opportunity, of course, you may take the initiative and add any related job knowledge that you may have gained from your avocations, hobbies, reading, and the like, to reinforce your qualifications.

Setting the Tone

Your answer to the first substantial question they ask you is very important; it sets the tone of the interview and is the basis for the interviewer's first formal assessment of who you are and where you will be taking him or her in the answers to come. You want to show that you will be the same person 'on the job' if hired as you are in your job interview. Don't give too short or abrupt an answer. When you know what you are talking about, give your answer 'in full' with conviction, then remain silent so the interviewer can comment on your answer or ask a follow-up question. To avoid appearing to be a know-it-all, you can preface your response with, "To the extent that I have had some exposure to that type of work, I would say…" Apply all the insight that we covered earlier into building great answers.

When asked about your interest in working for their company in particular, state your reasons with sincere enthusiasm. Don't be afraid to show that you're a warm, compassionate person. Show pride in your past job performances and accomplishments, and project self-confidence tempered with humility. Smile often with your mouth, cheeks, and eyes. Supervisors, peers, co-workers, customers, clients, family, friends, neighbors, and the public in general enjoy being around someone who seems happy in what he or she is doing and with life in general. Smiling conveys that image. It's good for business. Interviewers take note of it in their interview observations and assessments.

Any early negative or neutral image of you can be overcome by an outstanding interview performance during the remainder of your interview. Any early positive image can be destroyed by a poor performance during the remainder of time spent with the interviewer.

What They Can 'Quickly' Learn About You

The following is a composite of what a number of astute, seasoned interviewers said they were able to detect in their first five to ten minutes spent with job candidates. It's amazing how much very perceptive interviewers can learn about you in just that short length of time. They said that they confirmed, modified, or reassessed their initial observations during the course of the remainder of their interview…as they got to view the candidate more in depth.

- Dress, grooming and overall appearance
- Five o'clock shadow evident, or closely shaved
- Polished shoes
- Matching clothing—freshness in smell
- Fit and style of clothing worn
- Clean fingernails, manicured nails
- Type and amount of jewelry worn
- Brisk or slow walker—their gait
- How well trimmed their mustache, beard or hair was
- Hair combed
- Weak or strong handshake
- Strength of perfume/cologne/after shave lotion
- Fresh or bad breath—smell of tobacco or alcohol
- Hygiene concern—didn't appear to have bathed/showered that day or used a deodorant
- Amount of direct eye contact
- Display of facial expressions, gestures, other body movements
- Posture—sitting and standing
- Facial or body 'twitches' and other nervous mannerisms
- Display of irritation that the interview didn't begin on time
- Voice—loudness, pitch, clarity, diction, and pronunciations
- Extent of their vocabulary
- Whether fast or slow talking
- Ability to 'read the interviewer' and people in general
- Ease or difficulty in reading the applicant

- Applicant's awareness of time limitations, in answering questions, and length of interview
- Answers too long or too short
- Sense of timing in candidate's responses to questions—appropriateness
- Extent of 'openness' in expressing themselves
- Immediate liking or disliking of this person
- Ability to hold my attention throughout the interview
- Extent of interest in learning more about the job opening, department, and our company
- Level of comprehension and sincerity
- Degree of nervousness
- Energy level—high or low
- How frequently the person smiled
- Their laugh—type, timeliness, and appropriateness
- Overall warmth or coolness in personality and approach to others
- Degree of hyperness or sluggishness
- Fidgeting with hair and clothing
- Quickness to learn and adapt to new environments, people, conditions, and situations
- Degree of concentration on what is being discussed/happening and their comfort level (adjusting to me)
- Tolerance of others who don't agree with their beliefs or opinions
- Irritating habits and quirks
- Amount of attention paid to what I'm saying
- Extent of my interest in the applicant
- Quickness to grasp and understand each question asked
- Use of my name—too frequently, frequent, seldom, or never
- How easily distracted they are
- Initiative displayed in volunteering information and fostering a conversation
- Display of enthusiasm, ingenuity, tactfulness, sensitivity to others, and motivational level
- Evidence of tendency to interrupt, exaggerate, and blame others for their shortcomings
- Extent of their situational awareness, aggressiveness and willingness to assume full responsibility for all their actions
- Questioning of their honesty

- Evidence of reluctance to give others partial credit for their accomplishments
- Their criticalness of others and inconsideration of their needs
- Extent of 'exaggeration' in statements made
- Amount of diplomacy displayed
- Political astuteness and cleverness displayed
- Display of 'off the wall' comments, impulsiveness, sarcasm, and temper
- Abruptness and curtness in their responses to questions asked
- Ability to handle stress and remain calm
- Extent to which I'm enjoying interviewing this person
- Extent to which the applicant appears to be enjoying the interview
- How quickly and smoothly the interview is progressing
- How realistic' he/she seems to be
- Overall attitude and disposition
- Personality and character traits—those pleasing and irritating
- Sense of humor and wittiness displayed
- Type and extent of 'values'
- Degree of self-confidence shown
- Cooperativeness or arrogance displayed
- Extent of alertness, patience, maturity, and emotional control evidenced
- How impressed peers, co-workers, and other department supervisors will be with this candidate (if hired)
- Overall fit with job, supervisor, department team, and company

Experience in the real world has proved that if you can project yourself 'at your best' from the very start of your interview, as well as do it smoothly and make it seem natural, you will earn more points in the company's applicant scoring system.

Be sure to thank the interviewer for the opportunity to meet and to be interviewed. You might do this just before you are asked your first important question and again at the close of the interview.

■ ■ ■

People often spend more time trying to
justify what they do than finding the truth.

■ ■ ■

31

DRESSING APPROPRIATELY FOR YOUR INTERVIEW

Companies often hire people 'in their own image.' The dress and appearance of their personnel are important to this image. Your prospects of being hired are considerably enhanced by appropriate clothes, good grooming, and overall good appearance. Trends in dress come and go. Keep current, but stay moderate to conservative in your choices.

MEN

SUITS

When applying for a professional position, you should (ideally) wear a new or nearly new single-breasted suit of a good quality wool or wool blend. Conservative colors are navy blue, dark blue, or charcoal gray—you're playing it safe to stick with these. Wear a tan, camel, beige or brown suit only if you've been repeatedly told 'these are your colors.' If you are tall and thin and want to appear heavier, select a light colored suit (solid or patterned). If you'd like to appear taller, choose a subtle pinstripe. The cut and fit of the suit you choose should compliment your body size and build. Don't wear an old suit that still looks good but is out of style. If it has any shine or worn look to it at all, it's too old to wear to a job interview. Allow a half-inch of shirt cuff to show beyond the coat sleeves and the same amount of shirt collar to show above the back of the neck. The collar and lapels should hug your neck and body and not creep up when you bend forward. Your pant legs should hang straight without breaking (or only slightly breaking) over the tops of your shoes.

It's a good idea to dress as though you were going to your job interview and then visit one or two clothing stores that carry a better line of men's suits. Ask a seasoned salesperson if he or she feels that you are appropriately dressed, considering the position for which you're being interviewed. Ask if he or she has any suggestions for improving your professional image. Most of these people will give you an honest opinion. They may suggest a change in an accessory item. Dress well enough to reflect the image of a professional.

Unless your suit's brand new, have it dry cleaned before your interview. It's especially important to eliminate any odor of food or tobacco.

SHIRTS

Wear a new, preferably cotton, well-pressed, long sleeved, solid white or light-colored shirt with a standard collar. Button-down collars look nice when the shirt is new; if however, after laundering the collar 'buckles' when buttoned, don't use it.

TIES

Wear a new silk or partially silk tie that harmonizes with the color of your suit and has a high-quality appearance to it. A solid-colored tie with small matching patterns or narrow stripes would be appropriate—nothing too bold or flashy. Again, ask a seasoned men's clothing salesperson his or her opinion, or ask your spouse if he or she has great taste in helping you choose your clothes. The tie should not be so bold in design and color that it draws the interviewer's attention away from your face. The tie should be up-to-date in its width and knot, and long enough to cover part of your belt buckle when standing. The clips and tie tacks are no longer worn.

SHOES

The most appropriate dress shoes to wear to an interview are black, brown or burgundy wingtip slip-ons or oxfords with no pronounced decorative features, preferably recently purchased. If you buy new shoes just for the interview, allow a couple of wearings to break them in, so you're not distracted by uncomfortably stiff or tight shoes in an already stressful situation. On the other hand, don't wear your slipper-comfortable older shoes; even well-polished, they'll still look old.

Should you wear shoes with laces, be certain those laces aren't worn—if in doubt, purchase new ones. You don't want to experience a lace breaking and be distracted by it during your interview.

SOCKS

Wear new solid-color socks that match the color of your suit. No loud, bold patterns and colors. They should be over-the-calf length and fit snugly without slipping down during the course of your interview.

THE BACKUP
You could be asked to return the next day for further screening or additional interviews. Be prepared: Have a complete additional outfit available. Any element of your original outfit—suit, shirt, tie, socks, shoes— could be accidentally soiled or damaged in some way and you wouldn't have time for cleaning or repair. Plus, you don't want to appear to be wearing the same exact clothing—two days in a row.

BELTS
A new leather belt that matches the color of your shoes looks professional. The belt buckle should be a small or moderate size and traditional in style. Large, ornate belt buckles look unprofessional and are not appropriate.

RINGS
If you are married, of course you should wear your wedding ring. School rings (conservative in size and appearance) are appropriate. Wearing additional rings, bracelets, collar pins, or cuff links may appear inappropriate or dated to some interviewers.

WATCHES
Keep your wristwatch simple in appearance. Again, nothing huge, extravagant, gaudy or cheap looking. No trendy new style. The band can be leather or metal.

HAIR
Your hair length (for most professional jobs) should be moderate to short—a reflection of the accepted dress code for each particular employer. It should not (preferably) extend over the top of your ears unless it is acceptable to the interviewing company. The cut and style should be traditional/conservative, no 'brand new' looks, but in keeping with the current, prevailing style. Have your hair cut or trimmed approximately three days before your interview—allow for a little growing in should the barber cut it too short.

Moustaches should be kept trim and moderate in size. You may encounter an interviewer who does not like moustaches but will accept one if it is neat and trim—not one that is bushy. If you don't want to risk being interviewed by someone who frowns on moustaches, shave yours off. If, however, you have worn a moustache for years and would feel ill at ease with it missing, leave it be. If you have a tan, shaving it off just before an interview will leave you with a pale upper lip; get some sun beforehand so that your whole face has the same hue. Beards, goatees, and other facial hair are acceptable to some employers and not to others. Investigate beforehand to determine the company's policies and standards on dress codes.

If your hair loss is quite noticeable and ages you significantly, it's acceptable to wear a very well-made hair piece that fits well and looks natural in color and style. If your hair is graying and you wish to appear younger, you may want to use a coloring agent that matches your natural hair color. You don't want it to appear obvious that you colored your hair—perhaps leave a little gray at the temples.

A few added thoughts: keep your nails short and clean. Skip the aftershave lotion or cologne; the interviewer could be allergic to it. Be sure to use mouthwash the day of your interview. Carry mints with you as well.

GLASSES/CONTACT LENSES

Contact lenses can be worn—provided they fit well, are comfortable, and you don't blink steadily as though something was irritating your eyes. You can take your glasses along and put them on if you need to read and/or sign a document. If you have worn glasses for many years and would feel uncomfortable not wearing them, then just wear them. If you have several pairs, choose the one with a conservative looking frame that looks new and good on you. Wearing glasses, in most cases, is not an employer's concern. Avoid wearing very dark tinted glasses because interviewers rely on reading your eyes.

BRIEFCASE

If you plan to take paperwork to your interview, carry it in a briefcase or standard attaché case—one that is leather, a high-quality simulated leather, or sturdy nylon, and in excellent condition. The choice is yours, depending on how many items you'll be placing in the case. The color (ideally) should compliment the color of your suit. If you don't own one, consider borrowing a new looking one from a friend.

WOMEN

SUITS

To project a professional image, you should (ideally) wear a quality, tailored skirted business suit (wool or wool blend) in navy, dark blue, black, charcoal, or medium gray, brown or beige. Well tailored clothes have smooth seams and buttons are sewn on securely. A pants suit of similar quality can be worn when appropriate for the level of position applied for and the hiring employer's preferences. In most cases, you can't go wrong dressing conservatively.

It is advisable to purchase your suit at a better women's apparel store with an excellent reputation and a seasoned sales staff. Tell the salesperson that you are dressing for an important job interview and you want to appear professional. The higher the position, the more tailored the look.

Your suits should fit comfortably—not too loose or too tight. The style and cut should compliment your figure. Skirt hems should fall to a length in keeping with the current practice. When wearing a pants suit, your pant legs should hang straight without breaking (or only slightly breaking) over the tops of your shoes.

BLOUSE

Wear a well-tailored, solid white or light-colored long-sleeved silk or cotton blouse or one that appears similar to silk. Both the cut and buttons should be simple.

SHOES

Wear quality, low-heeled, plain dark-colored pumps or oxfords, preferably leather, with closed heel and toes. The toe of the shoes should not be overly pointed. Don't wear sandals. Avoid strapped shoes. Your shoes should also be quite comfortable for walking. The color should match or be compatible with the color of your suit. Choose from navy, dark blue, black, burgundy, brown, beige, or camel.

HOSE

Wear natural-color pantihose. Have several extra pairs available in your briefcase or purse in case you experience an unexpected run. Do not wear elaborately designed hose—save them for a night out.

COAT

If the weather requires a coat, it should be wool or wool blend with a plain collar, in a length that covers your skirt hem.

GLOVES

If you'll be interviewing in cold weather, wear dark-colored, close-fitting leather gloves.

HAIR

Ideally, your hair should be moderate to short in length—shoulder length at most—in a conservative, feminine style that compliments the shape of your face. Don't get an elaborate, attention-getting hair style. (Some jobs related to the modeling and the fashion industry and such are the exception.) If you look best with your hair pulled back in a bun or twist, then wear it that way. If your hair is prematurely graying, it's acceptable to color it the same shade as your natural hair color. Take your body size and shape into consideration when choosing your clothing, colors, and make-up.

MAKE-UP

Use a 'light touch' with cosmetics and avoid a heavy make-up look. Keep your eyebrows natural-looking; darken them slightly if necessary to accentuate them. You can use a subtle, tasteful amount of eye shadow or eye liner if you feel it enhances your appearance. The color/tone of your lipstick and make up should be compatible with your skin tone. Use lipstick sparingly.

NAILS

Keep your fingernails at a moderate length, using a colorless or subdued colored polish. Have your nails manicured just prior to your interview. Never enter an interviewer's office with 'chipped' or 'loud colored' nails. Artificial nails can be worn if they are relatively undetectable to the interviewer.

PERFUME

A slight scent of subtle cologne is acceptable. No heavy scented perfume —the interviewer might have allergies. If in doubt, don't use it.

WATCHES

Wristwatches should be simple in design. The size and shape should be proportioned to the size of your wrist. Both the watch and band should be high-quality in appearance.

GLASSES

Follow the guidelines for men. Interviewers seem to allow women more latitude in frame styles and size when appearing in job interviews.

JEWELRY

Wear a minimal amount of simple, finer jewelry, such as a thin gold or silver necklace and bracelet, or a single strand of pearls; perhaps some plain gold or silver posts if your ears are pierced, or conservative looking earrings. If you are married, of course you should wear your wedding ring. Engagement and dinner rings are also considered appropriate for a job interview. Wearing additional rings or bracelets is not recommended.

BRIEFCASE

Follow the guidelines for men. Women can carry an inconspicuous looking purse if they are not carrying a briefcase. Hopefully, you've applied your makeup before reporting for your interview. A very small purse or clutch bag with your 'basics' can readily fit inside your briefcase.

ADDITIONAL DRESS INSIGHTS (MEN AND WOMEN)

Dress according to what is considered appropriate dress wear for people in your profession and age bracket. Should you have a very youthful physical appearance and the employer is seeking someone heavily experienced, dress to appear older. On the other hand, if it is known that the employer is leaning toward hiring someone less experienced than yourself, you may wish to appear younger through your selection of clothing. You may also want to walk more briskly and avoid slower speech and actions. If you go overboard, the interviewer will think, "It's obvious that he/she is attempting to look twenty years younger than they are."

Your clothes should be wrinkle free when you walk into the interviewer's office; everything in place. There shouldn't be any dandruff or hairs on the shoulders of your suit. Don't eat any foods a day or two before your interview that will leave a smell of garlic or other strong smells on your clothes or breath.

Don't use aftershave [men] or perfume [women] with a heavy scent that can strongly linger on your face or hands long into and throughout your interview. To be on the safe side, ask the receptionist to direct you to the nearest restroom to 'freshen up.' Wash your hands, comb your hair, remove dandruff/hairs from your clothing, and use a breath mint. You might want to clear your throat or hum a few times to limber up your vocal chords.

Carry something with you (such as tissues) to wipe the perspiration from your hands before you meet and shake hands with the interviewer, something that isn't too bulky.

If you're reporting to your interview on a cold and/or rainy day, you can of course wear a topcoat or raincoat. If in doubt as whether or not to wear one...don't wear either. They're an inconvenience to carry around with you and also pose a problem to the receptionist or interviewer as to where to place it to be out of the way during your interview.

For certain positions, it would be acceptable for a woman to wear a professional-appearing, well-tailored dress to her job interview and for a man to wear a new pair of 'work pants,' short sleeve shirt (with or without a tie) and a quality, conservative looking jacket. Silk scarves and simple shell worn under a jacket may be appropriate for women to wear. Wearing a conservative-looking skirt and blouse with a matching jacket is also considered appropriate at many organizations.

Being well-groomed and dressed is crucial to a successful job interview. Your clothes must fit well and you must be comfortable in them. Your shoes must look new/well-polished. Be sure your shirt or blouse is tucked in well.

The clothes you choose to wear must not be so prominent that they draw more of the interviewer's attention than does your face and your expressions.

Some employers, especially smaller companies, allow casual/sporty clothes at work. Find out if the organization you're going to be interviewing with suggests job applicants come in dressed as their employees do while on-the-job. Dress according to the employer's culture.

Do not wear sunglasses during the interview—even if you're traveling to Hollywood for your interview.

Should your job interview be in the summer, choose a lighter wool/wool blended suit to wear. When you feel more comfortable in your interviewing clothes, you're more relaxed. In turn, you make the interviewer more relaxed.

Men should only carry a wallet, comb, and car keys. You don't want bulging pockets that are readily noticeable to the interviewer. Leave suspenders at home and avoid clothing mismatches, worn shoe heels, and excessively long or short ties.

You want to avoid walking into the interviewer's office with a noticeable tattoo or body piercing jewelry if the employer is conservative. Find out the company's attitude toward tatoos.

You want to display good manners along with your 'professionally dressed' image. Treat every job interview as your 'first interview' date.

It would be a good idea to phone the HR employment department receptionist at the company you're interviewing with to find out what he or she thinks would be most appropriate for you to wear, considering the position for which you are being interviewed. Most receptionists are very accommodating to job applicants.

No matter what job you're applying for, you want to look professional. You perform your job professionally—and should look that way as well. It will help you to 'feel professional' during your interviews.

"Al, you're a genius, how should I dress for my job interview?"

32

YOUR VOICE AND DELIVERY

The tone of your voice and the delivery of your answers—not only to the interviewers, but to everyone at the company with whom you come in contact—is extremely important. You can say something that you think is very appropriate and polite, but the listener can interpret or perceive it to be an inappropriate, negative thing if the tone is off.

You must sound clear, sincere, confident, and credible. Often *how* you say something can be more important than *what* you have to say. Interviewers are impressed with good answers presented in a convincing manner, as though you truly, enthusiastically believe what you're saying. The words you choose should paint a vivid picture of who you are and what you have to offer them. It is also important that you speak with good diction; not too fast or too slow. Smile often throughout your interview to reinforce what you are saying and your concurrence with what the interviewer has said. Avoid, however, continuously nodding in agreement with every statement the interviewer makes.

Show that you have a substantial, varied vocabulary; use the most appropriate and commonly used words by professionals to make your point. As we discussed earlier, try to avoid fillers like "and," "ah," "hmm," "oh well," "I suppose," "let me just say this," or "huh" while you're thinking of something else to say. Don't obsess on this,we all do it now and then. Avoid the clichés that many job applicants use: "I'm honest, hard working, a perfectionist."These are good points, but they've been used many times. Instead, make those points in a fresh way that will reflect your individuality. Don't use obscure expressions that the interviewer may not be familiar with and misinterpret, such as "That's like anchoring the wind."

When you don't sound confident in yourself or what you are saying, it projects uncertainty, timidity, or evasiveness. *A good answer made in an unconvincing manner is a bad answer.* If you come on too strong, you sound cocky and boastful. If you talk too loudly and quickly, you appear hyper. Talk too slowly, and the interviewer may think your mind moves slowly and that you can't think fast on your feet.

So what's the right pace? Seven words in five seconds is too slow; fifteen words in five seconds is too fast; ten is just about right. Try it out: jot down some of your best prepared answers and time yourself delivering them. You can always speed up or slow down a second or two to suit your natural delivery style.

A word on silence. It can be very stressful when the interviewer just sits there, not saying a word but looking at you intently. You may have an urge to talk when you haven't anything appropriate or worthwhile to say—don't! There is no need for you to fill every pause in conversation. If you do, the interviewer will say to himself or herself, "This candidate can't stand silence—can't handle the pressure, has to talk." Show you can handle the situation by merely sitting there quietly during the silence, occasionally smiling and looking directly at the interviewer—letting him or her know that you are not easily intimidated by the silent treatment. Wait calmly for the interviewer to ask you another question. When he or she does, answer his or her question and stop talking. Don't linger on. The interviewer will try the silent treatment approach again to find out whether you can handle it a second time. Prove you can.

If you don't pronounce your words clearly, you sound like a mumbler. Do you talk as well as you deliver results in your work? There's always some room for improvement.

Know when to vary your voice to emphasize an important point or underscore your descriptions: raise or lower it, slow down or speed up. Your voice should be like a wave, not a straight line. Consider it a musical instrument—learn to play it well and utilize its full range. If you have a high-pitched voice, practice lowering it and expanding your vocal range. Consider seeing a voice coach, attending a public speaking course, or joining a speaking group. You'll be surprised how well you can expand and improve your communication skills.

On the morning of the interview, before you leave your home/hotel room, do some vocal warm-ups. Talk to yourself or sing in the shower and on your drive to your interview. This will make your voice strong and clear during the interview.

33

SPEAKING WITH THE RIGHT 'BODY LANGUAGE'

Body posture and movements constitute a nonverbal language that interviewers understand, consciously or subconsciously. Your body language speaks as clearly as the words you use throughout your interview. Your body can say, "I'm an open, relaxed and professional person" or "I'm a tense, guarded, cautious person." Again, a word of caution: Don't wear sun glasses or heavily tinted prescription glasses. You don't want to hide your eyes—it will work against you.

Start off positively with a firm handshake, warm smile, and direct eye contact with the interviewer. Add a "Hi, I'm…, and I have been looking forward to meeting you."

Please Be Seated

Enter the interviewer's office with good erect posture and be brisk and smooth in your movements and actions. Display a high energy level and enthusiasm to show that you're delighted to have this interview. Sit down as the interviewer sits down—never before. If you're offered a chair quite far away from the desk or table that you are facing, or one not directly facing the interviewer, ask the interviewer's permission to straighten it and move closer in. Interviewers want to observe whether or not you will take the initiative to move closer to them—in a tactful manner. It's another way to add a few more points to your total score.

Take an erect seating position, with your bottom all the way to the back of the chair and your shoulders flat against the back. Don't sit at the edge or middle of the chair, and never slouch or slump. Suggestions: Men should sit with legs apart—about the width of the chair legs—with feet flat on the floor. If you need to release some pent-up energy during the interview, you can cross your legs for a while. Women can sit with legs crossed at the knees or with ankles crossed or uncrossed; shift position among these when you feel the need. All candidates should avoid frequent position changes—it looks 'fidgety.' Reposition yourself during times when you have answered a question and the interviewer is looking down at your resume or employment application—not while you are talking and he or she is closely observing you.

You shouldn't clasp your hands behind your head, chew gum, savor a mint, keep adjusting your tie, collar, or other clothing. Avoid the nervous habit of reaching up to straighten your hair with your fingers.

Ideally you should keep your fingers slightly coupled, with your left hand resting on your left leg and your right hand resting on your right leg. Many people want to know what to do with their hands and arms during a job interview. *Don't* fold your arms, clasp your hands tightly together, hold your hands up toward your face while talking, or touch the desk or table in front of you. Try to appear as open as you can. If you wish, you can bring the tips of your fingers together or place the fingers of your left hand loosely around your right wrist. Don't twiddle your thumbs or swing your foot or upper body back and forth. Avoid staring at any object in the room for a prolonged period of time as well as 'darting eyes.' You should release your pent up excess energy in your car, before walking to the front door of the company's facility; practice deep breathing and stretching at this time as well. Don't tap your fingers on the interviewer's desk or arm of your chair. Don't point to information on your resume or employment application in response to an interviewer's question. This could imply you're thinking, "Look—it's right there in front of you!"

Following these postural suggestions can definitely enhance the impression you make, but if obsessing about them undermines your ability to present good answers, focus on the answers.

Express Yourself

It's good to gesture and show enthusiasm, but don't go overboard—no sweeping hand or arm movements. Express your sincerity not only through gestures, but in your facial expressions as well. You don't want a 'dead pan' blank stare or 'closed' eyes at any time during your interview. Don't look at your watch. Smile often, move your head once in a while, and speak with your eyes. Loosen up! A tense, immobile body with little or no facial expression comes across as cold and insensitive. You don't want to be mistaken for a department store mannequin. It's fine to lean forward slightly as you begin answering a question—just don't overdo it or do it too frequently.

Interviewers observe both your verbal and nonverbal responses to their individual questions—such as scratching your nose, face, arm, neck or hand, twitching your nose, rapid blinking, raised eyebrows, throat-clearing, frequent tie adjustments, shifting in your chair while talking, abrupt or jerky movements, raised or lowered voice, faster or slower speech, or breaking eye contact. These are all indications that you have become uncomfortable; they alert the interviewer to dig further into the question that triggered the change. Were you lying or stretching the truth? Were you prepared for that particular question? Were you trying to think of something important you forgot to say?

Pay attention to the interviewer's body language, too. Are you holding his or her attention? If so, you are on target. If the interviewer begins changing his or her physical movements to 'shift gears' (in any area), it means he or she wants to move on to another question. Some will shuffle your paperwork, pick up or lay down a pen, or look away from you. When you see this, it's time to wrap up your answer.

Make Eye Contact

Your eye contact with the interviewer is very important. You should maintain eye contact most of the time (roughly 80 percent)—especially while you are being asked a question, gathering your thoughts, beginning your answer, and wrapping up your reply. The 20 percent of the time when you look away during your reply gives both of you a break; constant eye contact would get a little too intense! Break eye contact by moving your eyes, not your head. Look away diagonally upward to the left or right of the interviewer's face or gaze at his or her forehead.

When being interviewed by a panel or board, divide your eye contact equally among all the members. Resist the tendency to concentrate your attention on the person who seems most receptive, who smiles, nods frequently as though in agreement, or gives you undivided attention. If you direct your gaze too much to any one person, the others will feel ignored and be more critical of you in their scoring. While one interviewer asks you a question, focus your eyes on that person and remain focused as you begin your answer. Then alternate your eye contact among the other interviewers. End your answer looking at the person who asked the question.

Strong eye contact connotes strong interest. If another panel member interrupts you with a question, immediately look at that person and answer his or her question, then return to where you were in answering the original question, and finish answering it.

Some candidates frequently look away while answering a question because they find it stressful to gather and relate their thoughts when someone is looking them in the eye. The interviewer can almost read the candidate's thoughts, "Don't you have anywhere else to look? Your eye-balling me while I'm talking stresses me out!" Unfortunately, when you do this, it makes you look evasive—as if you're twisting the truth or lying—or as if you can't handle pressure well. Looking away frequently while the interviewer is talking to you may give the impression that you're not listening closely, are bored, indifferent, or losing interest in what is being said.

Don't drop your head and look down at the floor as though you're intimidated by the question, or tilt it back and look up at the ceiling.

Practice, Practice, Practice

If all these precise body-language requirements are just adding to your stress, you'd do well to practice them a few times with willing family members or friends. You can try this in the course of normal conversation, or you can enlist their active participation where they ask questions and you answer. They can help you achieve the right balance of eye contact and 'breaks.' Soon you'll feel more comfortable and secure in your eye-contact and body-language skills and they will come more naturally to you.

■ ■ ■

Decide who and what is important
to you each day you wake up.

■ ■ ■

"Is it hot in here or is it me?"

34

THE MESSAGES YOU'RE SENDING TO INTERVIEWERS

As you present the answers you've prepared to the interviewer, you're delivering much more than just a simple message of words. Whether or not you're aware of it, you are sending other messages—communicating in several essential ways:

- Conveying *information* (content), either in answer to a question asked or as a comment. Is this information accurate, applicable, and important? What should you include and exclude?
- Expressing your *attitude* toward the information that you are presenting to the interviewer—through your tone of voice, and overall conciseness or vagueness. Is this attitude positive, neutral, or negative? Are you aware of these signals?
- Speaking the unspoken through *body language:* your posture, how you arrange your hands, arms, legs, and feet; tension or relaxation in your facial expression; your gestures and body movements (whether holding still, or moving restlessly, at any point in the interview). Is your body language appropriate to the occasion and favorable to you? (Remember your performance on videotape.)

What's the effect of these multiple messages? They either support or undermine the case you are building for yourself as the best of the job candidates. All three may support one another or one may detract from the other two. Are all three of your communication techniques in sync? Are you believable?

You must be particularly aware of these three forms of communication when you are explaining to the interviewer any negative event you have experienced. While you strive to control your emotions in your choice of words, you may unconsciously express bitterness, resentment, guilt, and the like through your attitude or body language. We'll explore this more in the chapters ahead.

If you read the interviewer well, you can quickly adjust (not completely change) your behavior to be compatible with his or hers. When you concur with what the interviewer is saying, smile or nod your head. When he or she laughs, you can smile, laugh, or grin. Convey the silent message that you're on the same team. At the right moment, you can comment along the lines, "You must have a unique and interesting job. It must be challenging and rewarding choosing people who will determine your company's future—bet there's not a dull moment in your day." Don't overdo it—in just the 'right dosage,' you can make the interviewer feel good about himself or herself without thinking you're being patronizing.

Don't overestimate the importance of your interview with Human Resources (HR). Put equal or more emphasis on your interview with the hiring department because this is your potential 'new boss.' The 'feel' between yourself and your future supervisor is extremely important. There must be a good feeling on both sides or it's not a good match.

Display respect for everyone who interviews you and everyone else you come in contact with at the company. You don't have to 'look up' to them as superior to you, just show them the same respect you do to your family and close friends.

Taking notes during your interview could send the wrong message to the person interviewing you. Sure you are doing it to remember thoughts, names, etc. but the interviewer may think you're quoting him or her and building a good case for a lawsuit against the company should you be rejected. You may be viewed as being more focused on writing down information than you are on what the interviewer is saying. Instead, you should be concentrating on the answer you're giving to an important question. Practice retaining information without the need to take elaborate notes.

■ ■ ■

Ever wonder, "Why do I think...what I think...when I think it?

■ ■ ■

35

TACTFUL VERSUS TACKLESS
COMMENTS AND ANSWERS

Imagine this experiment: for one day, give everyone you encounter pure, honest statements about how you really feel about them without regard to tactfulness. Say exactly what you think. Then count how many people you may have offended by your remarks and how many feelings you may have hurt.

A tactful approach is as crucial in an interview as it is in your daily life. It is a highly-desired attribute that employers look for in every job candidate they interview. It is a quality that assures them that you will be able to get along with everyone you interact with at their organization throughout your career with them. It means you will also handle customers effectively. Fellow employees will look forward to working with you.

You must convince interviewers that you will be both honest and tactful with people, taking into consideration the specific situation/time, circumstances, and people involved. As you respond to an interviewer's questions, keep in mind that *an honest answer that isn't tactfully presented is a bad answer.*

Being tactful means considering the other party's viewpoint, needs, and expectations. A purely honest but tactless answer can convey a lack of concern for the others' past experiences, beliefs, values, opinions, and feelings. Tactlessness can destroy good teamwork. A blunt remark can easily cause a breach in a personal or professional relationship. How many friendships and marriages have been sheared or destroyed by a lack of tact in the communications between the exchanging parties?

There are many ways to give an honest answer. Choose the one that will be considered most tactful to a listening interviewer, and present it in the most effective possible manner. An interviewer may ask, "Why did you leave that company?" One candidate might answer, "I didn't get along too well with my supervisor—he was always criticizing me about something." Another may respond, "I had the opportunity to expand my job skills by taking a position involving greater job responsibilities, in more advanced areas for another company." Which answer seems most tactful to you?

Take this question: "Why did you decide to pursue your particular profession?" Option one: "I like the job status, hours of work, good salary, and benefits received in this line of work." Option two: "Everything I've learned about the profession and career field excite me—the people in it seem very satisfied. My interests and talents lie in this field and I felt I could learn a great deal, grow a lot, advance my career and at the same time, contribute to team success and the company's profitability. I'm excited by the thought of joining the people I have met at your company and their 'up attitude.' I'll have the opportunity to contribute new ideas and suggestions—you seem to encourage it." It only takes approximately 40 seconds to give option two as your answer. Even if you wish to cut the time and verbage in half, you've still delivered a strong message. Which answer do you think is the most tactful?

Keep in mind that the interviewer's background may be quite different from yours. The interviewer may have a degree unrelated to yours, and have an outstanding academic record. He or she may have been in the military, or be completely civilian trained and experienced. Perhaps their GPA may have been 'average.' You don't want to say anything that implies that your choices, education, training, and experience are the way to go, and any others are a weak second.

Don't go into an interview thinking that you're going to tell it just the way it is, regardless of the interviewer's background, or what he or /she thinks of my answers. This could cost you a job offer. You may feel you have impressive examples to offer, but if it becomes clear that these are not—for whatever reason—the most tactful ones to present, don't use them. *The interviewer's perceptions of you, based upon the interviewer's background, are the primary reasons why you will be hired or turned down—not the facts, in and of themselves. Facts are important—perceptions are crucial.*

Interviewers will often ask a question intended to measure your 'team' skills. They want to know whether or not you can tactfully approach a team of people to resolve a serious problem. This question is often presented in an interview as a role-playing situation in which you are the main character. Your behavior will be studied and evaluated carefully. Do you fully understand the problem you are facing? What are your options? What actions will you take? What decisions will you make? What will you say, to whom, and how? What motivational techniques will you use? Will you handle everything in the most tactful manner possible? Give this possible scenario plenty of thought, so you can respond confidently and impressively to the challenge you face.

Being tactful also means keeping to yourself those negative facts that could tarnish your image. Let's say you voluntarily mention that in college you did some heavy beer drinking and excessive smoking. You weren't interested in making good grades—just wanted to get a degree and have a good time. Unbeknownst to you, the interviewer frowns on heavy drinking and smoking. He or she worked hard to earn good grades and learn as much as possible about their major field of study. The interviewer can't justify rejecting your candidacy solely based on those personal feelings, but he or she may seek other, job-specific reasons to validate the rejection. Interviewers can rationalize like this once in a while giving good, legal reasons for rejecting an applicant, but not the real ones. You shouldn't have mentioned these particular experiences in the first place. It wouldn't be a very tactful thing to do. You initiated your own turndown.

Let's look at a few more cases that reflect tactless and tactful applicant responses.

Tactless Response:	**Tactful Response:**
It gets pretty hot and humid in that area of the country during the summer.	I don't have any problem dealing with heat and humidity; I quickly adjust to it each summer.
That city's cost of living is too high.	It's an interesting place to visit.
I don't care to be closely supervised.	Some bosses supervise their employees closely—some don't. You learn to adjust to both styles.
I don't care for the way he operates.	He's tough, but fair.

There are several things I don't like about that company and that's why I didn't apply with them.	They weren't accepting resumes then, but they are now. I'm sending them one, as a backup company, but your company is my top choice.

You'll need to exercise the utmost tactfulness when it comes to the matter of competing job offers. Interviewers recognize that many candidates are applying to several companies; there's no need to keep this a secret. However, be prepared to answer a question such as "Let's say you should get a job offer from another company while you are waiting to hear from us. You decide to accept it, and begin working there. Then two weeks later, we make you a job offer. What will you do?" Your honest response might be that you would immediately quit the company you just started with and accept employment with them—after all, they were your first choice! Honest, but not too tactful. The interviewer could certainly question your integrity. The competing company would have invested a significant amount of money and time in bringing you on board, indoctrinating and training you. That company trusted you and thought you were sincere in wanting to work with them. They probably felt you were making a commitment to stay with them for a reasonable period of time. They expected a good return on their investment in you. The interviewer who asked you the question would think that you don't have much of a conscience, and little integrity—that you could well do the same thing to them.

Never leave a company shortly after being hired—even to take a plum job with a competitor—without absolute justification. The next time you find yourself back on the job market, what sort of recommendation could you expect to get from the company that you left so abruptly? Think they will say that you are eligible for rehire? Not too likely! You could have contacted the company you preferred working for and explained your situation before accepting the job and starting to work. If it appeared that they were finalizing a job offer, you could 'hold off' the first company until you hear from the second—then make your decision on which job offer to accept.

Here are some typical interview questions with two possible answers from the same candidate (abbreviated to focus on the key differences). The first answer displays straightforward honesty; the second, honesty tempered with tactfulness.

Are we the only major company in our industry you have applied with?
- "Yes. I don't care to work for the others."
- "No, although you are my first choice by far. I felt it was important to have some backups. I realize you can't hire all of us, and I have to be realistic."

Why do you want to work for us?
- "There is one main reason…"
- "There are a number of very important reasons…"

Why didn't you apply with _____?
- "I didn't care for their location."
- "I am in the process of sending them my resume. They're another backup company with a good reputation."

Why did you choose that particular major in college?
- "I wanted to get my degree in the shortest amount of time possible—could in that area of study."
- "I believed it would help me, in several ways, in building my future career in _____ and in my personal life as well."

Why didn't you join the military after you graduated college and receive your training and experience with them?
- "I didn't care for the long commitment and regimentation."
- "It was a difficult decision to make. Both 'military' and 'civilian' have advantages of their own. Long range, I felt I would be happiest pursuing a civilian career."

Ever work with someone you didn't like?
- "Sure. Several of them. The reasons that I didn't like them were…"
- "There were one or two people who may have rubbed me the wrong way initially. But after taking the time to get to know and understand them better, we hit it off well from that point on."

Ever disagree with your company's rules, policies, practices, standards, or procedures?
- "Yes, and I pointed them all out."
- "The few times I did, would try coming up with a better way of

doing it backed with solid reasons. They accepted and implemented several of my ideas."

What didn't you like about that job?
- "The hours were long and it didn't pay much."
- "It didn't provide an opportunity to get into new and more challenging job assignments."

What did you think of the supervision you received?
- "It wasn't too good. They wouldn't listen to my complaints."
- "Overall, it was good. There were a few areas that could have been improved—but no major ones."

Why did you leave that job?
- "For more money and better benefits."
- "I had the opportunity to move up into supervision. I seem to have a knack for handling people well and getting them to work together closely."

What's one of your weak points?
- "It took me five years to finish college—longer than most people."
- "It took me five years to finish college, since I was working full-time. But I'm proud of the fact that I paid for my education and supported a family while earning my degree."

What would your last supervisor say about you?
- [Give only one or two favorable comments.]
- [Give three to five favorable comments.]

What are you especially proud of?
- "My many years of experience. It took a lot of work to accumulate that much time."
- "My job performance evaluations and promotional record. They went 'hand in hand.'"

Ever have an argument or personality conflict with someone you've worked with?
- "Yes, several. Some worked out okay. Several didn't."

- "I have had a few disagreements and conflicts, but didn't let them get out of hand and end up in a heated argument or personality clash. I let the person know that I understood how he or she felt and appreciated their position on the matter. One way or another, I smoothed them all out and got along well with those people from then on."

Why do you think you were turned down by that company?
- "I haven't the slightest idea."
- "My best guess is that the ones they ended up hiring had a stronger background in certain areas of qualifications that were very important to that company."

When have you said something you shouldn't have said?
- "When I told my boss that he was dead wrong. I lived to regret that one."
- "When I was critical of something a co-worker did. I should have realized he or she was too inexperienced to know better."

How do you give constructive criticism?
- "I tell the person what he or she did wrong, not to do it that way again, and show him or her the right way to do it."
- "I first point out what he or she did right and then the areas that need improvement. I help the person in every way I can, to figure out for themselves the best way to perform well."

If you suspect that your boss may have been drinking prior to reporting to work, what would you do?

- "I would straight out tell him to go home or I will 'turn him in'."
- "I look for all evidence present to confirm my suspicions and if convinced he was under the influence of alcohol, still seek out another reliable co-worker who might be nearby to obtain a second opinion, before reaching a conclusion and taking action."

What was the most important decision you made in the last year?
- "To buy a new house."
- "Whether or not to spend a lot of money and time getting an

advanced degree that might help me get ahead further in my career."

Do you have any questions for us?
- "No. I've found out everything I need to know."
- "Most of my questions have been answered through what you've told me, all the research I've done on your company, and talking to my friends who work for you. However, I do have one or two questions that relate to some very recent changes you've made, and would like to know today's status on them. I'm also interested in finding out more about your long-range goals."

Why should we hire you over all the other candidates we're interviewing?
- "I know that I can do a better job for you than anyone else."
- "We're all well qualified, I'm sure. I just hope that you will be impressed enough with my individual qualifications and track record to hire me. Compare what I've done with what the others have done, then make up your mind. That's all I ask."

■ ■ ■

Either you direct your life 'into the future'
or others will direct it for you.

■ ■ ■

36

HANDLING STRESS

Interviewers expect you to be able to handle the stress that you may experience while performing your numerous job tasks and interacting with other people in your department. They also expect you to prevent circumstances and situations from occurring that would adversely impact your job performance or reflect very negatively upon the company's public image. They not only expect you to handle stress well at all times, but to do whatever you possibly can to prevent stress from developing in the first place.

The stress-related questions interviewers ask are designed to find out different ways you control the level of stress you're exposed to, how you prevent it from occurring, and how you resolve it or reduce it to a minimum. Questions such as these:

- How do you cope with the stress in your life?
- What were the most stressful situations you've faced, both on and off the job? How did you handle and resolve them?
- What stressful situation are you facing today on your job?
- What sort of things cause you stress? Why?
- What would you do if you had an emergency occur that was so unique that there were no guidelines to cover it?
- What do you do if your boss does something in violation of company rules and policies?
- How did you handle that surprise layoff? Wasn't that a very tough situation to face? What did you do?
- How stressful is this interview? How do you feel right now? Why do you feel this way?

Each of us has a stress level that, if reached, causes us to make questionable decisions, say inappropriate things, or act erratically. Interviewers want to find out when you will 'step over the line,' how quickly you would reach that point, and what it would take to get you there. You should be prepared should an interviewer deliberately induce a little stress into the interview to test how well you handle it. Some people can cope with stress when everything is going their way (fair-weather people), but they start 'losing it' under difficult conditions and heavy pressure. Catch them off guard and it shows.

Stress-inducing interview tactics may be subtle. For example, an interviewer may say, "Speak up, I can't hear you," when she or he can actually hear you perfectly. The object is to observe your reactions and behavior. Even more deliberately, an interviewer may describe the kind of professional their company is looking for—someone with certain education, training, and job experience—none of which match your job qualifications. How well will you avoid becoming defensive?

A greater amount of stress is introduced into the interviw should the open position involve greater job responsibilities and assignments, where stressful situations occur frequently.

Many stress questions involve role-playing in difficult situations. Others will reveal how well you handle criticism, first praising you for something you did, then immediately questioning why you did something else. Do you seem upset?

Some interviewers will ask in-depth questions about a position you held many years ago, to find out how you react when you can't really recall detailed information about your job involvements back then. Some act like you must have padded your resume. Don't let it get to you. Stay calm. Don't react emotionally. Explain whatever the interviewer wants to know in a relaxed manner.

Fads in interviewing practices come and go. The well proven ones are retained. Certain stress-inducing questions and techniques may be 'in' at some companies but 'out' at others. Sometimes they're rotated from time to time within that company. Be prepared for as many as you reasonably can. Even an interviewer's critical look at you can be a test of your stress threshold. Don't let it shake you. Never adopt an attitude of, "I don't have to take that from anyone!" Pretend they just paid you a compliment.

You may be interrupted at times by the interviewer, a phone call, or someone entering the interviewer's office—all deliberately planned to observe your reaction. The interviewer may find fault or disagree with something you said, give you the silent treatment, question your honesty, suck you into a debate, unexpectedly request that you do something, such as "Tell me a joke." They may give false signals, such as pleasantly smiling when they're displeased with your answer, and frowning when they like it. At times the interviewer may act irritated and become abrupt— almost initiating an argument. They may appear to ignore you at times, mispronounce your name or seem to have forgotten it. They may not offer to shake hands when meeting you or act bored with something you're relating. He or she might stop having direct eye contact with you and notice if your behavior is affected by it. There might be a period of throwing questions at you—one after another—giving you very little time to answer them. They may switch unexpectedly from 'nice guy' to 'bad guy' or from asking a very easy question to an extremely difficult one. If you're prepared and you know you've given a good answer, 'stick to your guns.'

Identify 'stressors' in your life (personality conflicts, financial problems, etc.) and resolve them. Develop a healthier lifestyle. Engage in meditation, yoga, and biofeedback. [Many people turn to prayer.] Visit a massage therapist or take a hot bath or shower after experiencing a stressful situation. Take full responsibility for your actions—don't blame others. Take responsibility only for what you can control. Daydream at times. Eliminate tasks, appointments, and running errands that aren't critical. Ask for help more often. Focus on 'what you have'— not what you don't have!

There are a number of effective mind/body techniques for coping with stress. Deep breathing is a tried and true method. Take deep breaths, letting your abdomen (not your chest) expand, then exhale slowly. This technique slows your heart rate, lowers your blood pressure, relaxes your muscles, calms you down, and reduces your level of anxiety. Always allow yourself a moment to calmly assess a stressful situation and decide how best to resolve it. You can face a number of them in your interviews with HR and the hiring department.

Taking a fifteen minute 'power nap' in your automobile before you report for your interview can be quite relaxing and rejuvenating. Just make certain to set an alarm and look closely at your appearance before going in.

Prepare and plan daily for how to handle anything that is coming up soon in your work or personal life. Keep yourself in the best physical, mental, and emotional condition you possibly can, at all times, by getting a reasonable amount of sleep each day, eating properly, pacing yourself well, and exercising regularly. Work out, run, play your favorite sport—physical exertion is a great, lasting way to relieve stress.

Compartmentalize your life so that if something stressful occurs in your personal life, you don't allow it to carry over into your job assignments and working relationships, where it may have an adverse effect upon your decision-making and operational skills. Prioritize and put time frames around everything you need to accomplish. Follow through and don't overload yourself—know when it's time to delegate and ask for help. Talk to someone who you are very close to about the stressful situation you've experienced, or are anticipating. Just talking about what is bothering you can help a great deal.

When you've gone through a stressful experience, try to benefit in some way by considering whether there was there anything that you or someone else could have done to prevent that situation from happening. If so, consider what you should do the next time you're in a similar situation.

Relax after you have had a stressful day—put on your old clothes, sit in a nice comfortable chair, read something entertaining, turn on your favorite music to get your mind off what happened that day to produce tension. Watch a funny TV show or movie or talk about fun times you have experienced over the years with your spouse, family, and close friends. Laughter is great medicine for getting rid of feelings of stress. Step back from the stress-producing situation and look at the big picture from a broad perspective by saying to yourself, "When I think of all the major obstacles I have overcome in my life to get where I'm at, what happened to me today 'isn't a big deal' in comparison."

Stop holding grudges against people who may have offended or hurt you in some way. If you don't release the anger, you only hurt yourself and continue feeling stress when you think about what happened. Instead, focus on the future—*don't waste time on failed efforts in the past.*

Apply these techniques to expand your readiness for an important upcoming interview. Prior to that interview, avoid, if at all possible, heavy involvement in any area of activity with anyone that could create a very stressful experience. Don't eat a heavy meal and drink a lot of liquid prior to your interview, as well. Practice your favorite relaxation techniques regularly in the day or two before your interview.

37

DISPLAYING YOUR SENSE OF HUMOR

A good sense of humor is an important asset in dealing with people daily and especially throughout our work day. Humor is a safety valve, a tension breaker, a tool for easing or downplaying an embarrassing situation. It can make all the difference to a group of employees who are coping with a tense, critical work situation. Interviewers understandably look for a good sense of humor in their job candidates. By effectively demonstrating yours, you can score high marks.

It takes skill and good timing to successfully display a good sense of humor. Done without tact, it can backfire and end up being destructive. Your interview is not the place to try out risky new jokes or anecdotes, give flip responses or 'kid around' with the interviewers. They might come across to the interviewers as silly, sarcastic, cocky, inappropriate, or just plain weird. Try out your humor first on co-workers, friends, and family. Humor in good taste is a positive attribute. If your friends like it, then use it in your interview at the appropriate time.

Observe how well your interview is progressing. Watch and wait for the right time to inject a little humor. Your best bet is to follow the interviewer's lead. If he or she begins to instill a little lightness and/or humor in the conversation, it's the appropriate time to display yours. And be selective; underplay your sense of humor rather than going overboard. Remember, "If in doubt, throw it out!"

Should someone on an interview panel tell a joke or say something funny, all the interviewers will note your reaction; laugh along with them or at least grin or smile. Understand, however, that just because one of the interviewers joked or kidded around with you, it doesn't mean that you're a shoo-in to be hired. He might have observed your nervousness and was trying to put you at ease.

Some interviewers will ask you to tell them a funny story, just to see if you have a sense of humor. Make it part of your preparation to come up with a couple of good stories. Nothing sarcastic, controversial, or that might hit a little close to home for the interviewer (something related to that company, for example). Think short and simple, with a universal theme. Again, try them out on co-workers, family, and friends first.

Dry, ironic humor seems to go over well. At the right time, under-statements and exaggerations can be funny. Even serious situations can be described with a little humor if they happened 'long ago' and the inter-viewer can relate to them. Sometimes humor can make a tragedy more bearable.

You can find humor in everyday things that happen to you, your spouse, children, other family members, friends, and others around you. Think of the funny things that have happened to you over the years. Work on how you can tactfully turn these into funny stories for an interview.

Never make jest of anything said by an interviewer or panelist, even if you thought the comment was meant to be humorous. The person who made the remark might have been serious and resent your reaction. Self-deprecating humor is better. For example, "Boy, I did sort of a dumb thing when I was in college that I can laugh at now. Would you like to hear the story?" Don't relate a major blunder—just something the interviewers would probably chuckle about. This shows interviewers that you do not take yourself too seriously and can take some ribbing.

"Is he at least smiling a little?"

38

YOUR RELATIONSHIP WITH THE INTERVIEWER, UNDERSTANDING THE INTERACTION

Let's discuss your relationship with the interviewer in more depth—there's so much riding on it! In a way, it's very much like a student/instructor relationship—with you as the 'instructor' and the job interviewer as the 'student.' Your objective is to teach the student all there is to know about you that is important.

Like a student, the job interviewer asks you many questions in order to learn more about you. When you, playing the role of instructor, answer the questions thoroughly and extensively, the student feels well taught and quite impressed with the instructor. The student also feels confident to apply all his or her new knowledge to the important decisions ahead [who to hire], being well equipped with justification for those decisions. If the student believes that the instructor has taught much more than was expected, the student will enthusiastically recommend the instructor to every aspiring student. However, if the student feels short-changed by the instructor, the student won't recommend that instructor to anyone.

Which type of 'instructor' will you be in your job interview? Will you teach lots of good stuff or eke out only a very limited amount of valuable information—just enough to whet the student's appetite, but not enough to provide the expected full meal?

The Interviewer's Knowledge Advantage
There's one critical difference between the typical student/instructor relationship and the job interviewer/job candidate relationship: The job interviewer comes to the encounter knowing much more about you than you know about him or her. This is based on a review of your employment application, resume, letters of recommendation, and other pertinent documents. The job interviewer has been able to 'handicap' you; but you don't have the same advantage.

Armed with this extensive knowledge, interviewers often select questions that are tailored to your particular education, training and experience—the heavier your qualifications, the heavier the question. They feel that if you have that much background in your profession, it is fair to ask you tough questions. You are qualified to answer them and should do an impressive job.

Your lack of knowledge about the interviewer's background makes it particularly important to avoid careless negative remarks about any topic, which could backfire on you. For example, don't try to play up a choice you've made by playing down another option.

Candidate: "I chose electrical engineering as a major because I didn't want to waste my time studying something nontechnical like business or psychology that wouldn't be as useful to a career in engineering."

Interviewer: "That's funny; I had a business major and psychology minor. You must think I'm a real dummy to choose these two—yet here I am today, trying to decide whether or not we should hire you. Isn't that a blast?"

Your choice of what to say and how to say it is very important. Like most people, interviewers tend to make decisions based not just on a logical examination of the facts, but also on their feelings, opinions, and perception of the facts as well as the way you present them. The same facts can trigger irritation and resentment when you present them in a certain tone, but elicit sympathy and understanding when presented another way. Consider this less judgmental, more open-minded candidate approach:

Candidate: "I knew I wanted to be a design engineer when I chose my major. I asked professors and friends whether I ought to go for electrical engineering—which would directly apply, or a business or humanities major that would allow me to be more 'rounded.' They pretty much confirmed my feeling that an engineering major was the way to go and I followed their advice. But I sometimes wonder whether I couldn't have become more well-rounded with at least a non-technical minor."

The Jitters

There's nothing wrong with telling the interviewer, at the beginning of your interview that you are nervous. Everyone is—even job candidates who have been through many interviews. No two interviews and job interviewers are exactly the same, so you're venturing into the unknown, toward an outcome that can impact your entire future career and life. It is normal to show your nervousness in the first two to three minutes of an interview. When you admit this, any interviewer should empathize with you. You are, however, expected to calm down after that.

Candidates are often intimidated by an interviewer's dress, grooming, overall appearance, strong voice, and direct eye contact—all of which project a very commanding image. The more you focus on these, the less you'll be focusing on your answers. Keep your eyes on the target. If you have thoroughly prepared, you will have plenty of good answers on which to focus your attention.

Let's be Friends

A smiling, friendly demeanor helps set the right tone from the first handshake, and helps ease the natural nervousness and anxiety of the situation. Just don't overdo it. If you take a back-slapping 'old buddy' approach, the interviewer may think, "Do I know you? Have we met before?" Be pleasant, cordial, and patient. Follow the interviewer's lead. As you warm up to each other, the atmosphere will become more and more friendly; never, however, to a point where it becomes 'buddy-buddy.' You don't want to become so relaxed that you forget that you are in a job interview and start using slang expressions, poor grammar or say something you later wish you hadn't.

We all want to know how we are registering with the person or persons we're talking to. We look for signs of acceptance or rejection. Interviewers are no different. They expect applicants to respond to what they say or do as they conduct the interview: a smile or grin, a nod of concurrence, a "Yes, I see," and so on; not a blank stare. Don't ignore your interviewer. Even if you disagree with a comment, you can at least respond, "I understand what you're saying."

Should the interviewer not get around to asking you questions which would allow you to bring out your best strengths, attributes and qualifications, you can tactfully work them into your interview by interjecting, "Could I say something that I think is important to mention relative to my job qualifications for this position?" You don't want to sound imposing or direct in your approach.

Consider that the interviewer may be of an earlier or later generation than yourself. You don't want to say or do things that could offend someone of that generation. They have feelings associated with life experiences and are sensitive to any negative comments about people and events of that time period. The same can be said regarding their age bracket, education, job experiences, job practices, marital status, lifestyle, nationality, area of the country they grew up in, and such. You don't want to offend him or her with a careless remark. You should continuously show courtesy and respect to the interviewer and make him or her feel important.

As the interview proceeds, you get to know each other more and become more relaxed. You can reinforce the growing relationship by referring to "we," "us," and "ours," instead of "I," "me," and "mine," in your answers. This inclusive approach has helped a number of job candidates to identify themselves as team players.

Interviewers tend to want to hire people who make them feel comfortable. Bringing up part-time and summer jobs you held in school should strike a positive chord with the interviewer. For instance, "I held that job too when I was going to high school" or "I never did that type of work but wondered what it would be like." By mentioning your various hobbies, interest in sports, musical talents, writings, charity work, and so forth, you could hear the interviewer say, "I did some of those myself" or "Wish I had the ability to compose music and play the guitar." Many great sounding notes could be played in your favor.

When an interviewer spends a lot of time with you, telling you things about the job and company, it's likely that he or she is impressed with you. It's his or her way of selling you on the job and the company. Most interviewers don't spend a significant amount of time with someone he or she doesn't think will be hired.

Should the interviewer be very open with you on some of the drawbacks of this particular job [not all are ripe plums], and you really do want the job regardless of those drawbacks, tell him or her that you are already aware of them, thought about them, and that you're not concerned—giving the reasons you're not.

Don't be afraid to display your elation and excitement at positive things that occur. If the interviewer asks, "Can you come back to talk to our _____?" and you're pleased to have the opportunity, show it! "You bet! Anytime you want me to!" You're not only showing your excitement at having 'made the cut,' but you're showing heartfelt appreciation to the interviewer for the opportunity to be considered further.

In the end, the interviewer should feel he or she knows you, from everything you've said and done during the interview. You will feel better about yourself—even if you don't get hired—if you believe that at least the interviewer got to know you well before making the decision. You would hate to think that you remained an enigma because you didn't fully open up to questioning.

Interviewer Bias

Interviewers are not perfect—they're human, just like the rest of us. In an ideal world, they would all be perfectly objective. In the real world, they strive to be, but sometimes fall short. What the interviewer *feels* rather than *thinks* about you will ultimately determine his or her decision to recommend or reject you. When you do or say something that's displeasing, they can always find some legal reason or justification to turn you down, even though you have solid job qualifications. The interviewer can justify a decision that was actually subjective, with many rationales. For example, "He had a very good education, solid training and experience, but I just didn't like his attitude, self-centeredness, negative remarks, and inability to warm up. Plus he had an unimpressive GPA, an unrelated major, a correspondence degree, lacked directly-related job experience, had very limited exposure to advanced job assignments, and very few supervisory skills."

This can work both ways, of course. The interviewer who takes a liking to you is more likely to play up your strengths and play down your shortcomings, while giving significant credit to your stellar academic and career track record. Even if he or she likes you, if you don't have relatively solid job qualifications, it would be difficult to sell you to others involved in the assessment process. It wouldn't be wise for him or her to 'stick his or her neck out' for you. The decision, in both cases, was at heart an emotional one. Fortunately, companies weed out most job interviewers who allow a significant level of negative or positive bias to affect their decisions. Some employers still exhibit some of this 'halo effect' among their job interviewers because it's often difficult to spot. We see it happening frequently in our personal lives as well.

What can you do to address the possibility of interviewer bias sneaking into your interview? You need to quickly size up the interviewer, and then modify your approach to accommodate the differences in your styles. As the interviewer proceeds and you gain a broader, deeper perception and understanding of the interviewer's personality, outlook and preferences, keep 'observing and adapting.' You'll soon be able to create positive images of yourself in the interviewer's mind.

The orientation of interviewers varies greatly. You must understand what's important to them and what their perspective is. Knowing this, you can decide to focus your answers on certain areas most meaningful to them.

Many interviewers are primarily 'end result' oriented. Others center their attention on process and analysis. Some are action oriented. Others focus on new ideas and conceptualization. Certain interviewers are the 'touch-feely' type, while there are those who are strictly 'fact oriented.' You could be interviewed by someone who likes to talk about the past, or another who enjoys talking about future things. Observing this, you can modify your presentation to adopt to what is most important to them.

Notice if the interviewer dresses and acts conservatively, is more a listener than talker, likes to get 'straight to the point,' has a well-organized desk and office, displays family photos, certificates, and degrees—you get the idea. Most interviewers are combinations of these styles. It's very much like being assigned to a new boss: the burden's on you to adjust to him or her, not the other way around. You want the interviewer to feel comfortable conversing with you and being in your presence.

You must prepare yourself well when approaching job interviewers by making the assumption that they are as competent in their jobs as you are in yours. Anticipate a tough and demanding interviewer situation.

Stay Focused

There are times when you should 'stay focused' and times when you shouldn't. If the interviewer takes notes during the interview, don't focus on it—you could become so concerned with when and how long he or she writes that you lose your concentration on what you planned to say. Some job applicants hurt themselves by with obsessive thoughts such as, "Is he smiling or frowning? Why does she have that grin on her face? Why did he stop writing? Why did she put down her pen? Why that inquisitive look on his face after I said what I did? What did I say that made her suddenly look so serious?" You can't dwell on these and stay alert for the next question.

If the interviewer starts talking while you are answering a question, stop talking immediately and focus on what the interviewer is saying. Provide an appropriate response. Then return to completing the answer you were giving at the point at which you were interrupted. By the same token, you should never be so anxious to give your answer that you begin talking before the interviewer completes the last few words of a question or comment to you. Interrupting is an irritating habit and it will earn you a low score on your listening skills. Interviewers get irritated with applicants who ask for clarification of the question too often. You can do it once or twice—no more—and only if it's a rather complex or involved one. It's best to take responsibility for your lack of understanding, and say something like, "I seem to have difficulty understanding—could you help me?"

Interviewers also dislike competing for control of the interview with job applicants. Some applicants want to 'draw the interviewer out' on what they are seeking in job applicants. These applicants will ask numerous questions in an attempt to find out precisely what is most meaningful to the interviewer. Only weak interviewers lose control of their interview, and there aren't too many of these types around.

It's okay to offer to show the interviewers the results of your work. Key projects and programs that you were heavily involved in, patents you've received, articles and papers you've authored, awards you've received, and products you've designed often speak for themselves.

It bears repeating (from an earlier chapter): companies are asking job applicants for their best on-the-job examples to support what they say. Companies are also putting applicants in simulated 'real life' work situations to measure the results of their work behavior in handling problems, taking actions, using others around them productively, making decisions, and resolving controversial matters. All of this 'situational-based behavior' is carefully observed and evaluated by the job interviewers. It's an approach used to prevent interviewer bias in the selection process.

It's also a good idea to point out how you continuously grow by learning new things, adapting to innovations and changes, modifying your ideas and opinions, developing new job skills and techniques, and adjusting to changing working conditions, environments, problems, and challenges. Point out also how this has increased your maturity, your outlook on things, and how it has given you a truer and broader perspective on your life and the direction you're going.

Think of your answers to a question as a painting. The 'words' you choose to use are the colors on your pallet. How you choose to put them together and apply them to create the painting itself, is your 'delivery'—your paintbrush. The best artists win first place—they receive a job offer.

Tough Tactics

Remember the student/instructor comparison at the start of the chapter? Let's face it—as you sit there trying to cope with a dry mouth and stirring stomach, trying to remember all those answers you've prepared, you'll probably feel more like a defendant in court being cross-examined. Display an attitude of 'ask me anything,' and a willingness to discuss anything the interviewer chooses to talk about.

Even if you inwardly resent being asked a particular question or suspect a question's illegal, keep that feeling to yourself. You can safely say that you don't have any comments to make, rather than, "You can't ask me that—it's an illegal question!" or "That's getting too personal—why do you want to know that?"

Some interviewers will bait you by saying "We all have lots of weaknesses. Tell me about several of your biggest ones. Having them is no big deal." You bet it's not! Spelling out your worst traits, just might cost you the job. You're not going to beat your competition by convincing the interviewer that you have the 'biggest' and 'most' weaknesses of all the people being interviewed. Would you choose a doctor to perform a heart bypass on your spouse on the same basis?

Avoid getting into a debate with the interviewer. Even if you're right, you will lose because he or she calls the shots on whether or not to hire you. That's much more important than proving you're right. Sometimes interviewers deliberately bring up something that is considered controversial to see how tactfully you handle yourself. Is it easy to get you stirred up? How far will you go? You can give your opinion and then comment, "That's just my opinion, for what it's worth, based on my background and experience. I'm sure you've had a great deal more exposure to that area than I have."

Don't let the interviewer make you defensive. It's already been pointed out that some interviewers like to badger you with intimidating questions to find out how well you can handle stress and pressure. With this technique, the focus is not on the content of your answer, but on your emotional stability. Maintain your control and answer calmly, even if it kills you to do so.

It bears repeating that you must be prepared for the 'silent treatment' after answering a question. The interviewer may just sit there quietly, eye-balling you for several seconds. This is a test of your ability to handle the stress of a relatively long period of silence. Some applicants can't take it; they feel compelled to start talking, even if what they have to say is not that meaningful. If you do this, the interviewer may think you're hyper, impatient, or can't handle too much pressure. Again, keep your cool. Just sit there silently, looking pleasant, and wait for the interviewer to ask you the next question. He or she will admire you for your self-control and calmness.

Never put the interviewer 'on the spot' by asking a question they can't or won't answer and then pressuring him or her further to answer it. "Do you think I'm going to get the job?" or "Don't you think I'm more quali-fied than the other job candidates?" The deeper you go, the further you'll be from ever receiving a job offer. These are inappropriate questions to ask. You could be highly qualified for the job but relatively unimpressive in selling yourself in an interview.

Interviews with two people or a panel present additional challenges. You may be answering a question from one interviewer when another interrupts you with a new question. Then the first interviewer interjects, "You haven't finished answering my question." Stay focused on fully answering each question. Courteously ask the second interviewer to please hold that thought and you'll answer it as soon as you've finished answer-ing the first interviewer's question.

A pair of interviewers may also play the 'good cop/bad cop' game. One treats you as if you were his favorite relative; the other tears you apart with insinuations that you're lying or being evasive. Both are merely play-ing a role. They are evaluating how well you handle the stress of such extreme differences in treatment. Play your own role: stay calm, relaxed, and non-defensive.

Remember, no two interviews or interviewers are the same. Modify your approach in order to adapt to each interviewer you meet. Rely on your insight and select the best you can come up with—taking everything we have discussed into consideration.

■ ■ ■

We need the tears of laughter to ease the ones of pain.

■ ■ ■

39

HANDLING NEGATIVE QUESTIONS

It's always difficult for job candidates to talk (during the interview) about negative incidents that have happened in their careers or personal lives. They fear that if they don't handle it tactfully and convincingly, they could 'blow the interview.' There is no perfect way to do it but you can learn how to field these questions and still come out ahead.

As mentioned in an earlier chapter, when an interviewer asks you about your failures in performing your job responsibilities or as a leader, you should describe the least negative situation that occurred at a time when you had the least job training, experience, and time in the position. The more experience and training you have, the less interviewers expect to hear about screw-ups. They think a person with an extensive background has been around long enough to know better.

Downplay the incident—but tactfully, so as not to sound like you're trying to cover up something, or blame someone else for your mistake. Work on the wording of your explanation until you feel comfortable talking about it. Explain, step by step, what led up to it, why you made the mistake, how you decided to handle the situation, and what actions you took. Assume full responsibility for what happened. Don't give excuses, give explanations. Toward the end of your explanation, be sure to point out the lessons you learned from that experience and how you have applied them to improving your job performance.

Practice saying all this aloud, until it flows smoothly. Bounce it off your spouse and/or closest friend for their reaction. Modify as necessary. You may get emotional as you tell the story, and that's fine—now is the time to work through those feelings. You will find that the more you practice telling it, the more your own negative feelings will subside to a point where you can describe it as calmly as though it happened to someone else.

If the company already knows, or is certain to find out something negative about you, take the initiative to present it at the most appropriate time, in the least damaging way—say, in conjunction with a related question, or after you have scored many points with them. If they don't know about it, or could not discover it, don't initiate a discussion on it—especially early in the interview; the interviewer might write you off at that point, and not continue to cover all the questions for which you've worked so hard to prepare for. Let the interviewer bring it up.

You should however be prepared to give a calm explanation for such incidents, even if the chances of their coming to light seem remote; the interviewer could ask questions that you weren't expecting to be asked.

If you're asked about any conflicts you have had with supervisors, peers, or subordinates, make certain—before you relate an experience—that you fully understand the question. The word 'conflict' can mean a difference of opinion or point of view, a disagreement, an argument, or a personality clash. The latter two are the most negative. Companies in general feel that they undermine effective, close teamwork. Employees believe that differences of opinions and disagreements can be healthy if they don't get out of hand, but they are disinclined to hire someone with a record of frequently butting heads with other employees.

When asked to give an example of a conflict you have experienced, choose one stemming from a difference in style or opinion that has a happy ending. Point out how effectively you turned an initially negative relationship into a positive one in a relatively short period of time. You may be tempted to present a more exciting conflict story, but unless it ends with a resolution (thanks to your people skills), it's a bad story. Yes, conflict can be exciting—it's a mainstay of fiction and drama—but don't let that lure you into presenting a conflict you failed to resolve.

You need to be honest and tactful in selecting the negative experience you relate, and the manner in which you present it. Interviewers can forgive certain mistakes, but will not forgive any deliberate attempts to deceive them. However, don't voluntarily bring out something very negative about yourself just to prove how honest you are. You should explain any unusual circumstances beyond your control that may have accounted at least in part, for the incident. Do this effectively without sounding like you're making excuses and you may salvage a few points.

Realize that if you must explain several negatives, you will have to compensate for them with impressive positives in answering other questions.

All in all, most job interviewers will focus on these prodding questions that are legal to ask, and that are job related.

■ ■ ■

An idea should be based upon its merit,
not the status of the person proposing it.

■ ■ ■

40

QUESTIONS TO ASK INTERVIEWERS

During or toward the end of your interview, there is a good chance that you will be asked, "Do you have any questions for me?" The interviewer assumes that it is likely your discussions have 'sparked' some questions in your mind which you would like to address to him or her. Perhaps you've heard rumors about something that has happened, is happening, or is planned to take place at their company and would like to hear more about it…or would like clarification on something that was said earlier in the interview.

Interviewers don't expect you to ask about something they feel you should already know. For example, don't ask, "What products do you produce?" Nor will they appreciate an inappropriate question, such as, "How much vacation time would I get the first year of my employment with you?"

Interviewers are more impressed with candidates who ask one or two questions that show they are:

(1) inquisitive and like to learn more

(2) humble enough to realize they don't know it all

(3) appreciative of the opportunity to tap the minds of the interviewers

After asking so many questions themselves, interviewers appreciate being asked a good question, even if they don't have an answer for it. They respect your insight in coming up with it.

You can preface your question by saying something like "I don't have too many questions. I've found answers to most of the ones I thought of through my research and by asking friends who work for you. However, I would like to ask you…"

If you have listened to everything the interviewers seemed most concerned about during your discussions with them, you will have insight into what kind of questions you could ask them.

Throughout your interview with HR and the hiring department, you could ask several questions (appropriate to the job level) such as these:

- Could I see a copy of the job description for this position?
- To whom will the person filling this job directly report to? May I ask his or her job title?
- Could you describe typical job assignments?
- Could you describe a typical day on the job?
- How long has this position been open? When is the last time you hired someone for this position? How long has the present incumbent occupied this position?
- What amount of travel is likely? Is there overtime and weekend work?
- Are there relocation possibilities?
- Would you describe the department atmosphere and surroundings from your perspective?
- What would you say would be the most difficult or challenging aspects of this job?
- What would likely be my first big project if I were to be chosen for this position?
- What key projects, in the first six months, would the new hire in this position likely be involved in? Major responsibilities?
- Could you show me a department and company organizational chart? Could you describe the job family this position falls in?
- Can you point out the career path for this position?
- What are the promotional opportunities?
- How long does it usually take for someone in this job to move up to the next job level?
- What leadership/supervisory responsibilities would there be? How many subordinates would I manage? What are their job titles?
- Does the company have a management/executive development program?
- What are the department's growth expectations?
- What would you say are the department's strengths and limitations?
- What is this year's annual budget for the department? For the company?
- What other department(s) does this one closely interact with?
- Is there any department or company reorganization anticipated in the next two to three years?

- Could you tell me about the company's 'mission statement'?
- What share of this market do you hold in your main product areas?
- What was your annual profit growth over the past five years?
- What is the projected growth of the company over the next ten years?
- What is your projected employee growth over the next five years?
- How many employees and locations do you project you will have by [year]?
- Could I meet some of the people I would most likely spend my time working with if I were hired? Could you tell me a little about them?
- How long have you been with the company and in your present position?
- How would you [hiring department supervisor over the position] describe your overall management/supervisory style? Your philosophy as to how to best manage people? Your approach to delegating work and determining priorities on project assignments? How do you oversee progress being achieved on these?
- Do you have a long-range plan—say, ten years out—with major goals you hope to attain? If you do and are free to talk about them, I would love to find out more.
- What do you like most about your company?
- Can you [speaking to the hiring supervisor] tell me a little about your boss?
- You may be wondering why I _____. Could I address that subject to answer any concerns you might have?

Here are some possibilities for two or three questions to ask at or near the *close* of your interview:

- What significant changes have occurred at your company during the past five years?
- Are there any possible mergers and acquisitions? Reorganizations? Cut-backs? Downsizing? Outsourcing?
- What new products and markets are on the horizon?
- I heard a rumor that you may offer [a new product or service]—any truth to it?
- How do you envision the size and composition of your product line

changing over the next five to ten years? Any thoughts about phasing out your [specific product]?
- What is the biggest project the company's working on now?
- What training and development programs could I expect to attend?
- Could you briefly describe your tuition refund/educational development program?
- Do you have flex time arrangements? How are they handled?
- Do you fully cover relocation costs?
- Where could I obtain information on housing, schooling, shopping centers, public transportation, etc?
- Could you give me some idea of the salary latitude for this position?
- Are you free to discuss the salary range for this position, periodic performance and salary reviews?
- Can I see a copy of your employee performance appraisal form?
- Does the company have bonus plans, stock options, or deferred payment plans?
- What perks, if any, do you provide for people in this position?

Consider, also, gracefully turning the questioning opportunity back over to them:

- Is there anything else I could tell you about myself that might help you in assessing me?
- Do you have any suggestions on what I could do to further strengthen my qualifications and further increase my chances of getting hired by your company?
- For the fortunate few who get hired, what would be the most important word of advice you could offer them in order to succeed in your company?

Don't ask a self-serving question such as, "When will I hear from you?" (they will most likely let you know without your asking), or "When would I start training?"

If you ask too many questions relating to 'what is most important to succeed in the job' you're being considered for, or what they are specifically looking for in job applicants, the interviewer might reply, "That's why we invited you to this interview, to find out what you have to offer us. What do *you* think we're looking for?" It's a little like the applicant saying to the interviewer, "Tell me the answers you're looking for and I'll give them to you."

When the interviewer is done answering your questions, don't say goodbye just yet. The interviewer will let you know when the interview is over.

"I've asked you quite a few questions.
Want to ask me one?"

"I sure do!
Where is the closest restroom?"

41

SOME 'DON'TS'

Most of this book offers you advice on what to expect and what to do during your job interviews. It is also very important for you to know the essential 'don'ts.' Some of those already covered bear repeating; others are new.

- Don't drink too much liquid before or during your interview (for obvious reasons).
- Don't eat a heavy meal just before your interview.
- Don't chew gum or grimace periodically.
- Don't initiate the opening or closing of your interview—this is the interviewer's responsibility.
- Don't be too formal or informal.
- Don't mumble.
- Don't mispronounce the interviewer's name; if in doubt, ask for the proper pronunciation.
- Don't address the interviewers by their first names, unless they encourage you to do so.
- Don't start off asking questions—this will come later.
- Don't slouch—sit up straight.
- Don't fidget in your chair.
- Don't shout or get too loud (or soft).
- Don't answer a question with the first thing that pops into your head; stop and think first before responding.
- Don't get 'personal.'
- Don't get defensive or be inconsistent in answering questions.
- Don't give flip answers.

- Don't memorize your answers; remember key thoughts; the words will come to you and you'll sound more natural and spontaneous.
- Don't use slang or overworn expressions. Avoid excessive 'job jargon'.
- Don't interrupt.
- Don't give abrupt or curt answers. You can be brief without doing so.
- Don't sound 'cocky' or like a 'know it all.'
- Don't forget to display 'sincerity' in what you say—throughout your interview.
- Don't rush to give an answer—think a few seconds about what you plan to say before beginning to talk.
- Don't leave out one or two important key points you need to mention, just in order to keep your answer brief.
- Don't sound like you expect to be promoted and 'move up quickly' before you've proven you can perform well in the position for which you're being hired. (Other employees aren't going to 'step aside' to make room for your climb up the job family ladder.)
- Don't attempt to shortcut your answers by referring the interviewer to your resume or employment application.
- Don't talk down another company or their geographical location.
- Don't spend all your time elaborating on one or two good points and miss the opportunity to bring up several other important ones.
- If you don't have something positive to say, don't say anything.
- Don't exaggerate your qualifications and accomplishments. (Lies and falsehoods have a way of coming back to haunt you— just present honest responses in the best light possible.)
- Don't ask questions that might stump the interviewer.
- Don't debate or argue a point with the interviewer.
- Don't 'take over' the interview, at any time, for any reason.
- Don't display any signs of hostility toward the interviewer—no matter what he or she says. Never lose your cool.
- Don't be vague or show uncertainty in your answers. "Maybe it was...I'm not certain...I might have been..."
- Don't try to 'butter up' the interviewer.
- Don't look at your watch.
- Don't be afraid to admit when you're wrong if asked why you did something that appears questionable. (Don't shift the blame for your failures to others).

- Don't criticize a former employer—your prior supervisor, job, peer, co-worker, subordinate, job assignment, customer or client.
- Don't volunteer anything 'negative' about yourself or family health problems.
- Don't act like an 'I can do anything' person. No one's that invincible.
- Don't ask an interviewer to repeat a question unless you absolutely have to.
- Don't respond to a question with "What do you mean?" more than once.
- Don't respond to a serious question in a light manner, attempting to display a sense of humor.
- Don't joke around. You can display your sense of humor (in good taste) at an appropriate time.
- Don't say anything that might be taken as a sarcastic remark.
- Don't say or think about anything that you know will upset you emotionally and find difficult to talk about. (Enthusiasm is okay but letting out emotions that can get out of control isn't a good thing.)
- Don't wait too long before answering a simple "yes" or "no" question.
- Don't allow yourself to get angered by anything that happens during the interview, such as repeated phone-call interruptions.
- Don't repeat the question aloud before answering it.
- Don't repeat or summarize your answers; once you make your points and have answered the question, it's time to move on to the next one.
- Don't ask the interviewer how well you did in answering a particular question or did in general in answering all his or her questions; you may not like the answer.
- Don't play one company against another if you have received job offers from other companies as well; you may end up with none.
- Don't make your interview an unpleasant experience for the interviewer.

A final 'don't' that applies after you arrive back home from your interview: Don't say anything negative about the interviewers, the way you might have felt mistreated, or the interviewing process to anyone outside your spouse and closest, most trusted family members. If the interviewing company somehow got wind of this through a third or fourth party, it could come back to haunt you. Some people remember everything that was said to them by you about your interview but forget the "this is confidential" part.

■■■

Because we can't measure and understand it,
doesn't mean it doesn't exist.

■■■

42

SOME MORE 'DO'S'

Let's take a look at some more Do's that you want to think about in both your preparation for your interview and while you are presenting yourself. Some provide reinforcement to points made earlier—others will provide 'more to think about':

- Transition from a broad smile, to a moderate one, to a warm, pleasant, slight grin, to a straight face—off and on throughout the interview, at the appropriate time. Avoid abruptly going from a big smile to a very serious expression.
- Ask about the job responsibilities, typical job and project assignments of the open position early in the interview...or hope that the interviewer brings these out early. This will provide you with a great amount of insight as to how to pick and choose those job accomplishments you've achieved that will fit in nicely with those of the job that was described to you. The same applies to your job qualifications—you'll be able to choose wisely from among yours as to which to highlight.
- Adjust your style as quickly as possible to be compatible with the style of each interviewer you interact with. Don't completely change the image of who you really are. When you find yourself feeling quite uncomfortable, you've gone too far in adjusting. The things you want to make mental note of as you observe the interviewer are: his or her choice in dress, grooming, demeanor, vocabulary, voice speed, pitch, volume, and tone, talkative or quiet, seriousness or light heartedness, disposition, overall personality, eye

contact, mannerisms, gestures, and facial expressions. Observe their formality or informality, friendliness or 'distance kept' from you, sense of humor, directness or indirectness, openness, thoroughness, philosophies, listening skills, decisiveness, patience, frequency of interrupting you, and attempts to 'draw you out.' Is the interviewer rushing you to answer questions and initiating requests for feedback? How do they maintain control of the interview? How seasoned is the interviewer? To what extent is there use of intimidation and stress invoked? Are they 'people' or 'technically' oriented? What are their interests, likes and dislikes? How frequently do they smile and laugh? How comfortable are they conversing with you? Do they appear cautious? How assertive are they?

- Keep the palms of your hands dry. You can wipe them while you're in your car, getting relaxed for your interview. Use talcum powder and/or facial tissues. If they begin sweating again while you're seated in the employer's waiting room, ask to use their restroom and dry them again. Refrain from closing/clenching your hands— keep your fingers apart. Carry a very small pack of facial tissues with you at all times.
- Recent college graduates should try to get maximum mileage out of anything they have done which could be considered 'job related' —such as temporary, part time, or summer jobs; volunteer work; projects and term papers; internships; cooperative educational programs; planning social, sporting, fraternity/sorority activities; involvement in clubs, groups, and organizations; writing for the school newspaper and other publications; and work performed for nonprofit organizations.
- Be prepared to give the who, what, when, where, why and how of anything you're asked about.
- Gear your answers to your uniqueness—in all the positive ways you can envision. Point out how you are 'different' from the other job applicants applying for the same job opening.
- Spend sufficient time pointing out where you plan on going in your next two jobs in fulfilling your career objectives.
- Use a lot of 'action oriented' words such as: assert, assist, analyze, accelerate, record, evaluate, conceive, build, construct, develop, organize, research, discover, evolve, conduct, plan, direct, stimulate, transition, energize, establish, solve, condense, resolve,

generate, expand, focus, innovate, manage, monitor, motivate, participate, persuade, produce, provide, simplify, recommend, strengthen, train, educate, and systematize.

- Interject (at the appropriate time during the interview) the terminology used by the hiring company's management to reflect commonality and compatibility with their business culture. Consider such terminology as: company mission/statement/culture, profit-oriented, cost sensitive/containment/reduction, long-term impact, business repercussions, human resource availability, job requisites, sustained profitability, investment return, business necessity, corporate structure, organizational planning, outsourcing, downsizing, displacement and exit strategy.

- Disclose your ability to 'switch roles' effectively throughout your work day—from leader to follower, to devil's advocate, innovator, team builder, problem solver, investigator, salesperson, negotiator, counselor, trainer, evaluator, and so forth.

- Point out that you often volunteer to take on tasks and assignments that go beyond your job description—especially when it's evident that your peers/supervisor are being pressed for time to complete an important project. You're willing to take on assignments that others dislike or find a certain degree of risk involved.

- If non-degreed, bring up the fact that you have (or are pursuing) a certification in your field that is awarded by a reputable accredited university/college upon completion of numerous required courses. It's the next best thing to having a four-year degree with a 'major' in your field. Point out completed 'on-line' courses acquired, self-taught skills, and other training received in your profession.

- State that you believe in and follow the idea of 'self-management.' You don't have to be closely supervised, you know what your job responsibilities are and go about planning how and when to accomplish them, with limited direction from your supervisor.

- Focus primarily on things you do well, rather than on things you hope to improve in. Areas needing improvement are important to recognize—but not as important as your proven, existing strengths.

- When preparing at home for your upcoming interviews, recharge your mind periodically by stepping outside and breathing in deeply and letting it out slowly. Do this off and on for one to two minutes. You'd be surprised how refreshing it can be to invigorate your thinking and sharpen your thought process.

- Realize expressing your desire to change your behavior doesn't in itself cause it to change. It's repeating the new behavior over and over again that finally results in 'dropping the old' and 'establishing the new.' The same applies to job interviews. If you recognize that you need to smile more often during your interviews, you need to practice smiling often during mock interviews until it becomes ' natural' for you to do so. Apply this approach to all areas you need to work on—just as you do when you train on the job. Behavior is one of the most difficult things to change because it's so deep-rooted. The more you practice and become prepared, the more relaxed you'll become. If you don't feel good about *yourself,* how can you expect the interviewer to feel good about you?
- Remember that every occupation can be considered a 'professional position' when it is performed with the highest degree of 'professionalism.'
- Quantify (in dollars) every accomplishment you've had that impacts sales, profits, cost and time reductions, the number of customers and clients the company has, shorten manufacturing processes, new products and services, overcoming major obstacles, resolving critical problems, improving procedures, practices, policies, and quality standards.
- You might be in or have worked for organizations in which you spend 90% of your time directly serving the supervisors and managers of other departments who need your expertise and services. Your job performance and job worth to your company are a direct reflection of what the people you serve think of you—more so than your reporting boss. This type of accountability makes you more unique than other job candidates and you can provide the interviewers with many interesting stories about your job experiences.
- Realize that when an interviewer asks you a tough or sensitive question, he or she is only trying to determine how well you can handle stress—it doesn't mean that he or she dislikes you. Don't take it personally nor have it adversely affect your ability to perform well throughout the remainder of the interview.
- Have solutions to any problem situation you bring up for discussion. Interviewers look for astute problem solvers and decision makers.

- Be a 'we did' person—not a 'we need to do' one. Wanting and needing to get something important done isn't the same as actually getting it done. You would be surprised how often people can be falsely led to think something was actually accomplished when it wasn't achieved. (Sound familiar?)
- Small talk (limited) with the receptionist can often go a long way in gaining his or her support of you as one of the finalists.
- Practice 'being interrupted.' It's difficult to not show irritation when it happens. You need to work on this until you are able to treat it like a pause in giving your response to a question.
- Remember, 'team' comes first and 'individual' next in overall importance. Stress your team resource management (TRM) skills.
- Should you want to speak directly with one of the interviewers (sometime following your interview), try phoning their direct line prior to 'starting time' or after 'closing time.' He or she will most likely be there then. The receptionist or secretary will most likely not be there. (Hope their voice mail isn't turned on.)
- Have a slightly different 'few words of appreciation' for each panel interviewer when leaving the interview. For example, "It was a pleasure to have met you."… "Thank you for your time."… "I appreciate the opportunity to speak with you."… "Hope to see you again, soon." and such. Let them know you look forward to hearing from them and hopefully, the opportunity to work with them. Leave them by saying "I'm impressed with everyone I've met and what was discussed." Be certain that you have brought out your best job accomplishments and key job qualifications long before saying that last goodbye.

■ ■ ■

Where am I going? You ask yourself that
at the beginning, during, and end of your life.

■ ■ ■

43

REVIEW: THE KEY STEPS TO A SUCCESSFUL INTERVIEW

Let's review the key steps we've covered that are vital to achieving a successful job interview:

- Research the company and the job thoroughly.
- Be appreciative of the opportunity to interview with them.
- Listen closely to everything the interviewer is saying. Shows respect.
- Sell yourself in every way you can. Focus on 'selling'—not worrying about 'blowing this interview.'
- Smile often.
- Anticipate the questions you could be asked. Focus on the heaviest, most important questions first.
- Even if the question appears personal, don't take offense.
- Never rely on good answers 'coming to you' during the interview.
- Develop thorough, honest, tactful answers and present them in the best light possible.
- Prepare many significant key points and supporting points to present in response to each question you are asked.
- Make your points meaty, clear, and concise.
- Have plenty of good examples and stories of situational behavioral experiences, job accomplishments and problems solved to share with the interviewer. Begin with your most recent experience.
- Sound natural, spontaneous, sincere, friendly, and thoughtful.
- Remain calm and in control of yourself at all times.
- Use "we," "our," and "team" as often as you can.

- Display your enthusiasm, self-confidence and passion for the type of work you do.
- Show your sense of humor and your appreciation of theirs.'
- Eliminate negative thoughts and comments.
- Stress leadership, job results, teamwork, quality of work, customer satisfaction, profitability, and your commitment to each.
- At the close of the interview, emphasize that you hope to become an impressive professional and leader for them. Focus on the future.
- Practice mock interviews until you feel well prepared.
- 'Be yourself'—at your very best!

■ ■ ■

*Planning for the future is important...
enjoying what you have now even more important.*

■ ■ ■

44

INTERVIEWER REACTIONS TO APPLICANTS

Wouldn't it be interesting to know the numerous positive and negative reactions and comments of HR and hiring department interviewers about the candidates they just interviewed? These come from small and large sized companies across the country—including several of my own experiences over the years interviewing job applicants. Read their enlightening remarks [paraphrased]. No holds barred. See if you recognize anything that could be said about you. There are quite a few, but it will be well worth your time to read them all. Knowing what was said should give you a deeper and broader perspective of how to best present yourself in your next job interview.

First Impressions
Favorable
- "Displayed a positive attitude right from the start of the interview."
- "Seemed very appreciative of the opportunity to be interviewed. Acted excited to be there and meet everyone."
- "Has a great disposition."
- "Dressed and presented herself well as a seasoned professional— quite impressive, considering she had just recently graduated from college."
- "Had a great smile! Seemed to smile with his eyes—was one of the first things I noticed. His teeth looked well-cared for and his breath smelled fresh."
- "Dressed as well as one of our managers and what she wore was appropriate for the position applied for. Wasn't overdressed or underdressed."

- "Presented a very professional image in his overall grooming, speech, and actions."
- "His suit and shirt looked new and fit well. Tie, shirt, shoes, and socks coordinated well with his suit. His shoes were shined."
- "Everything she wore appeared new. Wore her makeup so well that you wouldn't have known she had it on—very natural and appealing. Her hair style looked good on her. The colors she chose in clothing went well with her skin tone."
- "The length of his hair was moderate. Looked as though he had a haircut recently and had shampooed his hair the night before his interview."
- "Now that was a firm handshake! Walked briskly and confidently —not too fast or too slow. Posture was good. Waited to be asked to be seated."
- "Sat up straight and in an open, unguarded manner. Seemed very relaxed and at ease."
- "Used their hand gestures and facial expressions very effectively. Seemed so natural and without effort."
- "Had excellent eye contact. Wasn't afraid to look me straight in the eye as I asked each question and when she began and ended each of her answers."
- "Their voice was strong, pleasant-sounding, and had a wide range. Spoke with good diction and at a moderate pace. Varied the tone and loudness at appropriate times. Had good timing too."
- "Established an immediate rapport with him that lasted throughout the interview. Very professional."
- "Was a good listener. Hung onto every word I said. Knew when to speak and when to remain quiet."
- "Projected the image of someone who is open, unbiased, personable, mature, enthusiastic, and focused. Seems to really care about people."
- "Would describe her as very warm and friendly, informative, concise, and tactful. Appears very honest as well."
- "He was a likeable, alert, and energetic candidate."
- "Knows how to set goals, timeframes, and action plans."
- "Appeared very interested in the job, working for me, in what our department did, and how it was operated. Also expressed a genuine interest in our company, it's products and services."

- "Did an excellent job of selling us on being the best candidate for the position."

Unfavorable

- "Didn't smile when I introduced myself. In fact, he very seldom smiled during the interview."
- "Thought just 'being nice' would get her the job. Made very little effort to impress me in any way."
- "Had dull-looking teeth and a tinge of bad breath."
- Too laid back—no spark, zip, or enthusiasm."
- "Was dressed too conservatively. Looked as though he was attending a wake following his interview."
- "Was overdressed. Looked as though she was going to a party later that day."
- "Seemed too casually dressed for the interview. His clothes had a worn look and didn't fit well on him."
- "Looked very pale to me—should get more sunlight or see a doctor."
- "His hair wasn't combed and both his moustache and beard needed trimming."
- "She should have worn a business suit instead of a mini-length dress, considering the position for which she was applying. Wore too much makeup and jewelry. Her earrings were too large for the size of her ears. Her perfume was overpowering."
- "His shirt was dingy looking and the collar was too loose around his neck—needed more starch. The shoulder pads on his suit coat drooped. His tie was out of style, too loud, worn looking, and the colors in it didn't blend well with the suit. Plus his socks were too short."
- "The style and cut of their clothing made them look overweight. They also needed pressing."
- "Had a weak handshake and clammy palms. Felt as though I had hold of a dead fish."
- "He flirted with our receptionist and took up too much of her time. She told me that she had to cut him off at one point and ask him to be seated."
- "Tried to 'kiss up' to me. Didn't work."
- "His eyes were bloodshot. Must have lost a lot sleep lately."
- "There was dirt under his fingernails and he needed a closer shave."

- "Her fingernails were too long and colored too brightly."
- "Must have a severe nail-biting problem—practically nothing left."
- "You would think that he would have dressed, acted, and presented himself as well as most of the other recent college graduates— certainly more appropriately for someone going into a job interview."
- "Walked so fast that she kept getting ahead of me."
- "Walked so slowly that I had to slow down for him to catch up with me. Seemed sluggish in general."
- "Wish that he would have unbuttoned his suit coat after sitting down. It made me uncomfortable wondering if he would 'pop a button.'"
- "Was not able to establish a strong rapport with him at the beginning of the interview. Felt more comfortable with him as the interview progressed—had to work at it."
- "Was a difficult person to read."
- "Was too casual in the way she conducted herself. You would think she was attending some social event rather than a job interview."
- "Had to ask them to get rid of the gum they were chewing."
- "Sat on the edge of his chair. Seemed round-shouldered and bent over. Fidgeted a lot."
- "Appeared quite stiff. Had the look of someone who was about to be attacked—hands clenched, knees and ankles close together. Had few gestures and facial expressions—looked almost like a statue."
- "She kept flinging her hands and arms around and continuously changing her seating position. Her eyes kept darting around the room. Seemed ill at ease."
- "Had a smirk and kind of cocky look on his face. Not very conducive to winning people over."
- "Sense that it wouldn't take much to upset him."
- "Kept tapping his fingers on the arm of his chair or on my desk. Would continuously sway his right foot from side to side, while his knees were crossed. It got on my nerves."
- "Would look away each time I began or finished asking a question. Whenever I confronted her with something, she would immediately break eye contact with me."
- "He periodically dropped his head and looked down at the floor."
- "Had a critical look, as though we were trying to trick them in

some way. Frowned and glared at me several times."

- "Directed most of his eye contact to just one member of our interviewing panel. Seemed quite frightened and overwhelmed having to face a panel of interviewers."
- "Has the habit of starring at people. It made me uncomfortable."
- "Didn't seem too mature for their age. Need to grow emotionally."
- "Kept forgetting my name and mispronouncing it when she did remember it."
- "No matter how serious we were or whenever we joked around, he kept the same somber facial expression."
- "Tried to take over the interview from the start. You would swear she was interviewing me."

Interview Preparation
Favorable

- "You could tell by her answers to my questions, that she spent a lot of time preparing for this interview. Seemed to know what we were looking for. She had good insight, a clear mind, and good focus on the things that really count."
- "Would pause to gather his thoughts before giving each answer— good planning. His answers were meaty, well-organized, well-worded and presented impressively. Many of the points he made sounded fresh and helped him to stand out from the other candidates."
- "Gave more important points and covered more areas than the others. Was well-prepared in answering both our technical and people-related questions."
- "Must have done a great deal of research on our company. Knew a lot about our history, our products and services, and what we're heavily engaged in at the present time. Even mentioned the key goals of our five year plan for expansion."
- "Asked our receptionist if he could briefly look at a copy of the job description of the position he was applying for and if it would be permissible to do so. Wanted to have as full an understanding of the job requirements and responsibilities as possible before going into his interview."
- "Was well-prepared to tell us about his most meaningful job accomplishments, in each major area of his job and project

assignments. Some were improvements in processes, procedures and practices. Others were in reducing costs, increasing sales, product advancements, and better customer relations."

- "Was fully prepared to explain to us how he happened to enter supervision, each supervisory and managerial position he held, and what he was able to accomplish during the time he held each job. A very resourceful person."
- "Was evident by her choice of words and the way she readily described her job achievements, that she had put in a great deal of time preparing for this interview."
- "Did a good job of summarizing what he had to offer our company at the close of the interview. Must have given a lot of thought to what he was going to say beforehand—good preparation."

Unfavorable

- "Was obvious that he hadn't spent much time preparing for his interview. Seemed taken off-guard by many of the topics discussed and the questions that were asked. Should have anticipated many of them."
- "Asked a direct 'yes' or 'no' question—got an evasive answer. They didn't even address my question."
- "Wasn't ready to discuss her major job accomplishments. Thought that just talking about her job responsibilities and assignments was enough. Didn't realize that what is of importance are the achievements and accomplishments made while carrying them out."
- "Seemed to have difficulty handling the stress of an interview. That concerned me. Should have practiced more before coming in."
- "Was too 'past-oriented.' Needed to talk more about the present and the future."
- "Didn't handle role-playing or situational behavior scenarios well."
- "Failed to review, identify, select, and effectively describe their major job accomplishments prior to reporting for their interview."
- "Should have taken a complete inventory of what they had going for them, long before coming in to see us. Played it by ear throughout the interview. Wasted a lot of our time trying to develop answers on the spot which should have been well thought out ahead of time."

- "Seems to have only small containers from which to draw their answers, instead of large boxes full of all sorts of good things from which to choose."
- "Made some good points but the examples and experiences she chose to use didn't bring them out very well. Her stories went on and on—she needs to practice closure."
- "Didn't have enough examples to support the key points he made—no stories to back them up."
- "Didn't seem to know too much about our company, its history, our products and services, or what we were currently engaged in."
- "Failed to place a strong enough emphasis on the importance of quality in work performed. Never mentioned the importance of profit or cost containment either."
- "Spoke about the importance of teamwork but didn't explain its role in some of the examples he gave. Also left out the importance of satisfying the customer's needs and how good teamwork is vital to customer satisfaction."
- "Didn't take long for her to run out of gas in answering several of our tough questions."
- "Needed more practice in what he had prepared to say when answering our questions. There were a lot of rough edges and loose ends."
- "Failed to prioritize the points she made (most important first) in forming her answers. All had the same worth to her. Wasn't able to determine what really was most important to her."
- "Would have been wiser to have spent less time elaborating on getting the interview and more time developing some good answers to anticipated questions. Left out a lot of good points which would have raised their score, and brought out a number which were trivial."
- "Went overboard bringing out the number of problems and conflicts he had with people over the years."
- "Didn't seem to take into consideration that we're on a tight interview schedule. Acted as though we could spend all morning with her."
- "Someone must have led them to think that there wasn't much to job interviews, judging by their lack of preparation."
- "Said he didn't have very much to say because he didn't want to

'sound corny,' giving the same answers that other applicants give. That statement in itself turned me off."

- "Each time I asked her what else she could add to her answer, she drew a blank."

- "Should have practiced what he planned to tell us out loud. I am certain he could have come up with something that sounded better than that."

- "Wasn't prepared to point out significant points in describing a problem—what caused the problem and the role they played in identifying and resolving it."

- "Didn't do too good of a job explaining the supervisory techniques he developed and applied over the years which made him successful in managing people effectively. Placed most of his emphasis on his technical know-how."

- "Suffered from underkill—too few important points, covering too few important areas."

- "Had difficulty remembering dates, events, places, and people's names. Should have gone over all of that before reporting for her interview."

- "Made two or three good points in answering a heavy question, then stopped thinking. Could have come up with one or two more and raised his score significantly. We weren't rushing him. What was he saving the rest of the good stuff for?"

- "Had a good middle to her answers but her beginnings and endings were too light. Bet she didn't spend much time planning how she would sell us on hiring her."

- "Used many cliche's and worn-out answers. They sounded copied from the ones his friends gave—word for word. Nothing unique or innovative. Good preparation takes time and he must not like hard work."

- "Got mostly 'yes' and 'no' answers. Didn't give much thought to how they would build full answers and best deliver them during their interview. Kept stalling for time to think of something meaningful to say."

- "Felt like telling him this wasn't a practice session. His answers weren't well-organized nor were they explained impressively."

- "Should have considered other situations that she had experienced and handled well which I'm certain would have scored more

points for her. Didn't think them all out before deciding which to present."
- "Despite all his years of experience in that type of work, he still screwed up something that shouldn't have given him any trouble."
- "Their answers were okay but not any better than those given by the other candidates. Didn't stand out from them in positive ways—mostly in what was lacking in their responses. No commitment to good planning, preparation, and practice for an upcoming interview."

Handling Questions
Favorable
- "Listened closely to each question I asked. Grasped what I was looking for quickly—didn't miss a thing."
- "Each of their answers was right on target—no shorter or longer than necessary. Only important points were brought out. They were given in a logical, prioritized manner."
- "Was so calm, you would have thought he had met us before. We felt relaxed talking to him. Weren't able to 'shake him' with a few tough questions or stressful role-playing situations."
- "Was surprised that she remembered all our names and could match each face with each name."
- "Impressed me at never being at a loss for a good example or explanation of their behavior in handling a difficult work situation. Didn't waste words or wander off the key points they were making."
- "Displayed strong situational awareness in addressing all of our questions."
- "Like the way she explained things—made something complex sound so simple to understand. We could use her in a training capacity as well."
- "Thinks well on his feet. Quite innovative in his answers. All he said made a lot of sense to me."
- "Projected a very favorable image of themselves in the manner in which they answered our questions. Appeared very professional but still 'down to earth.' Viewed things clearly about what's important and what isn't."
- "Clearly understood that we controlled the interview and deter-

mined what direction it should take."
- "Through the questions we asked her in our role-playing scenarios, it was evident that she had the ability to turn a negative situation into a positive one. Showed a great deal of insight."
- "Tells a good story. Got his main points across to us clearly and in an interesting and enjoyable manner."
- "Displayed her strong supervisory and leadership skills in explaining how she successfully resolved a very difficult subordinate problem."
- "Felt at ease talking to him—he was completely himself with no act or pretense. We were on the same wavelength."
- "Stated everything very thoroughly and clearly. We didn't need to ask her any follow-up questions."
- "Considering their limited training and job experience, they did very well in answering all our questions."

Unfavorable

- "Didn't listen closely to the questions we asked. Had to repeat several of them. Either has a hearing problem or doesn't pay close attention to what is being said. Seemed too wrapped up with what they were planning to say."
- "Had difficulty comprehending what we wanted to know. We had to reword the question we asked several times. All of the other candidates understood the questions."
- "Interrupted me several times. Must have felt that what he had to say was more important than what I was saying."
- "Asked so many questions (throughout the interview) that we weren't able to cover all the questions that we planned to ask. She tried controlling the interview a few times and we wouldn't let her."
- "Answered several questions quite abruptly. Didn't seem to want to say anymore than he had to."
- "Became argumentative when questioned for details on something she had said. Asked why we wanted to know that information. Seemed very sensitive to any question that she interpreted as being somewhat personal and none of our business."
- "Paused too long after hearing each question. Pausing two or three seconds would have been more appropriate to gather his thoughts before beginning his answer."

- "Didn't pause at all after being asked a question. Started talking before she knew exactly what she was going to say."
- "Seemed afraid of me. Appeared more concerned with my reaction to her answers than how well she was presenting them."
- "Was more concerned with how much he had done than how well he had accomplished it."
- "Spent too much time on one point. Should have moved on to other points that were more important than the one she dwelled on."
- "Was vague in covering many of the topics we discussed that related directly to his specific job expertise. Kept having to pin him down."
- "Would forget where she left off talking after she wandered off the question."
- "Had difficulty wrapping up some of his answers. Spoke in circles and repeated himself. Couldn't tell when he had finished giving his answer. Should have dropped his voice at the close of his last remark which would have been a good indicator."
- "Was startled and distracted when my phone rang. Acted uptight throughout our questioning and never really calmed down."
- "Should have taken advantage of the broad question I posed to bring out all sorts of good things about herself, but didn't."
- "Was often at a loss to find the right words to express a point he was trying to make. He seemed to have been caught off-guard several times and didn't quite know what to say."
- "We were surprised that she didn't sell us as strongly on her managerial leadership skills as she did in bringing out her technical insights and observations."
- "Tried to stump me by asking me a particular question. Put me on the spot because I was not at liberty to comment on the subject, especially to a job applicant."
- "Sounded as though she was making a speech at times instead of answering a question."
- "Acted as though he already knew what we were going to ask him and was becoming impatient waiting for us to finish our question."
- "Couldn't handle role-playing situations that we put her in.

Appeared to have all the know-how but lacked the ability to apply it when placed into a simulated work situation."

- "Wasn't able to change gears quickly enough when we switched our style and approach to interviewing her. Did well when we used the warm and friendly approach but became less impressive when we became somewhat critical and injected some stress into the interview."
- "Pressed me to find out if we had any mutual friends and common interests. It became obvious that he was trying to butter me up. I politely told him to focus on answering the questions."
- "Had that blank look on their face whenever we asked a question that wasn't on their prep sheet, especially the new ones we thought of this week."
- "Didn't pace herself well in answering our inquiries. Sometimes talked too fast and sometimes too slowly."
- "Suffers from both overkill and underkill. Will talk too long on one point and not long enough on another. Often brings up things that aren't important enough to mention."
- "Was often at a loss to find the most appropriate words to express himself. Would stumble over some explanation he was trying to give us in answering a relatively easy question."
- "Many of her answers to my questions were rationalized. Her answers sounded authentic but were not the actual reasons why she acted the way she did."
- "Kept quoting information from his resume. We wanted it straight from him, unedited and in his own words at that moment. Actually, he looked better on paper than in the interview."
- "Was trying to play games with us. Gave the appearance of having answered our question without really answering it."
- "Answers would have been totally acceptable for someone with much less education, training, and experience, but not for someone with their strong professional qualifications."
- "Came close to the core of what she was trying to get across to us but failed to reach it."
- "Started to forget that he was in a job interview and not hanging out with his buddies."
- "Had to ask her not to take notes during the interview, but to focus

completely on the questions. Had to wait for her to complete her notes once or twice. Was distracting and prevented a free flow of dialog between us."

- "Their answers sounded honest but not tactfully presented."
- "Was doing well up to the point when I asked her to address her weaknesses and the mistakes that she had made while performing her job responsibilities. It was downhill from then on."
- "Asked him a broad question and he gave me a narrow answer. Seemed too detail-oriented and lacking in having a wide perspective on many topics we covered."
- "Acted as though her job experience spoke for itself and it wasn't necessary to explain what she had accomplished. We had to rephrase our question to get her to elaborate on the subject."
- "Didn't manage their time as well as they should have in addressing the 'light' questions versus the 'heavy' ones. Had to interrupt them several times in order to move on to another area. Weren't able to get to other questions we had planned to ask."
- "Asked him a general question. Whey did he think it only applied to the job he had held and not to his degree, training, or his life outside his career involvements?"
- "Acted as though she was wasting her time answering silly questions. Had no grasp of the connections between our question and the extent of her job competency. Misinterpreted several of my questions."
- "Believed he might have had a number of good answers in his head but they sure didn't come out of his mouth. I'm not a mind reader. Ran out of gas quickly when answering several of my questions."
- "Her answers sounded memorized. Would pause at times, trying to remember the exact words she had planned to use."
- "Overstated their job knowledge and expertise at the beginning of the interview, then backed off as we asked in-depth questions about each area of their job experience. Avoided giving direct answers and made vague statements, implying that they had strong job knowledge."
- "Sounded as though he were reading off a checklist when answering many of my questions. Didn't sound spontaneous or authentic."
- "Seemed so afraid that she might say something that sounded stupid that she clammed up several times. Had to be encouraged to respond more fully to each question."

- "When asked a tough question, they appeared unsure of themselves. When asked for situational behavior examples to support the attributes they claimed to possess—why in the world did they choose those particular examples? Their choices certainly didn't strongly support what they were telling us or help to establish their credibility."
- "Was very sensitive to our probing questions as to her motives for taking certain actions. Seemed to think that we were questioning her integrity but we just wanted more facts."
- "Would guess when replying to certain questions instead of saying that he wasn't qualified to answer those questions. No answer would have been better than a bad guess."
- "When I asked her the same question our HR interviewer had asked earlier, she promptly informed me that she had already answered that question and couldn't figure out why I would ask it as well. Her doing so turned me off. Don't want someone working for me who is so shortsighted and lacking in tact."
- "Wasn't halfway through our interview when he began asking me about the starting salary and our benefits package. Seemed very premature to me."
- "Responded to my question by asking for further clarification of what it was that I was looking for. I guess if I allowed her to ask enough questions, I would have supplied the answers to her as well."
- "This candidate, as well as some of the others, needs to take some courses in psychology judging by the way he conducted himself in our role-playing scenarios. Didn't display good people skills."
- "Seemed anxious to end the interview. Must have had something 'more important' to do."

Personality and Character
Favorable

- "We clicked with one another immediately. Felt good chemistry between us. A very likeable person who went out of their way to be accommodating to our questions and our whole interviewing process."
- "Acted very enthusiastic about the job, our department, and our company. That's the way I want all my employees to feel."

- "Seemed excited to have gotten this interview. Thanked me for giving him the opportunity and he meant it."
- "Set high standards for themselves and put emphasis on their morals and honesty."
- "Was friendly, well-mannered, and displayed a good sense of humor. A fun type of person. Had a cheerful disposition and was quite witty as well."
- "Displayed a spirit of optimism and a positive attitude throughout the interview—even when tossed a stressful problem to resolve."
- "Isn't the least temperamental or self-centered. Controls their emotions well. The type that doesn't offend people."
- "Picked up quickly on everything I had to say. Didn't have to spoon feed him."
- "Could get to the heart of an issue in no time—very observant."
- "Displayed a great deal of self-confidence and believes in herself. Everything she said was done in a very convincing manner."
- "Would trust him an any work situation to tell me what really happened—the way it really was. He seemed to have a high sense of ethics and would never try to cover things up to make himself look good."
- "Isn't afraid of hard work. The type who doesn't take the easy way out. Very preservering in pursuing their career."
- "Acted very mature for her age considering that she just graduated from college and has no job experience directly in her chosen profession. She answered all our questions very impressively and beyond what we expected."
- "Conveys an image of someone who is patient and who has a lot of compassion for people with problems and pressing needs. You could tell by the way she went out of her way to help and counsel several of her peers and co-workers."
- "The type of person who is willing to admit when he's wrong."
- "During the interview, handled several stressful moments very well. Knows how to handle pressure and keep their cool."
- "The type that radiates excitement and enthusiasm. Motivates those around her to be their very best."
- "Their ways of looking at things would fit in well with our organization's image, philosophy, style and methods of operating."

- "Didn't try to overwhelm me with their extensive education and experience. Acted humble about the awards they received."
- "Has a good memory. Remembers things that happened to her years ago that most people wouldn't be able to recall."
- "Gave credit to others for many of his successes."
- "The type of supervisor with a personality that anyone would enjoy working for. Seems like a natural leader."
- "After interviewing her, I believe that 'what you see is what you get.' She is a sincere, loyal, realistic, caring person. The type of professional that I want working for me."
- "If I were to describe him in one word, it would be 'likeable'— to people at all job levels and those with vastly different backgrounds."
- "Wish we could have spent more time together. Is enjoyable to converse with and a real nice person. Would look forward to their joining our department."

Unfavorable

- "Didn't seem too warm a person. Didn't express a strong interest in the job or our company. Certainly didn't sense any feeling of excitement or enthusiasm for the interview itself."
- "Lacked the air of professionalism which must be projected regardless of the type of position or job level held."
- "Didn't take an immediate liking to him. Took awhile to establish a level of comfort between us. Seemed ill at ease and uncomfortable being in a job interview. Said no more than he had to. Couldn't bring him out of his shell."
- "Seldom smiled. Maintained a somber look throughout the interview. Displayed very little emotion—even at times when we introduced some levity into our interaction. Seems to have difficulty reading people."
- "Became too emotional at times. Needs more control over her emotions. Was quite moody and opinionated."
- "Lacked sincerity. Couldn't accept at face value what he said at times. He wasn't convincing."
- "Doesn't seem comfortable with himself and who he is."
- "Didn't seem to care what people thought of him. He felt he was

always right and couldn't understand why people didn't agree with him on every issue. Very set in his ways and has a short fuse. Quick to judge others."

- "Appeared to be the type of person who would try to cover up every mistake they made."
- "Tried to 'kiss up to us' several times. She would always agree with us no matter how she really felt. Once we deliberately made a debatable statement to observe how she would react and she agreed with us that time as well. She wouldn't take a stand on anything."
- "Didn't seem to see any humor in my kidding the other interviewer. Judging by the things he said, doesn't know the difference between humor and sarcasm."
- "Not certain if he is shy and quiet or just not too sharp. Was difficult to read and not assertive enough."
- "Can see where she can become upset easily by anything that isn't going the way she expects it should go. Displayed a lot of nervous energy. Seemed hyper and impulsive—a little 'off the wall' at times."
- "Thought he was being funny—I thought he was being obnoxious."
- "Was easily distracted. Appeared more interested in some minor things that were going on around us than in the interview itself."
- "Not too alert. Had to repeat myself several times. Appeared to be a slow thinker. Believe he suffers from depression—everything seems so serious to him."
- "Was uncertain of what she was about to say on several occasions."
- "Not very innovative in their approach to our problem-solving questions."
- "Was quite knowledgeable in many areas but didn't display a lot of common sense."
- "Acted conceited at times when it came to theoretical concepts."
- "Wasn't too impressive when it came to selling an idea."
- "Has good 'channel vision' on everything—how unfortunate."
- "Was eager to take credit when her performance results were note-worthy but reluctant to assume any blame when they weren't impressive."
- "Tends to exaggerate what happened to him over his career. Makes common experiences we've all had sound like 'big deals.'

- "Likes to be the center of attention. Can see where that wouldn't go over too well with the employees in my department."
- "Was too aggressive, direct, and blunt. His responses to our people problem scenarios showed a lack of insight into people behavior."
- "Would question his character—he's a little too slick. I think he's a phony."
- "The type of individual who could be easily intimidated. Doesn't like confrontation."
- "Seemed so blah—didn't impress me at all."
- "Appeared to enjoy 'beating up on people,' even when it was evident that they had tried their best but failed."
- "Her bias showed through in several comments she made—don't believe she recognized it. Tried to rationalize her beliefs, flaunting her professional credentials; failed to sway us as being objective. Was not flexible in changing her opinions, even when confronted with new facts."
- "Is not the type of person others would trust and enjoy working with no matter how technically well-qualified he is for the job."

Attitude
Favorable

- "Was a very positive-thinking person. Had a good attitude toward themselves, other people, and life in general."
- "Seemed excited picturing herself in the job and working for us. Appeared very confident that she would perform well for us if given the opportunity."
- "Pointed out that although she just received her bachelor's degree with a 3.5 GPA, she had a lot to learn and accomplish to prove herself in her chosen career field."
- "Considering that he just received his masters degree in a challenging technical field, with a 3.3 GPA, he was very humble in speaking about his academic achievements."
- "Reflected an image of someone willing to make whatever sacrifice necessary to get the job done."
- "Was completely open in discussing everything we covered. The type who is receptive to new ideas and ways of doing things."
- "Spoke about their job, supervisor, co-workers, and company in

positive terms. Focused on the 'ups' of their experiences over their career."

- "Didn't let setbacks get them down. They just put in greater effort to succeed the next time around. Were not easily discouraged."
- "Believed that people he worked for and with were sincere in wanting to help him perform his job well and in any way they could."
- "Talked up their company to their family, friends, and people in the community. A good spokesman for their employer."
- "No matter what topics we discussed, she would begin speaking in positive terms. Was reluctant to readily criticize anyone or the ways things were done."
- "Was fully supportive of his subordinates. Viewed them as a reflection of himself. Pointed out the techniques and skills he used to motivate each one individually and the group as a team. Was open and fair in discussing their strengths and weaknesses."
- "When I addressed the importance of meeting deadlines in our department, he made it clear that he was willing to work overtime or come in on a weekend in order to get an important assignment completed on time."
- "Her optimism was reflected in what she said and how she said it—throughout the interview."
- "Viewed everything that has happened to him throughout his career from a positive perspective."

Unfavorable

- "Seems to view everything that happens to them and around them from a negative perspective. Lives in their own black and white world. Doesn't think there are any gray areas."
- "Had no problem coming up with negative things to say about his last boss—volunteered bringing them up at times. Would probably say the same or similar things about me if I hired him."
- "Didn't care for their flip remarks. They seemed sarcastic to me."
- "Flaunted the fact that he had just graduated from a prestigious university. Didn't say anything about his C grade-point average."
- "The first thing on his mind was salary and benefits—not selling himself."
- "Didn't apologize for our having to reschedule his interview or

being ten minutes late for it."
- "Came on very defensively. Acted as though we doubted everything she told us and that we asked her many unfair questions."
- "Appeared to be the type who only does what he has to—no more, no less."
- "Has a yo-yo attitude—up and down, unpredictable."
- "What a lousy attitude! No wonder he's been unemployed for six months."
- "Sure was critical of his staff and his boss. Thought it made him look good that he knew what he was doing but that they needed lots of improvement. If he was so good, why did he draw a blank when we asked him about his own weaknesses."
- "In discussing her various job tasks and assignments, complained about how hard she had to work to please her supervisor. Told us that he expected too much of her and was overly critical of her job performance."
- "Didn't display a heck of a lot of enthusiasm when talking about the job, working for me, or our company. Showed very little excitement about anything. Not sure we really are his first choice among the companies he has applied to. Didn't have any questions for us."
- "Wasn't very polite or courteous. Quite abrasive and curt at times—another smart-ass."
- "Seems to expect more in return than for what she has to offer. Overrates herself."
- "Doesn't seem open to other people's opinions. A 'me' focused person."
- "Has a 'you must follow the rules no matter what' attitude, even if those rules appear outdated and ineffective in resolving unique problems and situations."
- "Believes that policies, practices, and procedures were meant for others but not them."
- "Appears to be an expert in 'losing.' Has a lot of experience in it."
- "When I asked why I should hire him, he said that he was better than all the other job candidates. How could he possibly know how strongly qualified the others are."
- "Was turned down for similar jobs by two major companies and hasn't the slightest insight as to why—I do."

Delivery
Favorable

- "Would be a good public speaker. Sounded like a TV news announcer—very articulate. Had a professional sounding voice and delivery."
- "Knew just how to pause and put the right amount of emphasis on certain words and points he was making. Had good timing throughout the interview."
- "Spoke at a nice moderate speed—not too fast or too slow."
- "Has an excellent vocabulary and didn't try to flaunt it to impress us."
- "Their voice wasn't too loud or too soft. It was easy on the ears."
- "Seemed very sincere and convincing—quite believable."
- "Was obvious that she was well-prepared to answer any questions we might ask her. Did her homework. Knew what to say and when to say it. Spoke in a natural-sounding tone and manner."
- "Remained calm no matter what question we threw at him."
- "Was a very interesting and enjoyable person to listen to."
- "Kept my interest throughout the interview. Time flew by talking to her."

Unfavorable

- "Started talking immediately after I asked a question and didn't give herself time to think."
- "Never once addressed me by my last name. Thinks everyone should be on a first name basis, even if it's a job interview."
- "Kept calling me 'sir' throughout the interview. Overdid a good thing."
- "Would pause at inappropriate times, making it difficult for us to really know what he meant to say."
- "Spoke too loudly and much too fast. Acted as though we were rushing her to give an answer to our question. Became overly dramatic at times."
- "Just didn't sound credible in what he was saying. Believe he was trying to tell us what he thought we wanted to hear and not how he really felt."
- "Could hardly hear what she had to say—was too soft-spoken and quiet. Seemed to have low self-esteem."
- "Spoke so slowly that we knew we would never get to cover all the

questions we had planned to ask him."

- "Talked a lot but really didn't say much that was meaty. Failed to score many points."
- "Was quite boring to listen to. We were anxious to get to our next job candidate."
- "Spoke in a monotone. Was difficult for us to really get enthused about what she was saying."
- "Wished he would have stopped saying 'uh huh,' 'you bet,' 'sure,' 'you know,' 'right,' and 'that's for sure.' It got on my nerves."
- "Their voice was very high-pitched—sounded like a teenager."
- "The statements he made sounded 'choppy,' not free-flowing. His voice cracked at times."
- "Sort of mumbled his words. His diction could have certainly been improved. It was difficult for us to follow what he was saying."
- "Came on too strong at times and too weak at other times. Her timing wasn't too good—she would laugh at the wrong time. Seemed to have a nervous laugh."
- "Spoke when he should have been listening and didn't say anything of great significance when given the opportunity to sell himself."
- "Didn't stop talking after making the main points—went on and on."
- "Tried to impress me with his extensive vocabulary. Felt it served as a cover-up for not knowing as much as he should have about the subject we were discussing—especially considering all the exposure he had to it."
- "Seemed to be talking down to her employees as she related how she would supervise and direct them in their job assignments. Lacking in today's skills and methods of motivating people to perform at their best."
- "In general, he failed to impress me with what he was saying. Had an impressive work background but wasn't able to sell himself and convince me to hire him."

Confidence Level
Favorable

- "Seemed very self-confident. Appeared to know who he was and where he was going in his career. The kind of person who isn't afraid to take risks in an area he's familiar with."
- "Like the way she was able to build her answers to create an image

of herself as someone who was confident that they could perform all the responsibilities of the job to our complete satisfaction."
- "Convinced us that he could overcome any obstacles faced in performing the job responsibilities of this position effectively."
- "Provided several examples of how she resolved problem situations despite having limited knowledge and experience in those areas."
- "Had never held a supervisory position before being promoted into her present position but has done a 'bang-up job,' judging by her written performance appraisals over the last two years."

Unfavorable

- "Had a long way to go to convince me that he felt confident enough to handle this job. Think it would be 'over his head.'"
- "Having just graduated from college, with an impressive record of accomplishments, expected her to express more confidence in herself than she did."
- "Seemed overly self-confident considering their past performance reviews weren't that impressive."
- Appeared more confident of their technical skills than of their leadership and supervisory knowledge."
- "Threw out the names of some of the people who work for us, as though they were close friends. Found out she only met them once."
- "Thinks he's a real hotshot professional. When he believes he has said something clever, astute, or witty, gets that 'hot stuff' look on his face. Doesn't have the track record of successful experience to support it. Seemed arrogant too. Hasn't a humble bone in his body."
- "Believed that knowing the son of one of our senior managers would give them an inside track in getting the job. Threw his name around several times."
- "Just because I was nice to her didn't mean I would hire her. I try to treat everyone that way. Acted like she aced the job."
- "Thought he would be hired as long as he didn't say or do anything wrong. Didn't try to sell himself at all."
- "Has been through several job interviews with other companies for a similar position and believes he's well-experienced in being

interviewed. Wonder why he hasn't received any job offers? Think I might know the answer to that question."

People Skills
Favorable

- "Displayed a thorough understanding of people—what motivates them and what turns them off. Knows how and when to compliment them."
- "Has both good communication and people skills—they go hand in hand."
- "Felt as though I was talking to a friend I hadn't seen in years. We seemed to hit it off right from the start of the interview."
- "Seemed like the type of individual who could get along well with people at all levels in our company. Could picture him interacting well with his supervisor, peers, co-workers, and employees from other departments."
- "Can see why she has done so well in supervision—has the ability to read people well and is very supportive of her employees. Treats them fairly and is very receptive to their ideas and opinions."
- "Appears very customer-oriented. Brought up the fact that he considers everyone he comes in contact with a customer that he is serving."

Unfavorable

- "Felt uncomfortable interacting with him throughout the interview. The type of person you could be around for years and still not be completely at ease with."
- "Didn't seem to feel comfortable with any of us. We extended ourselves to make her feel at ease but she still kept her distance from us by being very guarded in everything she said."
- "Can see where this candidate would have a problem dealing with certain personalities."
- "Plays up to us but down to our support staff. Gave my secretary a hard time."
- "Didn't spend as much time talking about his people skills as he did his technical expertise. Responded well to my technical questions but not to those related to his ability to handle people problems effectively."

- "Appears to cater to higher-ups over her immediate supervisor on every matter. Also has a tendency to look down upon people who have less formal education and hold positions at a level below hers."
- "Doubt if he would ever stand up to his boss, even if the boss did something unethical or questionable. Doesn't have the people skills necessary to handle such a sensitive area."
- "Doesn't seem to care what people think of him as long as he thinks he's right and can receive the credit for what was done. You would think there was only one way to resolve a situation— his way."
- "Sense a resentment of authority. Doesn't want to be told what to do without a great amount of justification for doing it. Questions the rationale for making changes—likes status quo."
- "Wouldn't take him too long to offend someone in our department. Doesn't express much empathy or concern for others. Can't seem to bend a lot to accommodate those who aren't as quick to learn as he is when given a new job assignment."
- "The type of person who can 'dish it out' but has difficulty being on the receiving end. Can understand why she's had several personality conflicts with people she's worked with. She has a very short fuse."
- "Should learn the difference between disagreeing and arguing with someone. Explains the reason why he's had several run-ins with his peers."
- "Treats customers the same as strangers. Doesn't realize that they are the reason why we're in business."
- "Resents younger people coming up with good ideas but have no suggestions to offer when asked for their input."
- "Seems to believe that anyone over 40 years of age is too inflexible and too set in their ways to view situations from a fresh perspective. Feels this group of people should take a back seat to the younger, more creative generation. Needs to take course at the 'school of life.'"
- "Treats everyone as though they should work, think, and act as he does. Doesn't recognize individual differences and thinks "I was able to do it, why can't he do the same?"
- "Is the type who would be determined to debate a point even if it cost her a job offer. Seems very hardheaded."

Self-Promotion
Favorable

- "Did an excellent job of selling me on how their education, train-ing, and experience tied in closely with this position."
- "Was especially convincing of how her major and minor—plus several other courses she took in college—were directly applica-ble to the job requirements and job responsibilities of the open position. Not too many recent graduates can do so that effectively."
- "Had an impressive way of pointing out how the job assignments in which he was engaged in over the last two years, were very similar to those of the position for which he was applying."
- "Seemed proud of both her people and technical skills. Discussed them with us in a very clear and credible manner."
- "Took credit for many job accomplishments without sounding boastful or egotistical. Stressed the importance of quality in every aspect of his performance."
- "Was able to work in a number of their achievements while answering my questions, in ways that seemed natural to bring up at that particular time."
- "While giving credit to a co-worker for a new idea to improve service to the company's customers, he did it in such a manner as to tactfully include the part he played in successfully implement-ing the idea."
- "Had an impressively unique way of being humble while dis-cussing how she planned and directed her career successfully, phase by phase. We never felt that she was bragging."
- "Must have thoroughly gone over everything he has ever done—prior to this interview—in order to have been able to come up with all the impressive answers he gave us."
- "Certainly did a better job of selling herself than other candidates who had much more job experience."

Unfavorable

- "Didn't give himself enough credit for all he had accomplished. Should have sold himself more."
- "Thought he bragged about some things he did that really weren't too impressive."
- "Sold herself well as a strong professional in general but failed to

bring up enough of her individual job accomplishments…which would have set her apart from the other strong candidates for the job opening."

- "Didn't sell their decision-making and problem-solving skills well."
- "Focused too heavily on their technical knowledge and experience and not enough on their insights into how to best handle people."
- "Overall, wasn't convincing enough to sell me as to why I should hire her over the other impressive job candidates I've interviewed for this position."

Interest in Their Profession
Favorable

- "Everything she has done seems related to her profession and career field in one way or another—she's really hooked on it. You couldn't buy her away from it. Loves the type of work, job responsibilities, and the people she works with."
- "Told me that as a teenager, he tried to read and learn everything he possibly could on the profession he went into. Spoke to family, friends, teachers, and career center counselors about his ambitions and what it would take to enter this field."
- "Had talked to several people who were currently in positions in this profession before committing herself to this career direction. She wanted the benefit of honest, firsthand assessments of what it was like from those who had been in it for some time."
- "Was told by many people to enter professions that paid more, but told them that the enjoyment of the work he was doing was more important to him than greater financial rewards at the sacrifice of less job satisfaction."

Unfavorable

- "Motivated primarily by salary and prestige—not a real love for their profession."
- "Brought up the importance of the business and financial aspects of their current employer's success before mentioning the company's impressive team of leaders and people throughout the organization who really made them so successful."
- "Think his dad talked him into becoming a computer design engineer. Didn't observe any display of enthusiasm and strong interest

in the job or field itself. Got indications that he would have enjoyed being an airline pilot more."

- "Spoke of how difficult it was to decide which profession and field to go into. Narrowed her choices to three. Believe, for one reason or another, the profession she's in was her second choice."
- "Only decided on sales and advertising after he flunked out of medical school."
- "Sure took him a long time to get started acquiring the education and training necessary to enter his chosen profession."
- "Appears more interested in teaching than performing in their profession."
- "For someone who says they love what they do, doesn't keep up with what's going on in their field in terms of innovations and research studies."
- "Was only halfway through the interview when she expressed interest in job openings in other professions in another department. Should have concentrated on selling herself as the best candidate for the position she had applied for."

Past Employment
Favorable

- "Am convinced that all of his past employers will speak well of him. The letters of recommendation from his last three immediate supervisors are very impressive."
- "Our background check and phone calls to her most recent employers revealed 'an excellent job performer' across the board. The type of person any employer would want to have working for them."
- "Spoke how well he enjoyed each of the jobs he has held, the supervision he received, and the companies he worked for since graduating from college."
- "Couldn't detect any hostility toward the management of any of the organizations she had worked for or the people she worked with."
- "Acted excited in telling us the things that impressed him most about each job he has held, each supervisor he has reported to, and the ways each company operated."
- "Didn't go overboard pointing out the strengths or shortcomings of each past employer. Seemed very objective and fair in their assessments."

Unfavorable

- "Was rather critical in talking about his past employers. Didn't have too many good things to say about them. Why did he stay so long with his last employer if he disliked the shoddy way they were operating?"
- "Has a record of job hopping—not all for good reasons. Doubt if she is eligible for rehire at several companies. Left them shortly after they put her through an extensive and expensive training program. Wasted time and money hiring and training her."
- "Wonder why he really left his last job? The reason he gave us didn't make a great deal of sense."
- "Should have found out more about that company before she decided to join them. Would have known they were about to fold."
- "Job rewards are more important to him than job challenges."
- "Really blasted his last supervisor and the way the department was run. Think that he overreacted to what was happening. Could do the same if he were working for us."
- "Was highly critical of the things their prior employer did that weren't successful but was never complementary of the employer's accomplishments."
- "Believe he was asked to leave or be fired by his last boss. Doesn't seem like the easiest type of individual to supervise. Have some serious doubts about adding him to my department."
- "Can't seem to be able to verify two of the jobs she was supposedly in. Her old boss isn't with that company any longer and no one else who works in that department remembers her performing in those jobs."
- "Wasn't able to account for several longer periods of time when he wasn't employed. Gave us a few leads to check as to his whereabouts but they didn't pan out. It's up to him to prove where he was and what he was doing during those time periods."
- "There must have been several short-term jobs that she held which she didn't list on her employment application. Most likely didn't perform too well or get along well with her boss or co-workers. Her job stories don't sound credible."
- "Claimed that he had an excellent performance and attendance record on his last job. Spoke to his supervisor by phone and she seemed hesitant to comment on his record in these two areas.

What she did say led me to believe that both his performance and attendance were marginal at best."
- "All of us on the interviewing panel felt that this candidate had inflated his job qualifications, experience, and accomplishments with prior employers. His answers to our questions did not coincide with what he led us to believe earlier in the interview."
- "Contradicted herself several times in telling us about the extent of her job involvement with several prior employers. We aren't even going to bother to check them out."
- "Our background investigation revealed someone who was quite unlike the person we thought he was. Past employers hesitated to recommend him and replied 'no comment' to several of the questions that were asked. Believe he was a good con artist who almost fooled us too."
- "There proved to be several major discrepancies in what he told us relative to the time periods, the type of work performed, and job titles regarding two relatively recent past employers. Spoke to him about the discrepancies but he only provided weak explanations."
- "Didn't do a good job of pointing out how each of their job and employer changes advanced their career."

Military or Civilian
Favorable
- "In talking to him, considering that his job experience is all in the military, was amazed that he spoke as though he had been working as a professional in the civilian world. Has picked up a great deal of civilian terminology and uses it very appropriately."
- "Was very open-minded in believing that military experience, in many cases, was equally as valuable to employers as civilian experience when comparing qualifications for a job opening."
- "Her military experience coincides closely with the job responsibilities of this position. All of her fitness reports and performance reviews over the past four years were excellent and her progression in positions held is impressive."
- "Even after serving with the military twenty years, he appears very flexible and adaptable to the civilian world of professionalism in his field and to this position."
- "Received a number of medals, awards, ribbons, and citations over

his years in the military and served in combat several times, yet acted very humble and gave most of the credit to his fellow servicemen and servicewomen. Was wounded in action—we can work around his disability."

Unfavorable
- "Used too much military jargon. Has a thick umbilical chord connected to the military—wish he would sever it and attach it to the civilian employers."
- "Judges everything by military criteria and standards. Has little insight into the way it's done in the civilian world."
- "Had a 'general discharge' rather than the typical 'honorable discharge.' Was reluctant to explain why. Offered a vague, fuzzy explanation. Still don't know the reason."
- "Was passed over for upgrading at his last review. Said he didn't know why. The military doesn't offer an explanation. Without knowing why, we aren't going to consider him further."
- "Should have realized that the remark he made about not caring to join the military would offend someone who was ex-military. Not a very tactful person."
- "Inferred that civilian professionals in his profession are better than those in the military—wonder if he knows that I'm ex-military."

Technical Expertise
Favorable
- "Considering her limited training and experience in that type of work, gave some very impressive answers to my questions."
- "Recently graduated with a technical degree which is directly applicable to our entry level job opening. Will consider offering her a starting salary that is higher than we would typically offer because of her strong GPA and thesis that addresses new research in our field."
- "His job experience is directly related to what he would be involved with in this position. If anything, the way he did it at his company is ahead of where we are now. Should be a valuable addition to our department."
- "Has considerable exposure to advance techniques in her field, through attending recent industry seminars, taking advanced

graduate courses, reading new books written on innovative approaches and concepts on subjects that are currently under discussion. Has also read articles written by leaders in her profession in technically-oriented magazines that she subscribes to. Has written a few such articles herself."

- "Threw some very tough, technical questions at him and he answered each of them impressively. Did as well, if not better, than one or two of my own employees."

- "Gave her a technical problem she could face in this position and asked her how she would approach and resolve it. Came up with some excellent insights. Explained them clearly."

- "Their technical expertise reflects their strong, in-depth perception and visualization capabilities, tied in with their intense curiosity to learn new things. Asked me several insightful questions about how we overcame a major obstacle faced by our company last year."

Unfavorable

- "Considering all of their education, training, and heavy job experience, was not as strong technically in their profession as they should have been."

- "Found it difficult for him to explain certain ways he would approach and handle a new job assignment. No doubt that he had it in his head—just couldn't seem able to describe it to others."

- "Needs more advanced training in her area of expertise. Should have taken the initiative to sign up for more lectures, seminars, and courses that were available."

- "Not enough exposure to complex job projects and assignments. Performed the same type of work over and over again—had limited challenges. Should have advanced technically by now, even if it meant changing jobs or joining another organization that could provide more opportunities for technical growth."

- "Should have completed his degree requirements by now. His grades in the technical courses he took weren't very high. Question his ability to grasp very complex matters."

- "As valuable as that type of technical training would be in advancing his career, he wasn't willing to spend the money to acquire it."

- "Should have been more selective in choosing her current job—doesn't sound as challenging as the last job she was in."
- "Was weak in describing some aspects of his decision-making process. Left out some important steps."
- "Didn't know (as well as she should have) the process that she was instructed to follow in carrying out her last job assignment. Forgot a significant procedure and it was an important project."
- "Acted taken off-guard and surprised that I would ask him a question on a technical subject that he had very limited exposure to. I wanted to know the extent of his knowledge in that area. In fact, there were several other questions I posed that he should have anticipated before coming to the interview."
- "Never managed a group of people in her area of job expertise. Didn't detect a thirst for supervising people—the main focus of this job opening. Enjoys technical challenges which reflect how well she has honed her technical skills. Thrives on individual rather than team accomplishments."
- "Most of her experience is in instructing others how to do the job—not performing the job responsibilities herself. Some people are more adept at explaining something than doing it themselves."
- "Is the type of person who will try to bluff his way through something he knows little about, through exaggerating what he does know and using his extensive vocabulary. We 'nailed him.'"

Education
Favorable
- "Made some wise decisions in planning the course of her education. Her degree is from a well-recognized university and her major is directly related to the field we are in and the position we have open. The electives she took compliment many of the aspects of what she would be doing for us."
- "Achieved an impressive overall grade point average and earned exceptionally high grades in his major. Continues to sign up for new after hours courses in his field. Working on an advanced degree."
- "Worked 30 hours a week and was still able to carry a full program throughout college, maintaining a 3.0 GPA."

- "Made good grades in school while being very active in sports, music, and several clubs and organizations."
- "Participated in an intern program with us in his last year of college. We know more about him firsthand than we do the other job candidates—what he's like to work with and supervise, how hard he works and how quickly he learns, his overall attitude, work habits and mannerisms, and how quickly he was able to assimilate to our culture and ways of operating."
- "Asked her a number of questions to bring out what she had gained in knowledge and direction, having received an associate, bachelor, and masters degree. Her answers addressed each degree and revealed her ability to grasp and retain many areas of knowledge that would apply to her chosen career. Had worked in her profession between receiving each degree, which gave her insight into the value of what she studied relative to the 'working world.'"

Unfavorable

- "Can't buy why he didn't finish college. Seems to have established a pattern of procrastination in other areas as well."
- "Never heard of that college—better check out its accreditation. Didn't clearly explain why he chose to attend that particular institution. Would suggest that he must have been turned down by those he had hoped to have attended."
- "Didn't satisfy me as to why she chose to major in that field. Think that her career interests were initially in that field but, for one reason or another, settled into her present profession. Believe that if we hire her, she might decide to change positions and go into another field within a short time after joining us. Have my doubts about her."
- "Am disappointed that his grade average is so low—seems rather bright. Acted as though grades have no real significance. Most likely wasn't willing to put in the time and effort it took to earn higher grades. Tells us something about his lack of motivation and commitment to working hard in order to do well."
- "Didn't relate the value of her major to her profession to my satisfaction. There were several ways in which she could have corre-

lated the two but she didn't take advantage of them."

- "Isn't very well rounded, considering the fact that he had a heavy educational background. I talked about several job-related topics and a few that have an impact upon his field and our industry. Asked for his assessments and comments but received very limited reactions from him."

- "Said he chose a psychology major because he didn't care for the business and technical courses he took. Told him that my degree was in electrical engineering with a minor in business administration. There was a long moment of deafening silence. Didn't apply what he learned in psychology too impressively."

Leadership
Favorable

- "Has just the right balance between being a good leader and a good follower. Can switch roles readily."

- "Seems to have a natural ability to excite and inspire people around him. Listening closely to him during the interview, I can see why."

- "Leads by example and the respect earned from those with whom she works. Has done so since high school and throughout college."

- "Was highly supportive of the leadership style of their manager and that of their company's top leaders as well. Gave me many reasons how and why these people are effective in motivating their employees at all job levels."

- "Pointed out examples of situations when she played an important leadership role (as a group leader) in motivating her peers and co-workers to meet project deadlines."

- "Took on department leadership responsibilities during the absence of his supervisor and was commended for the results he achieved in several areas."

- "Showed me recent performance appraisals which pointed out the times he successfully displayed his leadership skills."

- "Explained the various approaches, techniques, and skills that she uses to motivate the employees who directly report to her. They certainly are sound ones and provided impressive results for the program they were working on."

- "Has taken all the supervisory training courses and programs offered by their company, as well as several outside supervisory leadership seminars and courses offered by known consultants in the field and nearby university extension programs."

- "Will make a great future manager for our company. Has what it takes to manage people successfully. Has impressive leadership skills which is an extension of strong people skills—understanding people, why they feel the way they do, and what motivates them to perform their responsibilities to the best of their ability."

Unfavorable

- "Don't believe he has a full grasp of what leadership is all about. Seems to think that it's primarily ordering people to do things."
- "Can't envision her as a 'take charge' person. She seems insecure, hesitant, indecisive, and timid—needs to build her self-confidence."
- "Appears to be a very demanding individual—too forceful and impulsive. May be too rough on subordinates if he was their boss."
- "Just can't see leadership potential in him. Seems lacadasical and too laid-back. Isn't as team-oriented as he should be. Doesn't set an impressive example for people to follow."
- "Struck me as being overly critical of her subordinates, judging by the problem-solving story she told us regarding the resolution of a work discipline situation. Seemed overly critical of her boss as well. Sounded as though she were the only one who knew what they were doing."
- "Was apparent from the start that he was more concerned with salary and job title than with an opportunity to advance into supervision. Didn't act enthusiastic when I spoke about the possibility of this job leading to a managerial position."
- "Said she enjoyed the technical challenges of managing an important function more than she did managing a staff of people."
- "Their most recent performance appraisal ratings as a new department supervisor weren't as high on 'managing people' as they were on those reflecting their technical know-how."

Integrity
Favorable

- "Has very high professional standards and ethics. Her answers to my questions on several 'what would you do if...' situations brought these out vividly. Answered each in an open, straightforward, but tactful manner. I threw out some problem resolution approaches that would have stretched her work ethics, but she wouldn't take the bait. I like her stand on following what's being fair and the right thing to do."

- "Would trust him to level with me on tackling a problem that involves finding the true source of its origin within our own organization."

- "Tried crossing her up with questions from different perspectives on the same matter to see if I could trip her up on the stand she had taken earlier, but she came through with flying colors. Her logic, analytical ability, standards and ethics were all supportive of the stand she had taken."

- "Emphasized that one of his strongest and most important strengths was his integrity. Considering what he said in his stories in response to my questions requesting examples of how he handled sensitive situations, I would have no reason to question his integrity."

Unfavorable

- "Just didn't sound credible. Appears to be the type who would lie or stretch the truth to cover up something that reflected negatively upon himself."

- "Had excuse after excuse for everything she's done that didn't go well. Would never accept full or even partial responsibility for her actions or mistakes of any kind—no matter how minor."

- "Questioned his explanations in addressing several of our questions. Doubt if he gave us the real reasons. As with anyone who rationalizes, gave us reasonable sounding answers that many would accept at face value—not the true, real ones."

- "Gave me several instances as to why he had to deviate from company policies and practices, and from instructions from his supervisor. I asked him follow-up questions on each. All his stories sounded phony."

- "Sounds like a smooth con artist to me—wouldn't trust him."

Questions for the Interviewer
Favorable

- "Asked a few, very good questions. They were meaningful and reflected a sincere interest in the job, our department, myself, our company, and its future."

- "The questions she asked me were the type that showed she had done extensive research on our company but wanted to know even more about it. They coincided with her strong interest in the position and working for our organization."
- "Was particularly impressed with his question concerning ways to improve the process and system we now have in place which deals with reducing time and costs in manufacturing our products."
- "Realized we didn't have the time to answer more than two or three questions, so she picked out the most significant ones to ask. Said that she might ask more if she returned for a follow-up interview."
- "None of his questions related to the rewards he would receive working for our company—they centered on what more he could do to help us better understand his capabilities and accomplishments, as directly related to what we're seeking in the candidate who will fill this position."
- "Liked her question about our department's immediate and long-range goals and the role this position plays in successfully completing our current, most challenging program.
- "Asked for my perspective on our department's future and my thoughts on avenues that could lead to increased customer satisfaction. We had an interesting discussion."

Unfavorable

- "Didn't ask me any questions—I expected at least one. Surely there must be something he didn't know about us that we could have clued him in on."
- "Asked too many questions. After answering her first four questions, told her we didn't have time to answer any others."
- "Centered his questions around what we could do for him—not what more he could do to convince us that we should hire him."
- "Thought one of her questions was not appropriate—put me on the spot. There are certain things we might reveal to an employee but not to a job applicant. Plus, it was bordering on being personal."

- "Shouldn't have asked those questions. Expected him to have already acquired that knowledge about our products and services— didn't do his homework."

The Total Person
Favorable

- "Maintains a good balance between technical and people skills, their career and personal life. Seems to have things well under control. Spends most of their free time with their spouse, children, and close friends. Has several outside interests and club affiliations, but places family first."
- "Wish I had his energy level. Must eat the healthier foods, exercise, and work out on a regular basis."
- "Is the type of person who should fit in well with the employees in my department and with those of the other departments in our organization. Wouldn't have any problem adapting to our culture and philosophy."
- "Appears well-balanced in their job knowledge and skills. I don't anticipate any performance related problems."
- "Would be an interesting person to work and travel with. Keeps current with what is happening in their field, profession, and industry, around the company, world events, and community activities. Enjoys sports, music, and reading. Even has their own blog on the internet."

Unfavorable

- "Doesn't seem to realize that we're interested in the whole person —not just their technically-skilled half. Was weak on selling their people skills."
- "Looks like a loner to me. Has very few friends from what I could gather. Seems hesitant to confide in people."
- "Doesn't belong to any professional clubs or organizations related to his career field."
- "Has her mind on too many outside interests. Is stretching herself too thin. Sounds like she's not getting enough sleep and rest to approach her job each day at her best."
- "Was afraid he would doze off if I didn't prod him with another question. Either had a lack of interest in what I was saying or in

the job itself. In general, wasn't impressed with him."

- "Isn't doing anything of significance in terms of acquiring new knowledge to improve herself professionally."
- "Can't believe that he could successfully continue running his expanding side business and still do a good job working for us full time."
- "Didn't volunteer information about her family but readily spoke about her interest in surfing the internet on a daily basis."
- "Avoided saying much about his life away from his job. Wonder if he has something to hide."
- "Gathered from her remarks that she seemed to be starting and ending relationships continuously—both on and off the job. Seems to have difficulty maintaining close relationships."
- "In some areas of our discussion on various topics, he was very impressive in answering my questions. In other areas, I wasn't impressed at all. Runs hot and cold."

The Closing
Favorable

- "Briefly pointed out the key reasons why he would perform well for us if given the opportunity. Tied them in with the main job responsibilities of the job opening. Doing so separated him from the other candidates in a positive way."
- "Really appeared appreciative of the opportunity to be interviewed. Thanked each of us and said that she looked forward to hearing from us and hopefully working with us in the future."
- "Smiled frequently and seemed excited by the thought that he might be selected for the job. Shook hands with me vigorously as we concluded the interview."

Unfavorable

- "Started to say goodbye before I asked my last question. Should have waited for me to let him know when the interview was over—too presumptuous."
- "Didn't have a single final question for us nor expressed any appreciation for having been given the opportunity to present himself to us—not one thank you—must be that way with most things people do for him."

- "Failed to offer any final remarks or statement as to why we should hire her over the other well-qualified candidates we were considering for this position."
- "In wrapping up the interview, he mostly repeated what he had told us earlier—no fresh insights, twists, or ideas that would have highlighted the key attributes he had to offer. There was no fire or even a spark."

**"I see you studied many leadership styles.
Besides Attila The Hun, who else has impressed you?"**

45

WRAPPING UP THEIR INTERVIEW WITH YOU

We've already discussed two questions that interviewers often save for the end, just before wrapping up the interview: "How did you prepare for your interview with us?" and "Why do you think we should hire you over all the other well-qualified job candidates we have interviewed?" These should be two of your most complete, polished answers. Go over them again.

The interviewer may also ask you if you have any comments you would like to make before the interview is brought to a close. Should there be anything important that you forgot to cover earlier, this is the time to bring it up. You may also wish to modify, add to, or clarify something you said.

When ready to end the interview, interviewers will generally shuffle the paperwork, look at their watch, and start to rise from their chair. This makes it clear that the interview is now concluding. Your parting comments should include a sincere thank you for the time they spent with you and for providing you the opportunity to present yourself. Acknowledge the warm, fair treatment you received (if this be true), the meaningful questions you were asked, the sufficient time you were given to fully answer each question, and the thorough, fair evaluation you know you'll receive. Note how impressed you were with their facilities and atmosphere throughout your visit; how everyone you spoke to made you feel at home. Conclude by saying that as a result of this great treatment, you are more enthusiastic than ever about wanting to work for them.

Offer to provide any additional information the interviewer may care to have. He or she should feel free to phone you at home 'directly' any evening or weekend, or leave a message with your spouse or roommate should you be at work or on your voice mail. State your confidence that you would make an excellent employee for the position and how much you look forward to joining their team. Add something like, "I would never let you down," or "I hope that I was able to convey to you that I'm the type of professional you're looking for." Never ask "How did I do in the interview?"

As the interviewer begins to stand up to say goodbye to you, stand up at the same time. Shake hands firmly, smile, and say something like, "Thank you once more. I'm very excited about the position. I know I would feel very comfortable working for you and in this position. I hope that I will have the opportunity to see you again in the near future."

A Final Caution

Don't phone or e-mail the company a day or two later to find out the outcome of your interview. That is too soon. Employers frown on this kind of immediate follow-up. It takes up their time, keeps them from performing other job responsibilities, and ticks them off.

You can ask when you can expect to hear from them, although most interviewers will, at the close of the interview, tell you approximately when you can expect to hear from them as to your status. If you don't hear from them at or before that time, then feel free to contact them.

Do send a courteous, thoughtful thank you letter [the 'personal' touch] to each interviewer. It should be brief and reiterate some of your closing statements. Individualize each letter through your wording so as to not sound like you're sending the exact form letter to each person. This gesture seems obvious, but not every job candidate does it.

Be careful as to what you do or say to anyone after leaving the interviewer's office. You're still being watched, observed, and evaluated by people in the company with whom you come in contact. Don't let down your guard. Any contact and verbal exchange with the interviewers or support personnel is still 'on the record.' Some employers want to meet your spouse as well, to find out how she or he feels (in general) about the job, job title, salary, hours, overtime, travel, weekend work, distance and amount of travel time to and from the work location, work environment, housing costs in the area, the availability of schooling, churches, shopping, and recreational facilities. Be certain to alert your spouse of this to possibly avoid 'conflicting stories.'

■ ■ ■

Don't flow with the wind—create the breeze.

■ ■ ■

46

MAKING THEIR FINAL SELECTION

In large companies, job candidates who are under 'final consideration' will have the results of their written, technical, and psychological tests, interviewer's assessments, medical findings, and background investigations reviewed by a selection board made up of HR and hiring department people. The inputs of the company physician and consulting psychiatrist/psychologist are also considered. In small organizations, the hiring department supervisor or owner of the business makes the hiring decision. In some cases, the decision made must be passed up to the next management level for review and final approval. The pros and cons of each job candidate will be closely reviewed and discussed. Any questionable areas must be resolved. All factors are weighed. Each employer has its own format, process of evaluation, and scoring system. A forced ranking of final candidates by the assessment team may take place. Certain criteria and standards may be established with 'cut off' scoring of each job candidate. The candidate who scores highest above the cutoff point is hired. The more people and factors considered in making hiring decisions, the more validity there is in the eyes of the law and company management—and the less reliance on one evaluator's 'feelings.'

When there are only a few people on the selection team, all the members must approve the candidate for him or her to be hired. They don't want anyone on their team to have any serious reservations about any candidate.

When the selection team has many members, one dissenting member can be overruled by the consenting members, providing the objection is not very strong or in a very important area. A great deal depends on each member's status within the team and the importance of the factors being considered.

In reviewing the results of the background investigation, the stronger a candidate is rated by prior employers, the greater the chances of getting selected. Many employers will only verify the ex-employee's name, dates of employment, position(s) held, training received, and reasons for leaving. However, someone at the hiring company could have a good pipeline to someone in a prominent position with the candidate's former employer and use this contact to obtain 'off-the-record' information on this candidate's performance record. This is why it is so important for you to leave every employer on favorable terms and to encourage your ex-bosses to describe your performance record in the most favorable light possible, playing up your successes and positives.

Should your employment, education, and training credentials not check out, you won't be approved for hire. There must be confirmation of continuous good performance both in your job expertise and in dealing with people. Neutral responses, as well as cases in which the company is unable to readily confirm a particular, significant past employment, will weigh against you.

You may be informed of your status while you are still at their facilities or within several days to a week or two…depending upon the level of position being filled. Rejected applicants are generally sent a letter notifying them that another job candidate was chosen and that their employment application and resume [plus other paper work submitted] will be kept on file should another similar position become open. Each company has its own records retentions policy, in keeping with government legal requirements and their practices.

To avoid possible lawsuits by unsuccessful job candidates, companies will usually not reveal the reasons why candidates were not selected. The information is kept confidential, except if required by law to be disclosed.

■■■

Some people await their destiny—others create it.

■■■

PART THREE

What to Do
After Your Interview

"Who should we hire?"

47

RECAPPING YOUR INTERVIEWS

Reviewing Your Interview Performance

Phew! Your interviews are over! While they are still fresh in your mind, you may want to find a quiet section of a nearby restaurant, have a cup of coffee, and rehash all the things that happened during those interviews. Jot them down. They'll provide an inventory of what you accomplished, didn't accomplish but should have. By taking corrective action in future job interviews, you'll be even more prepared.

Your analysis of what happened, each step of the way, will open your eyes to a greater understanding of how well you performed in your interviews and your chances of receiving a job offer. Compare the results (as you see them) with the concerns you had going into the interviews—which were valid, which weren't?

By taking corrective actions, you will be even more prepared for future job interviews as you 'step up and up' your ladder of career growth and job advancement.

Here are some things you might want to recall and questions you might want to consider:

- Date of each interview.
- Did you arrive early, on time, or late?
- Did you forget to bring important documents/paperwork?
- The name and job title of each interviewer... the receptionist/secretary as well (for follow-up purposes), correct pronunciations of their names.
- How long each interview lasted.
- At the 'opening' and 'closing' moments of each interview, were your 'first impressions created' and 'closing remarks' as strong as they should have been?
- How were you treated by the 'support people' you met (receptionist,

security officers, secretaries, and others)?

- When the interviewer approached you, did you smile and shake their hand firmly?
- How long did it take to get over your nervousness and 'settle down'? Did the interviewers try to put you at ease? Did you exhibit any nervous mannerisms during the interview? Did you ever fling your hands and arms around while talking or keep them completely immobile?
- Were you able to maintain good eye contact with the interviewer—especially while being asked a question, and at the start and end of your answer? When appearing before their interviewing panel, did you divide your eye contact equally with each member?
- Did you look too serious or too casual?
- Did you smile often throughout the interview? Did the interviewer? Did he or she nod their head in agreement periodically and smile—or stay somber looking throughout the interview?
- How professionally did the interviewers conduct themselves? What were your first impressions?
- Was the interview itself too formal or too informal? Were you ever asked questions that were too personal? How well did you handle them? Did you ever become too personal with the interviewer?
- Did you express your appreciation, at the beginning and close of each interview, to each interviewer for being given the opportunity to be interviewed?
- Which questions were dwelled upon? Why? Did the interviewer ask follow-up questions?
- Did you speak too loudly or did you speak too softly? Too fast or too slow? Distinctly or indistinctly? Sound monotone?
- Did the interviewer seem highly interested in what you had to say—show excitement at anytime? Was there intense focus on you?
- Did you listen closely to everything the interviewer asked, said, or did? Did you display excitement from time to time over what was being said? Did you read the interviewer accurately? Did you study their approach to interviewing.
- Did you use 'and' and 'ah' too often? Did you use any slang expressions, or too much technical jargon?
- How often did you inject the interviewer's name in prefacing your response?

- When, if at all, were you at a loss for words as what to say?
- Did you express sincerity in everything you said?
- Did you misunderstand any of the questions? On which questions were you right on target and on which did you miss the target? Did any questions 'stump you'?
- Were you ever distracted during the interview by a phone ringing, people walking in to say something to the interviewer, and so on?
- Which of your answers were too long or too short? Were you too quick or too delayed in answering each question?
- At any time, were you curt and abrupt in your responses to the interviewer?
- Did you act as though you were excited about the job, department, and company? Do you now have a better understanding of the company's future, values, culture and personality?
- Did you show a sense of humor and laugh at something humorous that the interviewer said?
- Were there things you should have said and didn't. Were there things you shouldn't have said but did?
- How often were you asked a question that you failed to anticipate?
- Did you ask too many or too few questions?
- Did you ever interrupt the interviewer? Why? Did the interviewer ever interrupt you, saying, "We have to move on to another question?" or "We need to wrap things up?"
- Did you, at any time, take control of the interview away from the interviewer by asking too many questions, responding to a question asked with a question directed to the interviewer, or making too many ad lib comments?
- Did the interviewer show any signs of liking or disliking an answer you had given or a comment you had made?
- Were you ever asked to 'speak up?' When? How often?
- Did any of the interviewers appear impatient, waiting for you to finish answering their question?
- Were you asked to spend a few minutes touring the department and meeting some of the employees? If so, did you ask some of them what it was like working there? What were your impressions?
- Did the interviewer ask you what you had in mind as to your minimum salary expectations? Was anything else related to salary discussed? Were you given any indication as to what the starting

salary might be and of the salary range for the position? Were you shown a copy of the job description?

- Was there any mention of job perks or employee benefits?
- Were there any significant areas pertaining to your background, education, training, and job experience that the interviewer didn't cover with you? Why do you think they weren't covered?
- Which interviewers seemed to like you? Which didn't indicate? Which, if any, seemed to dislike you?
- Did HR or the hiring supervisor cover job responsibilities, typical job assignments, projects, people you would work with/lead/supervise, hours of work, overtime, weekend work, travel requirements, and other job-related factors?
- What were the key interview moments? What were things that threw you off and things you anticipated would happen? Were there any surprises? Where did you do well? Where didn't you do well? What were your best and worst moments?
- What are your overall impressions of the job, responsibilities and challenges, workplace, potential boss, the hiring department, their facilities, the caliber and friendliness of the people you met? Did the interviewer take the time to sell them to you?
- Was anything of concern said by any of the interviewers that would cause you to follow-up with a phone call addressing that concern? Did you offer to address any further questions they might think of at a later time?
- Did you welcome their conducting an extensive background check on you and your work references?
- Were you asked if you had any job offers pending and when you needed to give them an answer? Were you asked when you would be available to start work if they extended a job offer to you?
- Do you know when, how, and by whom you would be contacted as to the outcome of your interviews?
- How did you think you 'scored' with each interviewer?
- Did you thank each interviewer/panel member for their time and tell them that you look forward to meeting them again soon?
- As you were leaving, did the receptionist ask, "How did your interview go?" [That's usually a very positive sign that she's hoping it went well—she's 'in your corner'; otherwise she wouldn't ask].
- Do you think you'll get the job?

Should there be something important that you forgot to bring to the interviewer's attention, you can e-mail the information to him or her or phone if it's of a confidential nature.

Remember to write (within two days) a brief, individualized thank you note to each of the interviewers. Don't forget the receptionist/secretary of the hiring supervisor. Your spouse, mentor, and closest friend may have some questions to ask you about how your interview went. Cue them in.

Now you're in a position to be as realistic as you possibly can about your interview performance and chances of landing a job offer.

Do You Still Want the Job?

Your first priority is to receive a job offer. You second priority is to decide whether or not you still want the job— now that you know so much more about all the factors that go into 'sizing up' a prospective job and employer. Are they really what you're looking for? Were there any unusually pleasant or unpleasant situations that came up in your interviews? Are you now more or less impressed with the scope of the job, the responsibilities and challenges involved, typical job assignments and projects, the reporting supervisor's personality and management style? How do you feel about the job surroundings, people you will be working with, employee morale, the amount of overtime, travel, and weekend work involved, higher management's philosophies and the company's culture and plans for the future?

Weigh all these factors. Welcome the opinions of your spouse, mentor, and closest friends. They often have good insight into what's best for you. They can see if it is what you really want or if you are just temporarily excited about something. The decision is yours to make—just carefully weigh all the factors and input received. How do all these things sound to you in comparison to another job offer you just received and to the job you now have and your career future if you stay where you are? There are always risks involved in any significant change you make in your life. Do the advantages of making this change outweigh the risks?

You've done your homework! Now it's decision time—even before you've heard from the hiring company. You'll decide whether to take the the big step or stay put. Make your decision when you are relaxed and in a calm mood—by yourself. Once you decide – case closed. The 'lock-in' depends on how good the job offer/starting salary and benefits package are and the potential for future job and career advancement.

48

JOB OFFERS AND SALARY NEGOTIATIONS

Content of Job Offers

You receive a phone call, e-mail, or letter from the company you interviewed with—they made you a job offer! Great!! They stated the job title, the starting salary, salary grade, pay periods, to whom you would directly report (name and job title), the name of the reporting department, the conditions of employment, hours of work, employee benefits and perks, and other important information. The items covered will vary, employer to employer.

You will be requested to phone them ASAP with your response—acceptance or rejection of their offer, a request for further information on what was stated, or a discussion on the starting salary. Some employers have established uniform starting salaries for specific positions and state that figure in their job offer. Most have greater salary latitude.

Don't respond to their job offer immediately. Take at least a few hours to mull it over in your mind, compare it with the other job offer you received, and discuss it with those closest to you. You do, however, need to phone them the same day or the following morning. There may have been a 'runner up' candidate and they would want to get back to him or her quickly, should you not accept their job offer.

You must give the starting salary considerable thought. It will have a tremendous impact on future salary increases, annual income, and total earnings over your career. We're talking about tens of thousands of dollars in future earnings that are at stake. Realistically weigh every angle you can think of. Sure, we all want to earn as much money as we possibly can but need to be realistic when it comes to our *true salary worth (TSW)*.

What if They Don't Offer You a Job?

Should you not receive a job offer, it doesn't mean they didn't intend to hire you—they had just so many job openings to fill and couldn't hire everyone interviewed. Many well-qualified job candidates were considered—they selected how many they needed at that time. Those not offered the position go into their 'active file' for future reconsideration. Don't take it personally. Don't get discouraged—it's only the 'first round'... there will be many more 'interviewing rounds' coming up soon.

You're not unique—it's typical to be interviewed by several highly-desirable employers before receiving a job offer. Do you know anyone who received a job offer every time he or she interviewed for a job? I don't. In fact, most job candidates do not get hired! Employers typically interview four or more job candidates to fill just one job opening.

Candidates who aren't selected have not necessarily done anything *wrong* in their job interviews. Someone else may have barely beaten you out of the running. You may have done a good job in your interview, while the person offered the job did an excellent to outstanding job. You may have been a little lacking in certain areas or just a little short on credit hours if you're still completing your degree requirements. Your GPA may have been 'B' but the person hired held a 'B+' GPA. Perhaps you had the most total years of job experience but the person selected had the most directly-related job experience.

Companies often add promising candidates who were not hired on the first round to their 'on hold' list. When the company has a similar job opening to fill, these candidates are called back to be interviewed again, and often are hired.

Do contact the people who interviewed you to thank them again for the opportunity to interview with them. Let them know you are continuing to vigorously build your experience, credentials, and other important qualifications to match every aspect of their particular job candidate profile for that specific profession. You can state that you have your heart set on a career working for their company and are determined to succeed in filling all of the prerequisites and expectations. Sound upbeat and be optimistic that you'll eventually get the opportunity to work for their great company. Remember, you haven't lost a good job, you just haven't (quite yet) entered the one you want. Don't overreact. The company could have decided to fill the job opening with someone from within their organization, or changed the job requisites, or weren't able to meet your salary needs, or after giving it further thought decided not to fill the position at this time. Don't agonize over the situation. Vent your feelings with your spouse or closest friends if it will help you 'let go' of your disappointment.

Competition is keen. You will get a job you want with a company you really want to work for— it just may not happen overnight.

Company's Perspective on your Job Worth

Let's first look at salary from the employer's perspective. An organization has to establish salary ranges for each of their job classifications that will attract and retain productive employees. They have to balance salaries paid proportionate to each employee's job level, education, training, job knowledge, abilities, skills, job responsibilities and assignments, time in position, significant job accomplishments, 'end results' of their contributions, performance level, and other important factors—in order to establish a strong image of company fairness in its treatment of employees when it comes to salaries paid.

If they were to pay whatever salary figure it takes to attract someone to accept a job with their company, there would be 'uproars from within' if someone in the same job classification were to be hired who had less job credentials, but were offered a starting salary that was higher than theirs. Naturally the company has a certain amount of latitude in setting starting salary figures for its new hires, but cannot risk losing valuable present employees because of salary inequity.

Some employers are in a position to negotiate not only on starting salary but also on when they will receive the first salary review, certain perks and other benefits. This is especially true when it is a higher up position with only one job incumbent. Other employers have universally applied policies and practices that they closely adhere to. If current employees find out (and somehow they usually do) that a new hire in their job classification is receiving something they're not, they will want 'in on it' also.

It's important not only to negotiate the highest starting salary possible but also understand what will influence and/or determine your future salary growth if you accept the job offer. The company's perspective on compensation will greatly impact your salary future. How often will you receive a salary review? What size salary increase (approximately) can you expect to receive? How high can you advance in salary? What is the top salary paid at the company to someone in your position/job classification?

You need to have a basic understanding of a company's salary structure, practices and policies. Small-sized employers may not have a formal salary structure. They hire at a mutually acceptable salary figure and 'play it by ear' from there, negotiating each salary increase. Large companies establish salary grades and ranges for every job they have. Professional, supervisory, and managerial positions are analyzed and placed into established salary grades/ranges according to their 'job worth' to the company—the greater the worth, the higher the grade. Each grade (typically) has a salary range which can vary from company to company, from the minimum to the maximum salary paid for the job classification assigned to that grade. In some companies, the spread from the minimum of the grade to the maximum may be 35%; in others, it may be as broad as 60%. Each grade is divided into four quarters (quartiles). Job candidates seeking positions with their company are most often hired at salaries which fall within the 1st and 2nd quartiles of their salary range. A few may be hired at salaries within the 3rd quartile, but very seldom is someone hired at a salary falling within the 4th quartile.

Performance appraisals and salary reviews most often occur annually. As the job incumbent progresses into the 3rd or 4th quartile of his or her salary range, these reviews occur less frequently. The size of the salary increase varies according to the incumbent's rated performance level—ranging from acceptable and good, to excellent and outstanding.

Employers have to meet market competition when it comes to salaries, especially with its key competitors, but naturally they want to offer each perspective employee a starting salary that is the lowest a candidate will accept. The greater the company's need to fill the job opening, the fewer the number of well-qualified candidates available, the more valuable, applicable, and unique the candidate's background in the job classification, category, and career field in the company's industry, the more willing they are to offer a higher starting salary figure.

Perks and benefit packages can amount to as much as 37% more income to add to your base salary. These can include 'sign-on' and year end bonuses, commissions, 401k and other investment programs, stock options and awards, profit-sharing, pay in lieu of vacations, birthdays off with pay, comprehensive medical, dental, optical, and life insurance coverage, cafeteria insurance plans (choose and pick benefits), lucrative termination and retirement programs, flextime, casual dress allowances, personal/sabbatical leave, prearranged time off, comp days (time off) for unpaid overtime/

weekend work/business travel, working from home, assistance to spouse seeking employment in relocation area, childcare at company facilities, employee discounts, scholarships, tuition reimbursement, wellness programs, legal and financial counseling services, company car, health club, golf and other club memberships, season tickets to sporting events, attending conferences and seminars, and so forth.

Companies expect job candidates will 'high ball' their requested starting salary figure; job candidates expect companies to 'low ball' their offers. Agreement will be reached somewhere between the two.

Remember, your salary expectations are being considered by the company relative to the salaries of their employees who are in the same job classification/family you will be in. Their educational level, training, job knowledge, abilities, areas of job expertise, job and project assignments, end results achieved, and overall level of job performance are taken into consideration by the company—you should keep this in mind as well. Realize that the company must be concerned with the image of 'fairness' and 'balance' between the salaries paid to its current employees and those paid to new hires.

Your Perspective on your Job Worth

When asked, "What are you salary expectations?"... you can reply, "A starting salary that is fair and reasonable—one that takes into consideration my education, training, job skills, abilities and experience, current and prior job responsibilities, assignments, and project completions, job advancement/promotions, and salary growth. I know you will consider how closely these align to what the job calls for and consists of—and the salaries of your employees who are working in the same job family. You will certainly also consider how well I have performed my job responsibilities and assignments, as evidenced by my recent and past performance appraisals and salary increase amounts. I am certain that after you take all these factors into consideration as well as your salary grade and range for this position, you will come up with a realistic salary figure."

You may be worth more to one employer than another because of differences in job responsibilities, job and project assignments, as well as qualification requirements. All this has to enter the salary equation. Being currently employed in a secure position parallel to the available job and their need to fill the job within a certain timeframe will allow you more leverage and place you in a better bargaining position. *The salary offered will be based upon your 'job worth' to that particular employer— not on your financial needs.* The lifestyle you choose to live and your financial obligations have no bearing on your salary worth to them.

Smaller-sized employers often don't have formal salary grades and ranges, and standard benefit programs—so there's more room for negotiating. Larger-size employers will also have substantial room to negotiate with job candidates being considered for 'top level professional and managerial positions' when it comes to starting salaries, salary review periods, bonuses, perks, and benefits.

As you rise to higher professional and managerial levels and the more 'rare' your type of position is in their industry, the more latitude *you* will also have in negotiating starting salary. The more money an employer is willing to pay you, the more they expect out of you, so be prepared to deliver. It's much more difficult to negotiate benefits in large-size companies for 'most positions' because benefits are set and the same for all employees in equivalent positions and job levels.

Be careful that you don't negotiate yourself out of a job offer because you are not realistic in your salary requirements. You could be viewed as difficult to please in terms of future jobs and salary progression.

Some companies budget a certain annual amount for the position they're filling and can't go beyond that figure. Once they determine, after they've had an opportunity to learn all about you, what you could bring to the job, they can make a more realistic and meaningful decision on what salary to offer. Your 'market value' is important; it provides them with a *starting salary range* and gives you latitude to negotiate. If they want you badly enough, you might be able to get them to raise the salary grade one notch or create a new, higher level job classification to accommodate you and provide justification for offering you a higher starting salary.

Be realistic: If you've recently graduated from college and have very little or no job-related experience, you have less room to negotiate and less to offer. If you have an impressive GPA, bring it up. Bring up how much you got out of the key courses you took, your strong study habits, impressive term papers, project assignments, articles and thesis written, your strong 'people' and 'communication' skills, your ability to quickly and effectively adapt to new and unexpected situations, and your congenial personality, positive attitude, and strong character values. Sell whatever it is that you have going for you to compensate for not having the related on-the-job experience that others might have. Also consider the state of the economy and how tight or loose the job market for positions in your profession and career field is in your part of the country. At this time, what is the going salary for those in your profession, in your particular area of expertise?

Point out that you're not looking around for another job because your current job is insecure, or that you don't like your job, your boss, or the people you work with, the department, or company itself. You're looking for greater job responsibilities, accountabilities, and challenges, more diversified and challenging assignments, greater opportunity to contribute new ideas, greater advancement opportunities, and to further broaden your experience in your career field.

The employer knows if they offer you a starting salary below your job worth, then after you're on the job you may find out that others with the same or less qualifications and expertise are being paid significantly more and you'll become discontent.

Also, be cautious and aware that the employer could have plans to close the facility, sell out, outsource or phase out the job you're being offered (in the coming year or two)—as soon as things are 'straightened out.' Ask yourself, "Why are they offering me so much more than I'm really worth?"

Don't suddenly change your personality while negotiating a starting salary from 'real nice guy' to 'hard-nosed salary negotiator.' They may see another side of you that they don't care for and decide to rescind the job offer. You want to appear as a calm, objective person who wishes to be paid only what he or she deems themselves to be worth. To accomplish this, you must justify the figure you are asking for in terms of all of your job credentials.

Show you did a logical analysis of all the factors you've considered. The salary figure you came up with must be realistic. It represents your 'market value' to them—takes into consideration the type and level of position you hold, the length of time you've been in the position, type of job and project assignments, past positions, education, training, your salary grade level, where you fall in your salary range, your performance level rating, and how far you are from the top of your salary range.

An earlier definition of *intelligence* was 'the ability to successfully apply what you know.' That's what coming up with great 'end results' is all about. Your job knowledge and skills and abilities are the tools you use to 'make things happen' and get impressive results. It's a concept that relates to 'salary expectations' as well. Companies can be impressed with your job knowledge, job skills, and years of job experience, but they're most impressed with the major accomplishments and end results of applying them. How successful were those end results? The more successfully and the more consistently you achieve them, the more valuable you are to an employer and the more willing they are to pay you 'top money.'

A new, beautifully-designed automobile may draw everyone's attention but what counts is how well it runs and performs consistently. The extent to which you match, more than match, or less than match what the job they're offering calls for, will determine your job worth to the company and the starting salary they offer.

Check all available sources of information on salary surveys and data. There are websites that can provide or help you find the salary information you need. They will present a clear picture of what is happening relative to your job classification/category/family within your career field and industry, by general location in the country. Spend time talking to people at the library information reference section. They can offer you many leads. Find out what the salary grades and ranges are for your job classification at different companies, locations and industries. Learn what new trainees earn versus those who are among the top paid. Find out the top and the bottom of the salary range among companies in your area and industry for your type of work.

Check with the Bureau of Labor Statistics, state, city and local labor/government/HR departments, professional compensation organizations and consultants, associations in your profession, recruiters, outplacement and search firms, Society for Human Resource Management and other HR groups dealing with hiring personnel. Or you can read the *Wall Street Journal* and other prominent business newspapers, magazines and journals, advertisements for job openings, publications in your profession and industry. Consult nearby college and university placement/ career centers. These can provide you with further leads and insights to find the salary information you need.

Negotiating for the Highest Starting Salary

Negotiating a salary isn't a science—it's an art. You don't want to underprice nor overprice yourself as it could cost you a great opportunity. If you underprice yourself, a red flag goes up—"Why is he or she willing to work for such a low salary?" This is especially true if you have impressive job qualifications. On the other hand, if you overprice yourself, the reaction may be that you are too rich for their blood and out of their ballpark. They may opt to go with their 'backup candidate.' You don't want the hiring supervisor to say, "Hey, that's more than I make!" You need to understand how the salary negotiation game is played and what you need to consider before you come up with your 'asking salary.'

If you're not currently employed, indicate that you still came up with a salary figure that reflects your job worth. Don't count on going into a new job at a salary much lower than you think you are worth and expect that once they see how great you are, they'll give you a big boost in salary. It seldom works that way. If they did, other peers in your job classification at their company could get wind of it and ask for a good sized salary boost as well. Plus, it would appear that the company took advantage of you in the salary negotiations, significantly 'low balling' you.

In no way do you want to appear that you're almost 'begging for the job'—it reflects low self-esteem. Regardless of how high the bills are piling up, show that you still have a lot of pride and you are not desperate.

Keep in mind that you are typically paid for the extent and level of your job knowledge, skills, and capabilities [in addition to your overall level of job performance as observed] and how well you apply all these attributes when carrying out your job responsibilities, individual assignments, and projects—especially the 'end results' of your efforts, displayed through high impact achievements. These results are reflected in terms of increased sales, profits, cost savings, greater output in quantity and quality, new ideas/innovations, new and better products and services, increased customer contracts, and new customers and clients. They are also reflected in shortened procedures and improved practices resulting in time savings, increased consumer demand, more efficient production processes, and so on. You must point out how you have had positive 'results' in many of these as well as other areas, and can do the same for them. The more you tell them about your accomplishments, the more you increase your worth to them— and the starting salary they offer to you.

Recognize that most people never reach the top of their salary range. They usually move on to a higher position— within or outside their company. That's why it is so important to receive the highest starting salary you can, especially when companies are eliminating retirement plans and reducing benefits. If you compare the salary of two people in the same position and profession, with the same or very similar education, training, and job experience, the one who changed jobs periodically [not job hopping as such] for a 'higher position' will generally end up making much more money than the other who stays in the same position for many years.

Where do you fall in your present company's salary range for your job and at what point/salary figure within that range do you fall? Compare this with the company making you the job offer. Would your present salary fall above, at, or below where you would be [in their corresponding salary range] if you were already employed with them? Now estimate what your salary will be after receiving your next salary increase should you choose to remain with your current employer. Your 'point in the salary range' moves up a notch—so does your salary worth.

Also consider that salaries and the established size of a 'typical salary increase' ($ and %) are based upon a typical job performer—not an excellent to outstanding one. It's difficult to assess your own performance. It's too subjective a call.

Average out all your job appraisals/performance reviews/salary reviews over the time you've been in your current position/profession. Come up with an overall 'acceptable,' 'good,' 'excellent,' or 'outstanding' performance rating. What do you think someone now working in the same position you've been offered, working at the same performance level, would be earning? If he or she were considered an excellent to outstanding job performer with considerable job knowledge, skills, abilities and experience in their profession, that person would be in the top quarter of their salary range. Those in the bottom quarter of their salary range are generally considered junior in job knowledge and expertise, but performing well. Most people fall in the 2nd and 3rd quarters. Some people rise to the top of their quarter/quartile based upon 'longevity' in the job and total service time with the company. On some occasions, people who are considered 'average' performers with great longevity have entered the 3rd and even the 4th quartile of their salary range.

Your 'true salary worth' (TSW) is *what the hiring company believes to be your value to them,* weighing all the factors (ones we discussed) that are pertinent. It lies somewhere in the quarter of the new job salary range that corresponds to their best estimate of your overall performance level and the level of your job knowledge, accomplishments, abilities, skills, and overall capabilities.

You must follow the same approach and determine how closely your estimate of your job worth coincides with theirs as you establish your asking starting salary (range). Both you and the hiring company should be applying the same approach, using the same factors, but from separate viewing sites. You're looking at how they play the game, then applying the same rules.

If you're being considered for a supervisory/managerial position, you should have answers to the following questions if you want to consider important 'impact factors' when arriving at the starting salary you will ask for: Does the new job involve directly supervising, leading, counseling, or guiding others? Who [job titles] and how many employees will you be responsible for? What are their job responsibilities? What is the highest salary paid to someone who would be under your supervision? Who will you directly and indirectly [other supervisors/managers] report to? What 'equipment and tools' will you be working with? How much overtime, weekend work, and out-of-state travel can you expect? What specific projects and programs will you be held accountable for? What size budget will you manage? What level of decision-making will you have? How challenging will the job be in comparison to your present job? How much 'creative thinking' and conceptualizing are involved? Which job skills and abilities will you use most? What is their [hiring employer] performance appraisal system? What's the salary latitude (in the future) should you accept their job offer, in terms of how often you can expect to receive a salary review and the range of possible salary increases? What are the promotional possibilities? Do you expect to receive another job offer from another company shortly?

Use some of the answers to these questions to help formulate a starting salary figure that takes all pertinent factors into consideration. You'll be able to point out the logic of your analysis. You're trying to be fair and objective. Again, you're playing by their salary game rules.

Most employers have more flexibility on setting starting salaries than they are willing to admit. Having another job offer to consider at a higher salary than the one you've just been offered will help test that flexibility and place you in a better bargaining situation. Let them know this and that you're open to discussing salary further.

Try tactfully feeling out the person you're negotiating with. Ask to see or obtain a copy of the job description and the salary grade range. Asked to be given a rough estimate of the 'average' of all salaries paid to the people in the job classification and the typical size salary increase given to people performing at each of the performance levels. Don't push for the information. It would be ideal to know but if you detect any reluctance of the job offerer/hiring supervisor to reveal this information, back off immediately and just work with what information you have.

Don't sign any copy of a job offer until you have both agreed upon a final starting salary figure and it's put in writing. The closer your job knowledge, skills, abilities, and 'end results' of your performance correlate to those sought by the hiring company, the more accurately you can determine your 'true salary worth' (TSW) to that employer. If you project these and other very applicable job-related factors (all combined) to a point where it would fall within one of the quarters/quartiles of the hiring company's salary range for the *position you will be filling,* you will have a clearer picture of your 'true salary worth.' If you do this, you can approach the job offerer with sound rationale for how you came up with your starting salary figure. Set the figure that you calculated as realistically high as you can, to allow for 'downward' negotiation which you will most likely have to make.

Keep in mind that the first quarter of a salary range is reserved for job incumbents who have very little or limited job expertise in the job they're in. The 'end results' of their job performance may be at a level that is considered acceptable, good, excellent, or outstanding. 'Performance level' applies to all four quartiles. You can continue to expand your job knowledge and skills through 'longevity on the job' and move up further into your salary quartile, but you shouldn't expect to reach the 3rd or 4th quartile until your overall, consistent 'job results' are considered [by the company] 'excellent' to 'outstanding.' The higher your job-performance rating [based upon 'end results'], the faster you move to the top of your quartile. [Review salary progression chart.]

Should you be given higher job responsibilities and assignments, higher valued and more complex projects, greater people and budget authority, you will likely be placed in a higher quartile or promoted into a higher position. It is not unusual for another job 'peer' to have more job knowledge and job skills but not apply them as impressively— their end results aren't as impressive. Some people can perform at a very high job achievement level despite the fact that they have limited job knowledge, skills, and abilities—they're 'new-to-the-job' trainees.

Take into consideration the area of the country you will be working and living in should you accept a job offer. The same job in one area can warrant a much higher starting salary and salary grade/level than another because of differences in living costs.

Ask yourself "If I were performing the same job for the company that is making me a job offer, what would I 'guesstimate' I would be earning today?" How does that figure compare with what you're currently being paid? This should give you some further insight on what salary to ask for.

Don't forget that you can 'test the water' to find out how many of their perks and benefits are negotiable. If they aren't receptive because you aren't being considered for a high enough position within their pay plan, drop the topic.

No matter how disappointed you might be with the job/salary offer, never show your disappointment. If there is a significant difference in total perks and benefit values between those offered by the hiring employer and those provided by your current employer, adjust the salary figure you expect. Think and talk in terms of a 'total compensation package' and establish your own weighed value for each factor.

Let's get down to the starting salary figure you're going to ask for. Shoot for a figure that is at least 15-20% above what you're currently earning—more if you have the rationale to justify it. Establish a rock bottom figure [in your mind] which is not negotiable. Allow yourself latitude for negotiating but not beyond your rock bottom figure. Start with your ideal figure and be willing to come down to what you believe is your 'true salary worth.' It's expected that you are going to ask for a healthy salary increase over what you're now earning—you're not looking to make a 'lateral move.' You can point out that you believe you are worth more than what you're currently earning, considering your assessment of your job worth, using approximately the same factors that the hiring company uses. You're seeking greater job accountabilities and responsibilities, more challenging job assignments and projects, perhaps entering into supervision or a higher level management position, all of which your present employer cannot provide. These increase your value to them.

When the person making the job offer quotes a starting salary figure, pause several seconds [expressing 'deep thought'] and respond, "I had more of a range of $_____ to $_____ in mind." The lower end is your rock bottom figure and the upper end is 10% above your 'true salary worth' to allow for margin of error in your favor and in keeping with your goal of getting a 15-20% increase over your current salary. You can and are expected to 'come down' and compromise.

Stress that you gave a lot of thought to all the pertinent evaluation factors before you established your estimated starting salary range and feel that you were being logical and objective in doing so. Wait to see what their reaction is. Some employers will say, "We'll have to think about it," or "That is a firm offer," or "That is our final offer,"… or some might reply, "We'll go to $____, but that's it!" No matter what you're told, sit back calmly and say, "I appreciate your salary offer and want to give it full consideration. Changing jobs and employers deserves serious consideration. May I phone you with my decision?" Make up your mind by the end of the next day [recent college graduates are typically given 1 to 3 weeks to mull over an extended job offer.] Discuss the matter with your spouse, closest friends, and mentor. You want to get opinions from several realistic perspectives.

By asking for time to 'think it over,' you have the opportunity to phone any other company that also made you a job offer and let them know about the job offers you have received and that you need to give the other company an answer within the following day. They will appreciate your 'heads up.' Let the employers compete with one another—it helps to raise the starting salary figure. You, however, must decide which offer at which salary figure you will accept and say 'yes' or 'no thank you,' on your final phone call.

In salary negotiations, you don't want to tip your hand by not hesitating after they throw out a salary figure, or changing your facial expression to one of great elation to a figure that was much higher than you expected, or make any significant changes in your body language, voice or eye contact. The job offerer should not be able to detect your satisfaction or dissatisfaction with the salary figures being tossed around. He or she should keep their focus on the logic and reality of what salary figure you're proposing—based on 'facts' and the things on which job performance is judged. You and the hiring company must be flexible and fair in 'playing by the rules' of sound decision-making and not treat the other as though he or she were gullible.

Let's say both sides have reached their 'final salary offer' and you reach a stalemate. Then the question is, do you want them more than they want you? If they want you more, they will be willing to move up one small notch; if you want them more, you will be willing to move down one small notch. Again, compromise. No matter how it turns out—acceptance or rejection—end your discussions on a very positive, appreciative note. You might say, "I accept your offer and look forward to working with you" or "I really do appreciate the offer you've made and it was a difficult decision but I have decided to decline the offer. Thank you for inviting me to join your company and all the time you spent with me and the courtesy you extended to me." Convey this message by phone 'person to person with the individual extending the job offer' (not to someone who will take your message) and also in a personalized note or letter shortly afterwards. You'll appear professional in ending the relationship in the manner you did. It leaves the door open to unexpected future opportunities in which you might cross paths in business dealings or perhaps another lucrative job opening. Also, be sure to thank all the people who helped you (within or outside the company) get the job—in person or by letter.

We all tend to overrate our salary worth. We believe our employer/ boss doesn't truly realize how much we know, do, and contribute to his or her success and the success of our department and company. In reality, we might be well-paid in our current job, considering the factors we've talked about. This has to be recognized and taken into consideration in applying the 15-20% formula—especially if it's a job you want badly. Its easier to focus on how hard we work and all the things we do that the boss is not fully aware of, regardless of the results of that work. Did you ever stop to think that your boss might feel the same way about himself or herself? Everybody's in the same boat—rowing probably as hard, if not harder than you are.(The chart at the end of this chapter will illustrate the bargaining/negotiation process.)

Some people move ahead faster in job and salary growth than others. In many cases, it's a reflection of ingenuity, insight, ability, and lots of productive effort with noteworthy results. In other cases, it's being at the right place, at the right time, with the right people. Then there are the cases where it's a matter of a playing the game of 'company politics' well. Who you know and cater to may get you there. Life doesn't always deal people a 'good hand'—no matter what game we're playing.

Salary Negotiations, 'A Case Study'

HR and the hiring supervisor/manager have decided to hire you and need to come up with a reasonable salary offer. Both have reviewed your resume and employment application, letters of recommendation, test results, job reference checks, and background investigation report. They have also reviewed and assessed the results of their interviews with you, in terms of your job-related and directly-applicable education, training, job experience, skills and abilities (both technical and people), job responsibilities and accountabilities, job and project assignments and completions, noteworthy job accomplishments, and past performance levels. They have a good feel for your personality (attitude, sense of humor, disposition, openness), character, and job and personal values.

In determining what starting base salary they should offer to you, they consider your current base salary and what benefits/perks you now are receiving, their salary grade and range within their pay plan for the job classification you will be assigned to, and what they consider to be your true salary worth (TSW) to their company. They also consider all applicable job factor assessments and the overall performance record and salaries of their employees who are in the same position. Their objective is to offer you a starting salary and benefits package that you would accept.

Their next step is to project the bottom line of all these job-related factors to a point within the job's salary range for that grade level which they determine to be your TSW. Let's say the salary range extends from a minimum of $70K to a maximum of $109K annually—a spread of 55.7%. They believe your TSW to be $84.5K. Taking into account that the position they are offering you would be a step up in your profession from your current job, and that you are currently earning $72K, a salary offer of $82K would be appropriate and represent a 13.8% increase. It would most likely take at least two merit increases (approximately 2 years) to reach that figure if you remain in your present job. Sounds very fair to them. They have the latitude to compromise with you in direct salary negotiations and raise their salary offer closer to your TSW. Again, they don't want to overpay you and cause dissension among other employees in the same or closely related job classifications in the same salary grade. Should the company be desperate to fill the position and there is a critical shortage of well-qualified job candidates on the market, HR and the hiring supervisor/manager must consider going a little over TSW.

You in turn are very interested in the position offered but would like to receive a salary offer of $88K—a 22.2% increase over your current salary of $72K—taking you very close to the midpoint of the new position's salary grade range. You base this asking salary figure on your assessment of your salary worth using the same job factors which HR and the hiring supervisor/manager considered in reaching their salary conclusions. You center your thinking on the fact that you have greatly excelled in almost every area of your present and past job performance (as evidenced by the documented performance appraisals you have received)—all of which is directly applicable to the position being offered.

You must however also admit to yourself that you can't help but be somewhat biased in your favor in making your self assessment. We all are. Realizing this, you should be open to compromise and further negotiation. If you've been relatively fair and objective in thinking through this salary negotiation scenario, you will probably be willing to compromise at $85K—which represents a 18.1% salary increase going into a more challenging position with a better company. *You're playing the hiring company's salary negotiation game using their rules.*

If you have bargained for and received a commitment by the hiring company to grant certain benefits and perks to you which you requested, take this into consideration when arriving at your asking salary and during the compromising process. You must compare that part of the compensation package as well. Should the total benefits and perks part of the package represent more than you are now receiving, calculate the difference in worth to you and be more willing to 'give a little.' If the total is less, you're justified in upping both your asking and compromise/settling final salary acceptance figure.

In the end, it's a win-win situation for both you and the hiring company. The company is willing to up its salary offer to or slightly above your TSW to recruit the best job candidate available, and you are in turn, willing to lower your asking salary to (or close to) your estimate of your salary worth and receive the opportunity to work in a more responsible job with the company of your choice.

Choosing the Best Job Offer

If you have successfully applied all we've talked about in how to best sell yourself during your interviews, you may very well end up with two or even three job offers—all at the same time. Which will you choose to accept? Give it a lot of serious thought. 'Sleep on it' and make your decision when your head is clearest the next morning.

To help you decide which factors to compare in your analysis, here are a number of them which you might want to consider:

- Interest in the job offered, the responsibilities and involvements.
- Scope of the job and workload.
- Starting salary, frequency and size of increases expected, salary grade, salary structure/plans/policies, which 'quartile' will I be in.
- Frequency of job performance appraisals.

- Bonuses, commissions, stock options, and other forms of compensation offered.
- Paid sick leave and disability programs.
- Medical and life insurance plans provided and their cost to me.
- Perks and other benefits, such as company vehicle, flextime, financial planning and tax preparation help, expenses incurred in changing jobs covered (travel by air or automobile, meals, moving of personal possessions, help in selling home and purchasing another home, tuition reimbursement, membership fee coverages, etc.)
- Employment and termination contracts.
- Balance between job 'responsibilities' and 'authority.'
- Level, scope, and amount of decision-making/problem-solving involved.
- Level and number of job challenges to be taken on.
- Company's growth and expansion plans [the department's plans as well].
- Stability of the company, present and projected—likelihood of cutbacks.
- Stability of the industry (present and immediate future).
- Types of products and services provided—their customers and clients.
- Position and reputation of company among its competitors.
- Degree of comfort with company's management style, company values, culture, concern for its image, receptiveness to new ideas and innovations.
- Number, type, and job level of employees supervised.
- Budget and cost control accountabilities.
- Level of chemistry (projected) with immediate/reporting supervisor—how much I can learn from him or her.
- Company and department morale.
- Reputation in the industry and with the public.
- Job advancement opportunities—chance to advance into leadership roles, supervision, and management positions.
- Caliber of new boss, peers, and co-workers.
- Workplace conditions and atmosphere.
- Training and education programs provided.
- How well organized everything I've seen appears at every level.
- Amount of routine and repetitive job tasks.

- Amount and frequency of travel, overtime, and weekend work anticipated—typical working hours.
- Location—area of country, commuting distance to and from work, climactic conditions, closeness to schools, churches, and other religious places of worship, shopping centers, sporting events, recreational opportunities, desirability of city and neighborhood location [safety concerns], housing costs and availability, and proximity to family members and close friends.
- Amount of free time to spend with spouse, family, and close friends—as well as on own hobbies, sports, and other interests, including community involvement.
- My family's opinion of the 'overall package' provided by each job offer.
- Which job will be 'the most fun' and the one I feel most confident that I'm really good at.

You need to compare the job offers in areas of concern that are most important to you. One of the best ways is to make up a 'factor comparison' chart (see chart sample). List the most significant ones [to you] and assign a weighted value of importance to each factor, ranging from 1 (least important) to 5 (most important). Then rate each factor from 1 (least favorable) to 10 (most favorable). Multiply your rating on each factor by the weighted value of each factor to come up with a total score for that factor. Add up the total scores for a 'grand total' and compare one job offer's grand total with that of the others. Go with the winner!

"Any other questions?"   "Do you have a ski team?"

JOB OFFER EVALUATION GUIDELINES

	JOB OFFER			CURRENT JOB		
CRUCIAL FACTORS	SCORE	×	FACTOR WEIGHTED VALUE =	TOTAL SCORE	SCORE ×	FACTOR WEIGHTED VALUE =	TOTAL SCORE
• JOB (OVERALL)						
• STARTING SALARY (BASE)						
• BENEFITS (TOTAL)						
IMPORTANT FACTORS	SCORE: 1 (LOW) TO 10 (HIGH)			WEIGHTED VALUE: 1 (LOW) TO 5 (HIGH)		
• SPECIFIC JOB RESPONSIBILITIES AND ACCOUNTABILITIES (SKILLS AND ABILITIES EXERCISED, OPPORTUNITIES FOR CREATIVE/INNOVATIVE THINKING)						
• JOB AND PROJECT ASSIGNMENTS (TYPICAL AND KEY)						
• FREQUENCY OF SALARY REVIEWS (% & $) AND PERFORMANCE APPRAISALS						
• PROMOTIONAL AND PROFESSIONAL GROWTH OPPORTUNITIES						
• STIMULATING BOSS, PEERS, CO-WORKERS, AND WORK ATMOSPHERE						
• STABILITY AND GROWTH OF DEPARTMENT, COMPANY, PRODUCT LINES AND SERVICES						
• IN-HOUSE AND OUTSIDE TRAINING AND EDUCATIONAL OPPORTUNITIES						
• COMPANY REPUTATION AMONG COMPETITORS/THE PUBLIC						
• EMPLOYEE MORALE						
• DESIRABILITY OF COMPANY FACILITIES/LOCATIONS AND WORKING AREA						
• DAILY COMMUTE TO WORK (DISTANCE, TIME, AND COST)						
• FAMILY CONCERNS: DESIRABILITY OF THE AREA (CITY/TOWN/NEIGHBORHOOD), HOUSING AND RENTAL COSTS AND AVAILABILITY, LIVING CONDITIONS, CLOSENESS TO OTHER FAMILY MEMBERS AND FRIENDS, PLACES OF WORSHIP, SCHOOLS, ENTERTAINMENT, RESTAURANTS, SPORTING ACTIVITIES, PUBLIC TRANSPORTATION, PARKS, COMMUNITY CENTERS, LIBRARIES, AND SHOPPING CENTERS						
• CLIMATE AND TYPICAL WEATHER CONDITIONS (COMFORT AND ENERGY COSTS)						
BOTTOM LINE						

BASE SALARY OF JOB OFFERS SHOULD BE AT LEAST 15% – 20% ABOVE YOUR CURRENT SALARY. BENEFITS/PERKS OFFERED SHOULD EQUAL OR EXCEED THOSE NOW RECEIVING BY 5% – 10%. IF LESS, INCREASE YOUR ASKING AND COMPROMISE STARTING SALARY FIGURES ACCORDINGLY.

YOUR ASSESSMENT OF NEW JOB (CRUCIAL AND IMPORTANT FACTORS) SHOULD BE 20% – 30% ABOVE CURRENT JOB TO JUSTIFY CHANGING JOBS. [IF UNEMPLOYED SEVERAL MONTHS, LOWER YOUR SALARY EXPECTATIONS]. CONSIDER TRADEOFFS AND TOTAL PACKAGE NEGOTIATED BEFORE ACCEPTING OR REJECTING THE FINAL JOB OFFER.

SALARY NEGOTIATIONS WITHIN SALARY GRADE RANGE OF JOB CLASSIFICATION/POSITION OFFERED
GRADE SPREAD: 55.7%

MINIMUM	1ST QUARTILE THROUGH	2ND QUARTILE THROUGH	MIDPOINT	3RD QUARTILE THROUGH	4TH QUARTILE THROUGH	MAXIMUM
$70 K	$79K	$80 K	$89K $90 K	$99K	$100 K	$109K

- $72K: YOUR CURRENT SALARY

- $82K: JOB OFFER (13.8% INCREASE)

[$84.5K: YOUR "TRUE SALARY WORTH (TSW)" TO HIRING COMPANY]

- $85K: COMPROMISED FINAL SALARY OFFER (18.1% INCREASE) – AGREED UPON BY BOTH NEGOTIATORS

[$86K: YOUR ESTIMATE OF YOUR SALARY WORTH]

- $88K: YOUR ASKING SALARY (22.2% INCREASE) – FEEL UNDERPAID

HIRING COMPANY MAY EXTEND A SIGNING BONUS, IN ADDITION TO THE OTHER BENEFITS/PERKS INCLUDED IN THEIR JOB OFFER, TO ADD TO THEIR INITIAL JOB OFFER. DOING THIS, YOU WOULD BE EXPECTED TO COME DOWN FURTHER IN YOUR SALARY EXPECTATIONS.

THE NEED TO FILL THE POSITION CAN BECOME CRITICAL WHEN COMPETITORS FOR THE SAME OR SIMILAR POSITION FACE A TIGHT LABOR MARKET. SHOULD YOU APPEAR TO BE THE BEST JOB CANDIDATE INTERVIEWED, THE HIRING COMPANY MAY BE FORCED TO OFFER YOU A STARTING SALARY SIGNIFICANTLY ABOVE YOUR TSW. THIS IS PARTICULARLY TRUE IF THERE ARE ONLY ONE OR TWO OF THEIR EMPLOYEES, IN THE SAME JOB CLASSIFICATION, WHO HAVE LESS JOB EXPERTISE THAN YOURSELF, YET ARE BEING PAID MORE THAN YOU ARE CURRENTLY EARNING.

THE MORE DIRECTLY RELATED YOUR JOB EXPERTISE IS TO THAT REQUIRED BY THE HIRING COMPANY — TO PERFORM IMPRESSIVELY IN THE POSITION OFFERED TO YOU, THE MORE JUSTIFIED YOU ARE TO RAISE BOTH YOUR ASKING SALARY AND 'ROCK BOTTOM' SALARY FIGURE.

WHAT YOU DON'T GET IN YOUR COMPROMISED SALARY OFFER, YOU SHOULD STRIVE TO MAKE UP FOR BY OBTAINING ADDITIONAL BENEFITS/PERKS THROUGH FURTHER NEGOTIATIONS.

SALARY PROGRESSION WITHIN SALARY GRADE RANGE OF POSITION

FACTORS IMPACTING SALARY PROGRESSION

- YEARS OF EXPERIENCE IN POSITION
- PERFORMANCE LEVEL (OVERALL)
- JOB RESPONSIBILITIES AND ACCOUNTABILITIES
  — AMOUNT OF GROWTH EXPERIENCED
- SIGNIFICANT ACCOMPLISHMENTS AND ACHIEVEMENTS
- CONTRIBUTIONS TOWARD ACHIEVING DEPARTMENT AND COMPANY GOALS AND OBJECTIVES
  — IMMEDIATE, INTERMEDIATE, AND LONG RANGE
  — INCREASED SALES, PROFITS, MARKET SHARE, AND CUSTOMER SATISFACTION
  — REDUCED COSTS
  — NEW CUSTOMERS AND CLIENTS, PRODUCTS AND SERVICES
- SKILLS AND ABILITIES (POSITION RELATED)
  - TECHNICAL / TACTFULNESS
  - PEOPLE / EMOTIONAL CONTROL
  - COMMUNICATIVE / HANDLING STRESS
  - LEADERSHIP / INSIGHT
- WORKING RELATIONSHIP/INTERACTION WITH REPORTING SUPERVISOR
- GROWTH POTENTIAL/PROMOTABILITY
- KNOWLEDGE (JOB RELATED)
- EDUCATION (FORMAL AND CAREER RELATED)
- TRAINING (FORMAL AND ON-THE-JOB)
- CONTRIBUTIONS TO TEAM SUCCESS (PEERS, BOSS, AND CO-WORKERS)
- CREATION OF NEW IDEAS, TECHNICAL INNOVATIONS, AND TECHNIQUES WHICH HAVE BEEN ADOPTED BY DEPARTMENT AND COMPANY— INCLUDES PROCEDURES, PRACTICES, PROCESSES AND SYSTEMS
- FLEXIBILITY IN ADAPTING TO CHANGES WITHIN THE DEPARTMENT AND IN JOB ASSIGNMENTS
- MATURITY IN HANDLING PEOPLE IN JOB RELATED SITUATIONS
- SELF MOTIVATION AND INITIATIVE DISPLAYED

MINIMUM 1ST QUARTILE	2ND QUARTILE MIDPOINT	3RD QUARTILE	4TH QUARTILE MAXIMUM
UP TO 1½ YEARS	1½ YEARS TO 3½ YEARS	3½ YEARS TO 6½ YEARS	6½ TO 10 YEARS
MEETS ENTRY LEVEL PERFORMANCE EXPECTATIONS	GOOD TO EXCELLENT OVERALL JOB PERFORMANCE	EXCELLENT TO OUTSTANDING OVERALL JOB PERFORMANCE	OUTSTANDING OVERALL JOB PERFORMANCE
SATISFIES MINIMUM JOB REQUIREMENTS IN ALL FACTORS ASSESSED	STEADY DEVELOPMENT AND IMPROVEMENT IN ALL FACTORS/AREAS BEING ASSESSED		JOB SKILLS AND ABILITIES FULLY DEVELOPED & HONED GIVEN THE MOST IMPORTANT AND CHALLENGING JOB ASSIGNMENTS AND PROJECTS
RAPIDLY LEARNING ALL ASPECTS OF JOB RESPONSIBILITIES	MANY INCUMBENTS PROMOTED BEFORE REACHING THE 4TH QUARTILE AS ADVANCEMENT OPPORTUNITIES ARISE		ACHIEVES SIGNIFICANT JOB ACCOMPLISHMENTS ON A REGULAR BASIS
QUICKLY GRASPING JOB ASSIGNMENTS GIVEN AND ADAPTING TO TRAINING RECEIVED, PEERS, CO-WORKERS, SUPERVISOR'S MANAGEMENT STYLE, AND DEPARTMENT'S OPERATIONS	TIME INTERVAL BETWEEN SALARY INCREASES BECOMES GREATER IN THE 3RD AND 4TH QUARTILES		CONSISTENTLY EXCEEDS OVERALL PERFORMANCE EXPECTATIONS IN QUANTITY AND QUALITY OF WORK PERFORMED
ASKING MEANINGFUL QUESTIONS REGARDING JOB ASSIGNMENTS AND EXPECTATIONS			FREQUENTLY CONTRIBUTES SUGGESTIONS FOR RESOLVING PROBLEM SITUATIONS
BEGINNING TO MAKE POSITIVE CONTRIBUTIONS TO DEPARTMENT'S SUCCESS — FEELING GOOD ABOUT ACCOMPLISHMENTS			GENERATES NEW IDEAS FOR IMPROVEMENT IN MANY AREAS
			DOESN'T REQUIRE CLOSE SUPERVISION
			ADAPTS READILY TO CHANGING SITUATIONS AND CONDITIONS
			CONTRIBUTES TO THE ACHIEVEMENT OF THE GOALS AND OBJECTIVES OF SUPERVISOR, DEPARTMENT, AND COMPANY (DIRECTLY AND INDIRECTLY)
			STRIVES TO EXPAND JOB SKILLS AND ABILITIES BEYOND CURRENT JOB RESPONSIBILITIES
			PEERS SEEK THEIR ADVICE AND COUNSEL WHEN PERFORMING DIFFICULT JOB ASSIGNMENTS

A FINAL WORD FROM THE AUTHOR

If what has been brought out in this book does nothing more than give you greater self-confidence and greater determination to succeed, it is well worth the time you have spent reading it. If you apply only half of what you have learned to your upcoming job interviews, you can't help but significantly increase your chances of being hired. 'Apply' is the key word. Don't just store this knowledge—use it! If you visualize yourself doing a good job and using this new knowledge—you will get hired!

I sincerely wish you success in landing the job you want most—with your number-one company. You know you can do it!

Thank you for allowing me to share my thoughts, knowledge, perceptions, insights, ideas, and feelings about how you can succeed in getting hired with you. Now… Go get 'em!

INDEX

A

Accomplishments
  describing, 59–60, 84, 147
  interviewer's questions about, 112
Adaptability, 16
Affirmative action, 97
Age, 85
Americans with Disabilities Act
  (ADA), 50
Answers. See also Questions
  bluffing, 94
  building impressive, 80–81,
    137–51
  delivery of, 235–36
  examples in, 154–57
  key and supporting points in,
    139–42, 213
  length of, 152–53, 214–15
  memorizing, 82
  pauses before/during, 152–53,
    212–13
  presentation of, 203–17
  reserve, 150–51
  selecting and perfecting final,
    190–92
  situational awareness and, 76,
    77–78
  tactful vs. tactless, 244–51
  underkill vs. overkill in, 135–36
Appearance, personal, 149, 226–34
Applicants
  common misconceptions
    among, 2–3

desired attributes for, 1–2, 12–20,
  53–58
inexperienced vs. experienced,
  163–64
interviewers' reactions to,
  286–326
military, 31–32, 99–100, 184–86,
  315–16
relationship between interviewer
  and, 258–66
screening process for, 33–51
selecting among, 329–30
Applications
  as crutch, 205
  reviewing, 145
  updating, 8
Attitude
  importance of, 12–13, 205–6,
    242
  interviewers' reactions to, 303–5
Attributes
  physical, 176
  quantitative vs. qualitative, 10
Availability, 185

B

Background investigations, 50–51,
  313–15
Benefit packages, 341–42
Board interviews, 42–43, 239–40,
  266
Body language, 55, 237–40, 242
Briefcases, 229, 232

C

Campus screening, 37
Career
    choices made in, 84, 98–100
    commitment to, 13, 55, 83, 312–13
    goals for, 124
    questions to ask yourself about,
        86–88
    selecting, 45–46
Character, 124–26, 171–72,
    299–303
Coaches, 188–89
Commitment, importance of, 55
Communication
    forms of, 242–43
    skills, 17, 55, 90
Compromise, 215
Conflicts, 111
Consultants, 23
Contacts, 46
Convictions, 215
Courtesy interviews, 45
Criminal record, 50–51, 101
Criticism, constructive, 111
Customers
    concerns of, 123–24
    recommendations from, 27

D

Decision-making skills, 84, 115–17,
    142
Degrees, 100–101, 318–20
Delivery, 306–7
Determination, 13–14, 360
Disagreements, 111
Disappointments, 112
Diversified hiring, 97

Dress, appropriate, 226–34

E

Education, 100–101, 318–20
Emotions
    role of, 67–68
    thoughts associated with, 71–73
Employee/management relations,
    122–23
Employers
    current, 25
    questions about previous, 104–9,
        145, 313–15
    recommendations from prior,
        25–26
    researching potential, 21–24, 144
Enthusiasm, displaying, 237, 238
Eye contact, 239–40

F

Feelings. See Emotions
Filler expressions, 191, 235
First impressions, 218–25, 286–89
Flexibility, 16
Focus, importance of, 263–65
Follow-through, 144
Free time, questions about, 126–27
Friends
    advice from, 3, 337
    recommendations from, 26–27
Future growth, potential for, 85, 127

G

Gestures, 238–39
Goals
    interviewer's questions about, 124
    unrealized, 180–81

Grade point average (GPA), 7–8, 318–20
Grooming, 226–34
Group interviews, 44–45, 160–62

H
Hair, 228–29, 231
Hiring department supervisors, 42
Honesty, 244–51
Human Resources (HR), interviews with, 40–41, 243
Humor, sense of, 18, 256–57

I
Image, importance of, 54–55, 148–49, 218–19
Influence, 17
Integrity, 321–22
Intellectual strengths, 170–71
Intelligence, 66–67, 68
Interviewers
    addressing, 204, 219–20
    bias of, 262–63
    objectives of, 47–48, 93
    questions asked by, 92–127
    reactions of, to applicants, 286–326
    relationship between applicants and, 258–66
    roles of, 2
    styles of, 206–8, 279–80
    thanking, 328, 337, 339
Interview preparation
    with coaches, 188–89
    importance of, 79–80, 82
    impressing with, 145–46
    interviewers' reactions to, 290–94

with prep sheets, 187–88
    strategy for, 80–85
Interviews. See also Answers; Questions
    approaches to, 48–49
    arriving for, 201–2
    for career selection, 45–46
    closing, 128, 325–28
    courtesy, 45
    'do's' and 'don'ts' for, 275–83
    dressing for, 226–34
    first five minutes of, 218–25
    following up after, 328
    group, 44–45, 160–62
    with hiring department, 42
    with HR, 40–41, 243
    importance of, 79–80
    key steps to successful, 284–85
    messages conveyed during, 242–43
    obtaining, 46–47
    panel/board, 42–43, 239–40, 266
    paperwork to bring to, 193–94
    phone, 33–36
    for promotions, 62–65
    relaxing during, 206–8
    reviewing performance in, 333–37
    scoring points in, 3–4, 56–57
    short, 54
    silence during, 236, 266
    skills for, 88–90
    of spouse, 43–44, 328
    tone of, 222–23, 260–62
    traveling to, 195–97
    understanding process of, 52–58
    videotaping mock, 189, 192

Intuition, 73–74

J

Job fairs, 36–37
Job leads, 46–47
Job offers
    competing, 247
    content of, 338
    evaluating, 337, 354–57
    lack of, 339–40
Job responsibilities, 103–4
Job worth. See Salary

L

Leadership, 14, 117–20, 320–21
Learning ability, 15
Letters
    of recommendation, 25–32, 193,
        194
    thank-you, 328, 337
Listening skills, 264
Loyalty, 145

M

Management, relationship with,
    122–23
Medical condition, 101–2
Medical examinations, 49–50
Military applicants
    availability date for, 185
    interviewers' reactions to,
        315–16
    questions for, 99–100
    sample letter of recommendation
        for, 31–32
    tips for, 184–86
Mind
    conscious, 68, 69–71

managing, 68
subconscious, 69–71, 73, 74–75,
    138–39
thought-feeling associations in,
    71–73

N

Negatives, handling, 149–50, 217,
    267–69
Nervousness, 207, 260

O

'On hold' list, 339
Overkill, 135–36

P

Panel interviews, 42–43, 239–40,
    266
People skills, 16–17, 83–84, 144,
    172–76, 309–10
Performance factors, 6–8
Personality, 124–26, 172–76,
    299–303
Personal life
    questions about, 90
    as strengths, 176–77
Phone interviews, 33–36
Physical attributes, 176
Positive attitude, 12–13
Posture, 237–38
Prep sheets, 187–88
Prescreening interviews, 33–37
Problem-solving skills, 11, 115–17
Professionalism, 15–16, 114–15,
    164–67
Promotions, 62–65
Psychological tests, 38–39
Psychologists, evaluation by, 129–33

Q

Qualifications
  exceeding basic, 53–54
  performance-related, 6–7
  questions about, 110–11
  updating, 6–7
Questions. See also Answers
  art of fielding, 210–13, 294–99
  asked by interviewers, 92–127
  asked by psychologists, 129–32
  to ask interviewers, 127–28,
    270–74, 322–24
  to ask yourself, 86–90
  legally prohibited, 85, 92–93
  negative, 267–69
  repeated, 48, 216
  trick/intimidating, 94, 209,
    215–16, 253, 265–66
  types of, 208–10

R

Rapport, establishing, 94–95
Receptionists, 201, 218, 337
Recommendations and references,
  25–32, 193, 194
Rejection, handling, 143
Relaxation techniques, 254–55
Research, 21–24, 144
Resumes, 136, 145, 193
Role-playing scenarios, 120,
  158–59, 161–62

S

Salary
  company's perspective on,
    340–42
  negotiating, 35, 345–54, 358
  progression, 359
  questions about, 97–98
  your perspective on, 338, 342–45
Screening process. See also
  Interviews
  background investigations, 50–51
  campus interviews, 37
  job fairs, 36–37
  medical examinations, 49–50
  phone interviews, 33–36
  tests, 38–40
Search firms, 36
Selection process, 329–30
Self-confidence, 16, 307–9, 360
Selling yourself, 59–61, 204–5,
  311–12
Silence, 236, 266
Situational awareness, 76–78,
  114–15
Situational-based behavior
  examples of, 154–57
  negative, 155–56
  role-playing, 158–59, 161–62
Smiling, 60, 238, 279
Spouse
  interviews of, 43–44, 328
  support of, 83, 217, 337
SPSRP approach, 157
Strengths, 113, 163–77
Stress, handling, 14–15, 113–14,
  149–50, 252–55
Subconscious, 69–71, 73, 74–75,
  138–39

T

Tactfulness, importance of, 244–51
Team orientation, 15

Technical expertise, 102, 143–44,
   316–18
Tests, 38–40
Thank-you notes, 328, 337
Thought-feeling associations,
   71–73
Total person, concept of, 90,
   324–25
Training, 100–101
Traveling, 195–97
True salary worth (TSW), 338,
   347–49

U

Underkill, 135–36
Unemployment, questions about,
   93, 109
Update submissions, 8

V

Values, 171–72
Visualization, 74–75
Voice, tone of, 235–36, 306–7

W

Weaknesses, 113, 178–83
Work locations, 97

Your Key Thought Reminders

Your Key Thought Reminders